ISBN 978-1-331-53366-5
PIBN 10202284

1 MONTH OF
FREE
READING

at

www.ForgottenBooks.com

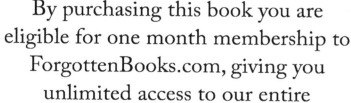

By purchasing this book you are eligible for one month membership to ForgottenBooks.com, giving you unlimited access to our entire collection of over 700,000 titles via our web site and mobile apps.

To claim your free month visit:

www.forgottenbooks.com/free202284

A Series of English Texts, edited for use in Elementary and Secondary Schools, with Critical Introductions, Notes, etc.

Addison's Sir Roger de Coverley.
American Democracy from Washington to Wilson.
American Patriotism in Prose and Verse.
Andersen's Fairy Tales.
Arabian Nights' Entertainments.
Arnold's Sohrab and Rustum.
Austen's Pride and Prejudice.
Austen's Sense and Sensibility.
Bacon's Essays.
Baker's Out of the Northland.
Bible (Memorable Passages).
Blackmore's Lorna Doone.
Boswell's Life of Johnson. Abridged.
Browning's Shorter Poems.
Mrs. Browning's Poems (Selected).
Bryant's Thanatopsis, etc.
Bryce on American Democracy.
Bulwer–Lytton's Last Days of Pompeii.
Bunyan's The Pilgrim's Progress.
Burke's Speech on Conciliation.
Burns' Poems (Selections).
Byron's Childe Harold's Pilgrimage.
Byron's Shorter Poems.
Carlyle's Essay on Burns.
Carlyle's Heroes and Hero Worship.
Carroll's Alice's Adventures in Wonderland.
Chaucer's Prologue and Knight's Tale.
Church's The Story of the Iliad.
Church's The Story of the Odyssey.
Coleridge's The Ancient Mariner.
Cooper's The Deerslayer.
Cooper's The Last of the Mohicans.
Cooper's The Spy.
Curtis' Prue and I.
Dana's Two Years Before the Mast.
Defoe's Robinson Crusoe. Part I.
Defoe's Robinson Crusoe. Abridged.
De Quincey's Confessions of an English Opium-Eater.
De Quincey's Joan of Arc, and The English Mail-Coach.
Dickens' A Christmas Carol, and The Cricket on the Hearth.
Dickens' A Tale of Two Cities.
Dickens' David Copperfield. (Two vols.)
Dickens' Oliver Twist.

Dryden's Palamon and Arcite.
Early American Orations, 1760–1824.
Edwards' Sermons.
Eliot's Mill on the Floss.
Eliot's Silas Marner.
Emerson's Early Poems.
Emerson's Essays.
Emerson's Representative Men.
English Essays.
English Narrative Poems.
Epoch-making Papers in U. S. History.
Franklin's Autobiography.
Mrs. Gaskell's Cranford.
Goldsmith's The Deserted Village, and Other Poems.
Goldsmith's The Vicar of Wakefield.
Gray's Elegy, etc., and Cowper's John Gilpin, etc.
Grimm's Fairy Tales.
Hale's The Man Without a Country.
Hawthorne's Grandfather's Chair.
Hawthorne's Mosses from an Old Manse.
Hawthorne's Scarlet Letter.
Hawthorne's Tanglewood Tales.
Hawthorne's The House of the Seven Gables.
Hawthorne's Twice-told Tales (Selections).
Hawthorne's Wonder-Book.
Holmes' Autocrat of the Breakfast Table.
Holmes' Poems.
Homer's Iliad (Translated).
Homer's Odyssey (Translated).
Hughes' Tom Brown's School Days.
Hugo's Les Miserables. Abridged.
Huxley's Selected Essays and Addresses.
Irving's Knickerbocker's History.
Irving's Life of Goldsmith.
Irving's Sketch Book.
Irving's Tales of a Traveller.
Irving's The Alhambra.
Keary's Heroes of Asgard.
à Kempis: The Imitation of Christ.
Kingsley's The Heroes.
Kingsley's Westward Ho!
Lamb's Tales from Shakespeare.
Lamb's The Essays of Elia.
Letters from Many Pens.

A SERIES OF ENGLISH TEXTS, EDITED FOR USE IN ELEMENTARY AND SECONDARY SCHOOLS, WITH CRITICAL INTRODUCTIONS, NOTES, ETC.

·oln's Addresses, Inaugurals, and
· ·tters.
.hart's Life of Scott. Abridged.
·ɹdon's Call of the Wild.
Longfellow's Evangeline.
Longfellow's Hiawatha.
Longfellow's Miles Standish.
Longfellow's Miles Standish and Minor Poems.
Longfellow's Tales of a Wayside Inn.
Lowell's Earlier Essays.
Lowell's The Vision of Sir Launfal.
Macaulay's Essay on Addison.
Macaulay's Essay on Hastings.
Macaulay's Essay on Lord Clive.
Macaulay's Essay on Milton.
Macaulay's Lays of Ancient Rome.
Macaulay's Life of Samuel Johnson.
Malory's Le Morte d'Arthur.
Milton's Minor Poems.
Milton's Paradise Lost, Books L and II.
Old English Ballads.
Old Testament Selections.
Palgrave's Golden Treasury.
Parkman's Oregon Trail.
Plutarch's Lives of Cæsar, Brutus, and Mark Antony.
Poe's Poems.
Poe's Prose Tales (Selections).
Poems, Narrative and Lyrical.
Pope's Homer's Iliad.
Pope's Homer's Odyssey.
Pope's The Rape of the Lock.
Reade's Cloister and the Hearth.
Representative Short Stories.
Roosevelt's Writings.
Rossetti's (Christina) Selected Poems.
Ruskin's Sesame and Lilies.
Ruskin's The Crown of Wild Olive and Queen of the Air.
Scott's Guy Mannering.
Scott's Ivanhoe.
Scott's Kenilworth.
Scott's Lady of the Lake.
Scott's Lay of the Last Minstrel.
Scott's Marmion.
Scott's Quentin Durward.
Scott's Rob Roy.
Scott's The Talisman.
Select Orations.

Selected Poems, for Required Reading in Secondary Schools.
Selections from American Poetry.
Selections for Oral Reading.
Shakespeare's As You Like It.
Shakespeare's Coriolanus.
Shakespeare's Hamlet.
Shakespeare's Henry V.
Shakespeare's Julius Cæsar.
Shakespeare's King Lear.
Shakespeare's Macbeth.
Shakespeare's Merchant of Venice.
Shakespeare's Midsummer Night's Dream
Shakespeare's Richard H.
Shakespeare's Richard III.
Shakespeare's Romeo and Juliet.
Shakespeare's The Tempest.
Shakespeare's Twelfth Night.
Shelley and Keats: Poems.
Sheridan's The Rivals and The School for Scandal.
Short Stories.
Short Stories and Selections.
Southern Orators: Selections.
Southern Poets: Selections.
Southey's Life of Nelson.
Spenser's Faerie Queene, Book I.
Stevenson's Kidnapped.
Stevenson's The Master of Ballantrae.
Stevenson's Travels with a Donkey, and An Inland Voyage.
Stevenson's Treasure Island.
Swift's Gulliver's Travels.
Tennyson's Idylls of the King.
Tennyson's In Memoriam.
Tennyson's The Princess.
Tennyson's Shorter Poems.
Thackeray's English Humourists.
Thackeray's Henry Esmond.
Thoreau's Walden.
Trevelyan's Life of Macaulay. Abridged.
Virgil's Æneid.
Washington's Farewell Address, and Webster's First Bunker Hill Oration.
Whittier's Snow-Bound and Other Early Poems.
Wister's The Virginian.
Woodman's Journal.
Wordsworth's Shorter Poems.

THE MACMILLAN COMPANY
NEW YORK · BOSTON · CHICAGO · DALLAS
ATLANTA · SAN FRANCISCO

MACMILLAN & CO., Limited
LONDON · BOMBAY · CALCUTTA
MELBOURNE

THE MACMILLAN CO. OF CANADA, Ltd.
TORONTO

THEODORE ROOSEVELT

ROOSEVELT'S WRITINGS

SELECTIONS FROM THE WRITINGS
OF THEODORE ROOSEVELT

EDITED WITH INTRODUCTION AND NOTES

BY MAURICE GARLAND FULTON

ASSISTANT PROFESSOR OF ENGLISH,
INDIANA UNIVERSITY

New York
THE MACMILLAN COMPANY
1920

IN REMEMBRANCE OF

R. B. F.

1849   1919

FROM WHOSE SUGGESTION
THIS BOOK ORIGINATED

" Methinks, 'tis prize enough to be his son."
Shakespeare, 3 Henry VI

PREFACE

My aim has been to bring together passages of appreciable length selected from Theodore Roosevelt's Autobiography and from his more significant writings in the fields of history, adventure, public questions, and natural history. It was in these diverse fields that his wide interests, his intensity and enthusiasm and his habits of clear thinking led him to write vigorously and with authority. In these selections, moreover, are revealed the characteristics of his mind and spirit.

Americanism can best be studied concretely through the careers of great Americans. For such a purpose few lives will be more useful than that of Roosevelt. If this book stimulates among the present and future generations of young Americans an interest in this great man's life and leadership and in his ideals for democracy practically applied, it will have fulfilled my purpose.

My especial thanks are due to Mrs. Edith Carow Roosevelt for permission to use generously material from *Theodore Roosevelt, An Autobiography*, without which this book would have been incomplete.

M. G. F.

BLOOMINGTON, INDIANA.

CONTENTS

INTRODUCTION

ROOSEVELT'S CAREER

ROOSEVELT'S career is so fully presented in the selections from his autobiography included in this book that it is needless to attempt here a sketch of his life. Nevertheless it may be helpful to give the landmarks of his career by the simple but convenient means of a table showing the notable dates.

Born in New York City, October 27, 1858.

Graduated from Harvard University, June 30, 1880.

Married Alice Hathaway Lee, October 27, 1880.

Served in New York State Legislature, 1882–1884.

His first wife died, February 14, 1884.

Spent several years on ranch in North Dakota, 1883–1886.

Candidate for Mayor of New York City, 1886.

Married Edith Kermit Carow, December 2, 1886.

United States Civil Service Commissioner, 1889–1895.

President of the New York Police Board, 1895–1897.

Assistant Secretary of the Navy, 1897–1898.

Lieutenant-Colonel First Volunteer Cavalry, United States Army ("Rough Riders"), May 6, 1898 (later became Colonel).

Elected Governor of New York State, November 8, 1898.

Elected Vice-President of the United States, November 4, 1900.

Succeeded to the Presidency upon the death of President McKinley, September 14, 1901.

Elected President, November 8, 1904.

Awarded Nobel Peace Prize for efforts in connection with the Russo-Japanese Peace Treaty, 1906.

Retired to private life upon expiration of Presidential term, March 4, 1909.

Became contributing editor of *The Outlook*, 1909.

Sailed for Africa on a hunting trip, March 23, 1909.

Returned from African trip, arriving at New York, June 18, 1910.

Announced candidacy for a second nomination for the Presidency, February 25, 1912.

Broke with the Republican Party and formed the Progressive Party, June 22, 1912.

Nominated for President by the Progressive Party, August 7, 1912.

Shot, at Milwaukee, by John Schrank, October 14, 1912.

Defeated for Presidency by Woodrow Wilson, November 5, 1912.

Started on hunting and exploring trip in South America, October 14, 1913.

Discovered and explored the River *Theodore* in Brazil, February to April, 1914.

Returned to New York, May 19, 1914.

Declined Progressive nomination for Presidency and supported Hughes, the Republican nominee, 1916.

After declaration of war with Germany, offered to raise an army division, but the War Department declined his offer, 1917.

Died at Sagamore Hill, January 6, 1919.

A record such as this, even though stripped of all detail

and enlargement, constitutes a most impressive career. But it represents inadequately the variety of Roosevelt's achievements. To do this, it should evidence his knowledge of history equalled by few, his hunting trips and explorations which made him familiar not only with remote parts of his own country but also with two of the less well-known continents, his standing among scientists as an authority on the habits of big game in America and in Africa, his popularity and effectiveness as a speaker, his wide range of reading to which might be applied De-Quincey's description of his own accomplishment. Finally his books and other writings sufficient in number and quality to give him an enduring reputation in the field of letters irrespective of his other achievements. Furthermore his domestic life was filled with the manifold responsibilities of a husband and father, responsibilities which he felt as intensely as those of his public life, and discharged as faithfully. Such diversified ability as this seems to justify the statement made of him that "since Cæsar, perhaps no one has attained among crowded duties and great responsibilities, such high proficiency in so many separate fields of activity."

ROOSEVELT'S PERSONALITY

On more than one occasion Roosevelt said of himself that he was simply a man of ordinary abilities who had made the most of the gifts that were his. He was doubtless sincere in this opinion, but he was undeniably the possessor of native endowments such as come to few men. The elements of his extraordinary personality have been so sympathetically and fairly set forth by his life-long friend, Senator Henry Cabot Lodge, in a memorial address before Congress, that it is desirable to make a lengthy extract.

"Theodore Roosevelt always believed that character was of greater worth and moment than anything else. He possessed abilities of the first order, which he was disposed to underrate because he set so much greater store upon the moral qualities which we bring together under the single word 'character.'

"Let me speak first of his abilities. He had a powerful, well-trained, ever-active mind. He thought clearly, independently, and with originality and imagination. These priceless gifts were sustained by an extraordinary power of acquisition, joined to a greater quickness of apprehension, a greater swiftness in seizing upon the essence of a question, than I have ever happened to see in any other man. His reading began with natural history, then went to general history, and thence to the whole field of literature. He had a capacity for concentration which enabled him to read with remarkable rapidity anything which he took up, if only for a moment, and which separated him for the time being from everything going on about him. The subjects upon which he was well and widely informed would, if enumerated, fill a large space, and to this power of acquisition was united not only a tenacious but an extraordinarily accurate memory. It was never safe to contest with him on any question of fact or figures, whether they related to the ancient Assyrians or to the present-day conditions of the tribes of central Africa, to the Syracusan Expedition, as told by Thucydides, or to protective coloring in birds and animals. He knew and held details always at command, but he was not mastered by them. He never failed to see the forest on account of the trees or the city on account of the houses.

"He made himself a writer, not only of occasional addresses and essays, but of books. He had the trained thoroughness of the historian, as he showed in his history of the War of 1812 and of the *Winning of the West,* and nature had endowed him with that most enviable of gifts, the faculty of narrative and the art of the teller of tales. He knew how to weigh evidence in the historical scales and how to depict character. He learned to write with great ease and fluency. He was always vigorous, always energetic, always clear and forcible in everything he wrote—nobody could ever misunderstand him—and when he allowed himself time and his feelings were deeply engaged he gave to the world many pages of beauty as well as power, not only in thought but in form and style. At the same time he made himself a public speaker, and here again, through a practice probably unequaled in amount, he became one of the most effective in all our history. In speaking, as in writing, he was always full of force and energy; he drove home his arguments and never was misunderstood. In many of his more carefully prepared addresses are to be found passages of impressive eloquence, touched with imagination and instinct with grace and feeling.

"He had a large capacity for administration, clearness of vision, promptness in decision, and a thorough apprehension of what constituted efficient organization. All the vast and varied work which he accomplished could not have been done unless he had had most exceptional natural abilities, but behind them was the driving force of an intense energy and the ever-present belief that a man could do what he willed to do. As he made himself an athlete, a horseman, a good shot, a bold explorer, so he made himself an exceptionally successful writer and speaker. Only a most abnormal energy would have enabled him to enter and conquer in so many fields of intellectual achievement. But something more than energy and determination is needed for the largest success, especially in the world's high places. The first requisite of leadership is ability to lead, and that ability Theodore Roosevelt possessed in full measure. Whether in a game or in the hunting field, in a fight or in politics, he sought the front, where, as Webster once remarked, there is always plenty of room for those who can get there. His instinct was always to say 'come' rather than 'go,' and he had the talent of command.

"The criticism most commonly made upon Theodore Roosevelt was that he was impulsive and impetuous, that he acted without thinking. He would have been the last to claim infallibility. His head did not turn when fame came to him and choruses of admiration sounded in his ears, for he was neither vain nor credulous. He knew that he made mistakes, and never hesitated to admit them to be mistakes and to correct them or put them behind him when satisfied that they were such. But he wasted no time in mourning, explaining, or vainly regretting them. It is also true that the middle way did not attract him. He was apt to go far, both in praise and censure, although nobody could analyze qualities and balance them justly in judging men better than he. He felt strongly, and as he had no concealments of any kind, he expressed himself in like manner. But vehemence is not violence nor is earnestness anger, which a very wise man defined as a brief madness. It was all according to his nature, just as his eager cordiality in meeting men and women, his keen interest in other people's cares or joys, was not assumed, as some persons thought who did not know him. It was all profoundly natural, it was all real, and in that way and in no other was he able to meet and greet his fellow men.

"The feeling that he was impetuous and impulsive was also due to the fact that in a sudden, seemingly unexpected crisis he would act with great rapidity. This happened when he had been for weeks, perhaps for months, considering what he should do if such a crisis arose. He always believed that one of the most important elements of success, whether in public or in private life, was to know what one meant to do under given circumstances. If he saw the possibility of perilous questions arising, it was his practice to think over carefully just how he would act under certain contingencies. Many of the contingencies never arose. Now and then a contingency became an actuality, and then he was ready. He knew what he meant to do, he acted at once, and some critics considered him impetuous, impulsive, and, therefore, dangerous, because they did not know that he had thought the question all out beforehand. Very many people, powerful elements in the community, regarded him at one time as a dangerous radical, bent upon overthrowing all the safeguards of society and planning to tear out the foundations of an ordered liberty. As a matter of fact, what Theodore Roosevelt was trying to do was to strengthen American society and American government by demonstrating to the American people that he was aiming at a larger economic equality and a more generous industrial opportunity for all men, and that any combination of capital or of business, which threatened the control of the Government by the people who made it, was to be curbed and resisted, just as he would have resisted an enemy who tried to take possession of the city of Washington. He had no hostility to a man because he had been successful in business or because he had accumulated a fortune. If the man had been honestly successful and used his fortune wisely and beneficently, he was regarded by Theodore Roosevelt as a good citizen. The vulgar hatred of wealth found no place in his heart. He had but one standard, one test, and that was whether a man, rich or poor, was an honest man, a good citizen, and a good American.

"All men admire courage, and that he possessed in the highest degree. But he had also something larger and rarer than courage, in the ordinary acceptation of the word. When an assassin shot him at Chicago he was severely wounded; how severely he could not tell, but it might well have been mortal. He went on to the great meeting awaiting him and there, bleeding, suffering, ignorant of his fate, but still unconquered, made his speech and went from the stage to the hospital. What bore him up was the dauntless spirit which could rise victorious over pain and darkness and the unknown and meet the duty of the hour as if all were well. A spirit like this awakens in all men more than admiration, it kindles affection and appeals to every generous impulse.

"Very different, but equally compelling, was another quality. There is nothing in human beings at once so sane and so sympathetic as a sense of humor. This great gift the good fairies conferred upon Theodore Roosevelt at his birth in unstinted measure. No man ever had a more abundant sense of humor—joyous, irrepressible humor—

and it never deserted him. Even at the most serious and even perilous moments if there was a gleam of humor anywhere he saw it and rejoiced and helped himself with it over the rough places and in the dark hour. He loved fun, loved to joke and chaff, and, what is more uncommon, greatly enjoyed being chaffed himself. His ready smile and contagious laugh made countless friends and saved him from many an enmity. Even more generally effective than his humor, and yet allied to it, was the universal knowledge that Roosevelt had no secrets from the American people.

"Yet another quality—perhaps the most engaging of all—was his homely, generous humanity which enabled him to speak directly to the primitive instincts of man.

' He dwelt with the tribes of the marsh and moor,
    He sate at the board of kings;
He tasted the toil of the burdened slave
    And the joy that triumph brings.
But whether to jungle or palace hall
    Or white-walled tent he came,
He was brother to king and soldier and slave,
    His welcome was the same.'

"He was very human and intensely American, and this knit a bond between him and the American people which nothing could ever break. And then he had yet one more attraction, not so impressive perhaps as the others, but none the less very important and very captivating. He never by any chance bored the American people. They might laugh at him or laugh with him, they might like what he said or dislike it, they might agree with him or disagree with him, but they were never wearied of him and he never failed to interest them. He was never heavy, laborious, or dull. If he had made any effort to be always interesting and entertaining he would have failed and been tiresome. He was unfailingly attractive because he was always perfectly natural and his own unconscious self. And so all these things combined to give him his hold upon the American people, not only upon their minds but upon their hearts and their instincts, which nothing could ever weaken and which made him one of the most remarkable as he was one of the strongest characters that the history of popular government can show. He was also, and this is very revealing and explanatory, too, of his vast popularity, a man of ideals. He did not expose them daily on the roadside with language fluttering about them like the Thibetan who ties his slip of paper to the prayer wheel whirling in the wind. He kept his ideals to himself until the hour of fulfillment arrived. Some of them were the dreams of boyhood from which he never departed and which I have seen him carry out shyly and yet thoroughly and with intense personal satisfaction.

"He had a touch of the knight errant in his daily life, although he would never have admitted it; but it was there. It was not visible in the medieval form of shining armor and dazzling tournaments but in the never-ceasing effort to help the poor and the oppressed, to defend and protect women and children, to right the wronged and succor the downtrodden. Passing by on the other side was not a mode of travel through life ever possible to him; and yet he was as far distant from the professional philanthropist as could well be imagined, for all he tried to do to help his fellow men he regarded as part of the day's work to be done and not talked about. No man ever prized sentiment or hated sentimentality more than he. He preached unceasingly the familiar morals which lie at the bottom of both family and public life. The blood of some ancestral Scotch covenanter or of some Dutch reformed preacher facing the tyranny of Philip of Spain was in his veins, and with his large opportunities and his vast audiences he was always ready to appeal for justice and righteousness. But his own particular ideals he never attempted to thrust upon the world until the day came when they were to be translated into realities of action.

"When the future historian traces Theodore Roosevelt's extraordinary career he will find these embodied ideals planted like milestones along the road over which he marched. They never left him. His ideal of public service was to be found in his life, and as his life drew to its close he had to meet his ideal of sacrifice face to face. All his sons went from him to the war and one was killed upon the field of honor. Of all the ideals that lift men up, the hardest to fulfill is the ideal of sacrifice. Theodore Roosevelt met it as he had all others and fulfilled it to the last jot of its terrible demands. His country asked the sacrifice and he gave it with solemn pride and uncomplaining lips.

"This is not the place to speak of his private life, but within that sacred circle no man was ever more blessed in the utter devotion of a noble wife and the passionate love of his children. The absolute purity and beauty of his family life tell us why the pride and interest which his fellow countrymen felt in him were always touched with the warm light of love. In the home so dear to him, in his sleep, death came, and—

"So Valiant-for-Truth passed over and all the trumpets sounded for him on the other side."

Roosevelt as a Writer

Of the many sides to Roosevelt's activity, this volume aims to present merely one—his literary work. It has been well said of him that if he had any profession in private life it was that of literature. His fondness for writing began even in college and continued until his death. He enjoyed his literary work thoroughly and always hoped that it would take a larger part in his life than other duties usually permitted. But these other matters were so pressing that Roosevelt could seldom give to his writing more than his spare time. Nevertheless he was able in the midst of manifold duties to accomplish a great deal.

An illustration in point is the way in which he wrote his account of the Rough Riders. Upon his return from Cuba in the summer of 1898, Roosevelt engaged to write an account of the part his regiment had taken in the Spanish-American War. The story was to appear first in *Scribner's Magazine*, and later to be published as a book. A few weeks after agreeing to write the account, he began his vigorous campaign for the Governorship of New York, but neither the campaign nor duties after he took office prevented him from delivering the monthly instalments on schedule time. Of almost every one of his books it might be said that it was written in the spare moments of his busy life as a relaxation from public duties. This circumstance gives force to the remark of John Morley, the English statesman and author, that "Roosevelt was a man of letters temporarily assigned to other duty."

In a survey of Roosevelt's literary achievement, the first impressive feature is its quantity. When Roosevelt's many other activities are taken into consideration, the quantity of his work becomes more significant. The list of his books on page xxxv shows over thirty titles—an accomplishment which in the case of a man giving un-divided attention to writing would be remarkable as an output for a period of about forty years. And when to these books, his major productions, are added the scores of speeches, state papers, magazine articles and newspaper editorials, which as yet are largely uncollected into book form, his work becomes more impressive even when considered merely in respect to quantity.

But a still more striking feature of his literary work is its range. Few writers have equalled Roosevelt in the production of works so varied in kind. He wrote history—*The Naval War of 1812, The Winning of the West, A History of New York*. He wrote biography—lives of Benton, Morris, and Oliver Cromwell. He described in books of travel and adventure his hunting and exploring trips in the Rocky Mountains, in Africa, and in South America. His more important magazine articles and speeches dealing with problems of government and citizenship were collected into volumes such as *American Ideals, The Strenuous Life*, and *History as Literature*. He wrote also much on natural history—*The Deer Family in America* and *Life History of African Game Animals*, being notable books in this field. In addition to all these different types of books, mention must be made of his autobiography, his lectures, his orations, his state papers, and his editorials.

With all their extent and variety, Roosevelt's writings would not deserve attention unless they were solid and important contributions in their several fields. That most of them have permanent value of this kind seems to be the verdict of those competent to judge. In particular is this true of his work in history and the kindred field of biography. Of his several books in this field, the four volumes of *The Winning of the West*,—a brilliant and accurate account of the deeds of the frontiersmen in Kentucky, Tennessee, and the Old Northwest, covering the closing years of the eighteenth century and the opening ones of the nineteenth, are alone sufficient to establish Roosevelt's position as an historian. This book deservedly ranks with the best historical writings that America has produced.

Roosevelt's books of travel and adventure also possess unquestioned value. Those relating to his experiences in the Far West contain unique pictures of the vanished frontier life, this being especially true of the volume *Ranch Life and Hunting Trail*. The books treating of his African and his South American trips contain not only interesting adventures but also valuable scientific information. Upon this point, Sir H. H. Johnston, an English explorer and authority on Africa whose opinion is entirely unprejudiced, says with reference especially to *African Game Trails*, "We should like to see Mr. Roosevelt's book take its place in the ranks of Bates's *Naturalist in the Amazons*, Schillings' *With Flash Light and Rifle*, and works of that character. He is a good zoölogist and a peculiarly accurate and discriminating observer. Although he has traversed lands visited by some of the greatest naturalist explorers of the world, he has still made discoveries himself, or through others, and records a great many facts not hitherto known about the life history of beasts and birds in Equatorial East Africa." A similar statement could be made regarding the interest and scientific value of his later book, *Through the Brazilian Wilderness*.

The above quotation suggests the standing which Roosevelt's observations on the habits of mammals and birds have among naturalists. Most of his writing in this field was done incidentally to his accounts of his hunting trips. There is comparatively little of this material in his earlier writings, such as *Hunting Trips of a Ranchman, Ranch Life and the Hunting Trail, The Wilderness Hunter,* but there is more and more of it in the later books, such as *Out Door Pastimes of an American Hunter, African Game Trails* and *Through the Brazilian Wilderness.* Roosevelt was regretful that he did not devote more space in these first books to natural history. "I vaguely supposed," he said in later life, "that the obvious facts on the habits of the animals were known and let most of my opportunities pass by." Books especially devoted to this subject, such as *The Deer Family in America,* and *Life Histories of African Game Animals,* contain important contributions to natural history and show that Roosevelt possessed the qualifications of a naturalist,—keenness of observation, clearness of mind, accuracy in deduction, and absolute regard for truth. Roosevelt was, of course, not a scientist or a biologist in the narrower sense of the term. He cared nothing for the so-called "closet" study of natural history, but made his interest the study of the living animal in its habitat. As John Burroughs says of him, "He was a naturalist on the broadest grounds, uniting much technical knowledge with knowledge of the daily lives and habits of all forms of wild life." One result at least of Roosevelt's natural history writings has been to remind his countrymen of the spirit of love, of zeal, and of intelligence with which they should approach nature in any of its wonderful aspects.

When we turn to that section of Roosevelt's writings containing his addresses, essays, state papers, and miscellaneous writings, we come to the part of his work which has the least merit in a literary sense. Nevertheless these productions constitute a body of political idealism which the future will not overlook, the underlying ideas of which have been well summarized by Mr. Harold Howland as follows: "First he believed in a sternly moral standard of conduct. Right is right and wrong is wrong. It does not make wrong right to say that it is done in defense of property, on the one hand, or, on the other, done in behalf of the people. . . . Secondly, he believed in democracy. He believed in it, not in any theoretical, doctrinaire fashion, but with peculiar concreteness and directness. . . . Thirdly, he laid a compelling emphasis upon the responsibility of the individual citizen as the primary condition of national progress. . . . Lastly, he held to the golden middle course, not tepidly or timorously, but with the zeal and the conviction of a crusader. He was a middle-of-the-road man, not because he was unwilling or afraid to commit himself to the position on either side, but he found the way to truth to lie midway between the two extremes. He was a zealot and a fighter for the truth, justice and righteousness. He found no monopoly of any one of these precious possessions in the camp of the extremists on either side. . . . This was the fourfold structure of his creed: righteousness, democracy, individual character, and the true balance between opposing forces." [1]

Against the underlying ideas in Roosevelt's speeches

[1] "Theodore Roosevelt and his Times," *Independent*, January 19, 1919.

and essays the charge of commonplaceness has sometimes been brought. The truth of the charge may be admitted, but it must be added that it was no ordinary and dull use of the commonplace. With Roosevelt the ordinary took on the air of extreme novelty because he imparted to it energy and passion. In regard to his ability to do this, it has been said, "He did not content himself with a bare statement that children ought to love their fathers and mothers. In his hands the obvious became a flaming sword. He would wave it vehemently above his head and defy the world to deny that crime ought to be punished and virtue rewarded. Such zest and joy did he put into his vigorous enunciations of what all sane men agree to be true, that he somehow appeared, even when uttering platitudes, a great moral and political discoverer." Such ability to vivify ordinary routine thoughts and sentiments connotes high mental talents and a rush of soul of a kind to which not inaptly might be applied the term genius. Certainly many of the world's writers who have been most influential with the mass of mankind have had a gift of this kind, and it ought not be derogatory to Roosevelt's work that he was successful in this way.

Another charge brought sometimes against Roosevelt's work is its redundancy. It is asserted that he was always reiterating the same ideas, and it is easy to perceive that especially in his speeches, Roosevelt nearly always boxed the compass of his favorite ideas. This makes much reading in the speeches tedious, but in apology it may be said that it was the method best adapted to the purpose of Roosevelt. He clearly felt himself to be a teacher to his generation, and he used, as all similar leaders have done, the teacher's method of line upon line and

precept upon precept. Wearisome though the method
may be, yet this drawback must be overlooked in the light
of the results. As Colquhoun, an English student of
Roosevelt's life and work remarks, "But what Roosevelt
has accomplished in awakening a public conscience, and
when we remember that this was primarily one of his aims,
we can forgive the redundancy of some of his public utter-
ances. There is no better way to make truth believed by
the masses than that suggested by Lewis Carroll: 'He said
it very loud and clear; he went and shouted it in my ear.'
Roosevelt's success as a propagandist has been due to his
saying things very loud and clear."

From this mass of speeches and articles Roosevelt himself has selected what he cared to preserve in book form,
and has included it in the three volumes, *American Ideals*,
The Strenuous Life, and *History as Literature*. Of these
books, *American Ideals* is in large measure the repository
of many of Roosevelt's favorite political ideas. *The
Strenuous Life* deals with ideals of conduct and citizenship in a larger and more general way. *History as Literature* is more significant than the other two books. While
it presents also ideals of citizenship, it has a wider range
embracing especially comments on books and writers
of such searching character as to give force to the remark
someone made in connection with Roosevelt, "We have
half or more than half a suspicion that an admirable
literary critic was lost to the world when Mr. Roosevelt
became a public character."

We have seen how in the diverse fields of history, adventure, natural science, and political discussion, Roosevelt has left solid and substantial contributions. But this
sketch must not close without reference to another book

which is in some respects the most important single volume he produced. This is his autobiography entitled *Theodore Roosevelt, An Autobiography*. Written a few years after Roosevelt had returned to private life, the book was too close in time to the excitement of the writer's political career, and accordingly it is in large measure a justification of measures and policies. Nevertheless it will continue to attract readers not only because of its value as a record of a very significant political period from the pen of the one who was the leader in it, but also because of the intimate and attractive revelation of the man Roosevelt.

Herein are clearly exhibited his different interests. Herein are uncovered the characteristics of his mind and spirit. As Brander Matthews has remarked, "It is a very human personality that is so disclosed; very engaging and very energetic; tingling with vitality, endowed with the zest of life and the gusto of living; not unduly self-conscious; interested in himself, no doubt, like the rest of us, but scarcely more than he is interested in many others; possessed of abundant humor and good humor; able to take a joke even when it is against himself; and enriched with an unsurpassed gift for friendship."

It seems possible that the Autobiography will as time goes on be ranked with that of Franklin. These two happened to be the most interesting Americans of their generations, the one at the close of the eighteenth century, the other at the close of the nineteenth and the beginning of the twentieth. It must, however, be borne in mind that the conditions of composition of the two autobiographies were different. Franklin in his old age wrote out his recollections, not for general publications, but for his children. Roosevelt in the midst of his career wrote his memoir largely to justify his political actions. Possibly in this difference may be found the cause why Franklin's sketch of himself will exceed Roosevelt's in general interest, but if the latter were freed from the weight of the explanations of political matters and left with merely the passages of more direct autobiographical interest, it might rival Franklin's book in popularity. Even as it is, the Autobiography drew from an American critic, Professor W. P. Trent, the statement that it belonged "to the very small group of books—witness Dr. Johnson—which a reasonable man could wish longer."

ROOSEVELT'S STYLE

BECAUSE Roosevelt wrote so much and that usually under the most unfavorable circumstances, there is the inpression in the minds of many that he dashed off his work with little or no effort. Nothing, however, is farther from the truth. Roosevelt was painstaking and conscientious in his writing not alone in those things he wrote with a feeling of their importance as literature but even in those he wrote in more or less of a routine way. When he was doing editorial work for *The Outlook*, he did articles with great care although knowing that in most instances they were ephemeral in their appeal. "No one knows how much time I put into my articles for *The Outlook*," he once said to a friend. Then, pulling a manuscript from his pocket, he continued, "Here is an article that I am going over, as I have opportunity, correcting and recasting it."

Father Zahm who accompanied Roosevelt on the

South African trip and who had opportunity to see his methods of work in writing in the field for magazine publication the account of that trip, gives testimony of the same sort. "Colonel Roosevelt," he says "did not by any means write as rapidly as is generally supposed. He was too careful a literary craftsman for that. Nor had he the facility sometimes credited to him. He put into his magazine work far more thought and labor than is usually imagined. After an article was written, he revised it carefully, correcting, changing, amplifying and excising until certain of the pages were scarcely decipherable." [1]

This carefulness in expression extended also to his speeches, especially in the case of the more important. Mr. D. W. Lewis gives in his *Life of Theodore Roosevelt* an instance of this thorough preparation in the case of the important Carnegie Hall address delivered in New York City, March 20th 1912. Mr. Lewis and another friend had been invited to Oyster Bay for a conference over the matter. Says Mr. Lewis, "We found that the speech was already in manuscript form. I think the copy we used was the second or third revision. At any rate, the Colonel himself had already made numerous corrections in pencil." Roosevelt was ready to accept criticism and take suggestions,—in fact almost too ready to do so, thinks Mr. Lewis. "He read the typewritten sheets aloud," continues Mr. Lewis, "not minding in the least if one or the other of us interrupted him before he had completed a single sentence. When some time after twelve o'clock, we had apparently reached the end, he said: 'I shall have to sit up and go over this again tonight.'"

Further interesting insight into Roosevelt's methods of

[1] Roosevelt as a Hunter-Naturalist. *Outlook*, 121: 438.

composition is given in a vivid account by Mr. F. E. Leupp.[1] "Most of his original composing is done on feet, pacing up and down the room and dictating to a stenographer. He does not even see how his periods hang together till they have been reduced to typewritten form and the sheets laid upon his desk. Then, when an interval of reduced tension comes, his eye falls upon the manuscript and lingers there. . . . His left hand lifts the top sheet while the right gropes for a pen, and in a moment the author is quite buried in his work, annotating between the lines as he reads.

"The friend who is with him probably respects his mood and subsides into a sofa-corner, or warms his hands before the fire, or amuses himself at the window till the first force of absorption has spent itself and Mr. Roosevelt lifts his head to remark, 'Now, here is where I believe I have made a point never before brought out,' and proceeds to read aloud a passage and descant upon it. If this impromptu enlargement transcends certain bounds, the speaker is on his feet again in an instant and pacing the floor as he talks. Sentence follows sentence from his lips like shots from the muzzle of a magazine-gun—all well-timed and well-aimed in spite of their swiftness of utterance. The chances are that one of them will recoil to impress its author afresh with its aptness, and back he will slide into the vacant chair to put that idea into visible form with his pen and wedge it in between two others."

Roosevelt's methods of composing help us to understand certain features of his style. In general it is clear rather than elegant, and like the man himself, characterized by force and emphatic power rather than by

[1] *The Man Roosevelt*, Chapter XVII.

polish and rhetorical refinement. The oral method of composition that has been mentioned is perhaps responsible for two of its noticeable defects,—looseness of structure and frequent repetition. A third defect,—extravagance of statement, is probably temperamental. To quote again from Mr. Leupp, "Mr. Roosevelt fairly lives in an atmosphere of superlatives. He will speak of a 'perfectly good man with a perfectly honest motive,' where all he intends to say is that the man is well-meaning. He is 'delighted' where most of us are pleased. The latest visitor is 'just the very man I wanted to see,' and 'nothing I have heard in a long time has interested me so much,' is the passing bit of information. A fourth defect, encountered occasionally, is some slight grammatical lapse— a too great use, perhaps, of the split infinitive, an ambiguous use of pronouns or participles, or some other carelessness in syntactical matters. These, however, are simply evidences that Roosevelt rated the expressiveness of language above its correctness, and he would have been ready to take refuge behind the words of Thomas Jefferson, 'Whenever by small grammatical negligence the energy of an idea can be condensed or a word be made to stand for a sentence, I hold grammatical rigor in contempt,' or the remark of Henry Ward Beecher to the person who was speaking of grammatical faults in one of Beecher's sermons, 'Young man, when the English language gets in my way it doesn't stand a chance.'"

But what stamps any writer as great is not freedom from faults but abundance of powers. Roosevelt's style has its positive excellencies. Foremost of all, it possesses the quality of energy and vividness. He always shows the artist's eye for the concrete and picturesque, and avails himself of this gift not only in his narrative writings but as well in his essays and speeches. At times the reader becomes conscious of a great pent-up force of feeling and enthusiasm expressing itself in some striking and eloquent passage such as those which may be found in several of the selections in this book. He had also the gift of terse, epigrammatic expression which gave currency to many of his expressions in a widespread degree that was most remarkable. Sometimes he would dredge up from the past a word or phrase and give it modern use. An instance is the expression "muck-raking." This was as old as *Pilgrim's Progress*, but it was Roosevelt's use of the word that put it into everybody's vocabulary. More frequently the words or phrases were of his own coinage. "Malefactors of great wealth," "the big stick," and "weasel words" are a few samples of the dozens of such expressions that might be given.

A fitting close to these remarks on Roosevelt's style is the comment made by Professor Trent of the English department of Columbia University in a review of *The Winning of the West:* " When he is at his best, Mr. Roosevelt writes as well as any man need desire to write, who is not aiming at that elusive glory of being considered a master of style. The truth of this statement will be plain to any one who will take the trouble to analyze the impression made by a rapid reading of the chapter describing the fight at King's Mountain. The effect can be summed up in a brief sentence—You are at the battle. Surely this is a better test of the quality of a man's style than can ever be furnished by minute rhetorical analysis, which would, I suspect, convict Mr. Roosevelt of offences at which a pedant would shake his head."

BIBLIOGRAPHY

ROOSEVELT'S BOOKS

The Naval War of 1812 (1882).
Hunting Trips of a Ranchman (1885).
Life of Thomas Hart Benton (1887).
The Wilderness Hunter (1887).
Life of Gouverneur Morris (1888).
Ranch Life and Hunting Trail (1888).
Essays on Practical Politics (1888).
The Winning of the West, 4 vols. (1889–1896).
New York City. A History (1891).
American Big Game Hunting (with George Bird Grinnell) (1893).
Claws and Antlers of the Rocky Mountains (1894).
Hero Tales from American History (with Henry Cabot Lodge) (1895).
Hunting in Many Lands (with George Bird Grinnell) (1895).
American Ideals (1897, enlarged 1907).
The Rough Riders (1898).
The Strenuous Life (1900).
Oliver Cromwell (1901).
Addresses and Presidential Messages (1904).
The Deer Family (1902).
Outdoor Pastimes of an American Hunter (1906).
Good Hunting (1907).
African Game Trails (1910).
Realizable Ideals (1912).
Conservation of Womanhood and Childhood (1912).
History as Literature (1913).

Theodore Roosevelt, An Autobiography (1913).
Life Histories of African Game Animals, 2 vols. (1914).
Through the Brazilian Wilderness (1914).
America and the World War (1915).
A Booklover's Holidays in the Open (1916).
Fear God and Take Your Own Part (1916)..
The Great Adventure (1917).
Theodore Roosevelt's Letters to his Children (edited by J. B.
    Bishop) (1919).

BIOGRAPHIES OF ROOSEVELT

Douglas, G. W., *The Many-Sided Roosevelt.*
Hagedorn, H., *Boy's Life of Roosevelt.*
Iglehart, F. C., *Theodore Roosevelt: The Man as I Knew
    Him.*
Leupp, F. E., *The Man Roosevelt.*
Morgan, J., *Theodore Roosevelt, the Boy and the Man.*
Lewis, W. D., *The Life of Theodore Roosevelt.*
Riis, J. A., *Theodore Roosevelt the Citizen.*
Street, J. L., *The Most Interesting American.*
Thayer, W. R., *Theodore Roosevelt.*
Thwing, E., *Theodore Roosevelt.*
Washburn, C. G., *Theodore Roosevelt, the Logic of his
    Career.*

MAGAZINE ARTICLES RELATING TO ROOSEVELT

The following selections from the magazine writing
about Roosevelt give interesting details about various
aspects of his career:

The Man

"Roosevelt—A Character Sketch" (Julian Ralph), *Review of Reviews*, Vol. 12, page 159.

"Estimate of Roosevelt" (G. Horton), *Reader*, Vol. 4, page 19.

"Keynote of Roosevelt's Character" (B. Gilman), *Review of Reviews*, Vol. 46, page 303.

"Characterization of Roosevelt's Personal Qualities" (Mark Sullivan), *Collier's Weekly*, Vol. 42, page 21.

"Theodore Roosevelt" (A. R. Colquhoun), *Fortnightly Review*, Vol. 93, page 832.

"The Personality of Roosevelt" (W. G. Brown), *Independent*, Vol. 55, page 1547.

"Roosevelt in Retrospect" (M. F. Egan), *Atlantic Monthly*, Vol. 123, page 676.

"Theodore Roosevelt" (C. G. Washburn), *Harvard Graduate's Magazine*, Vol. 27, page 451.

"My Neighbor, Theodore Roosevelt" (H. Garland), *Everybody's Magazine*, Vol. 41, page 9.

The Politician

"Roosevelt as a Practical Politician" (Brander Matthews), *Outlook*, Vol. 122, page 433.

"Roosevelt, A Force for Righteousness" (W. A. White), *McClure's Magazine*, Vol. 28, page 386.

"President Roosevelt" (H. T. Peck), *Bookman*, Vol. 23, page 300.

"Theodore Roosevelt and his Times Shown in his Own Letters" (J. B. Bishop), *Scribner's Magazine*, Vol. 66, pages 257, 385, 515, 650.

"High Lights of Roosevelt's Two Administrations" (Anon.), *Century*, Vol. 77, page 954.

"Roosevelt the Politician" (F. E. Leupp), *Atlantic Monthly*, Vol. 109, page 843.

"Theodore Roosevelt and His Times" (H. H. Howland), *Independent*, Vol. 97, page 83.

"Roosevelt and the National Psychology" (Stuart P. Sherman), *Nation*, Vol. 109, page 599.

The Out-of-Doors Man

"Roosevelt—Cowboy and Ranchman" (W. T. Dantz), *Harper's Weekly*, Vol. 48, page 1212.

"Roosevelt as an Outdoor Man" (H. B. Needham), *McClure's Magazine*, Vol. 36, page 231.

"Roosevelt the Athlete" (A. Day), *Putnam's Magazine*, Vol. 4, page 659.

"Roosevelt the Greatest Outdoor Man" (A. K. Willyoung), *Outing*, Vol. 74, pages 273, 355; Vol. 75, page 21.

"Roosevelt the Husbandman" (H. J. Forman), *Review of Reviews*, Vol. 42, page 173.

"Roosevelt as a Volunteer Soldier" (H. E. Armstrong), *Independent*, Vol. 53, page 2277.

The Naturalist

"Colonel Roosevelt as an Explorer" (V. Stepansson), *Review of Reviews*, Vol. 59, page 165.

"Theodore Roosevelt as a Hunter Naturalist" (Father Zahm), *Outlook*, Vol. 121, page 434.

"The Wilderness Hunter" (Anon.), *Atlantic Monthly*, Vol. 75, page 286.

"Camping with Roosevelt" (John Burroughs), *Atlantic Monthly*, Vol. 97, page 585.

"Roosevelt as Nature-lover and Observer" (John Burroughs), *Outlook*, Vol. 86, page 547.

"Roosevelt as an Explorer" (Anon.), *Littell's Living Age*, Vol. 282, page 189.

"Theodore Roosevelt as a Naturalist" (H. H. Johnston), *Littell's Living Age*, Vol. 281, page 373.

"Roosevelt's Visit to South America" (Father Zahm), *Review of Reviews*, Vol. 50, page 81.

The Writer

"Man of Letters in the White House" (J. B. Gilder), *Critic*, Vol. 39, page 401.

"Roosevelt as a Man of Letters" (H. A. Beers), *Yale Review*, Vol. 8, page 694.

"Writings of Roosevelt" (G. R. Johnston), *Book Buyer*, Vol. 18, page 5.

"Roosevelt as a Journalist" (Lyman Abbott), *Outlook*, Vol. 107, page 642.

"Mr. Roosevelt as a Letter Writer" (J. B. Gilder), *Bellman*, Vol. 26, page 103.

"Roosevelt as a Historian" (W. P. Trent), *Forum*, Vol. 21, page 566.

"Roosevelt as a Reader" (Anon.), *Century Magazine*, Vol. 69, page 951.

ROOSEVELT'S WRITINGS

ROOSEVELT'S WRITINGS

AUTOBIOGRAPHY

BOYHOOD AND YOUTH [1]

On October 27, 1858, I was born at No. 28 East Twen-tieth Street, New York City, in the house in which we lived during the time that my two sisters and my brother and I were small children. It was furnished in the canon-ical taste of the New York which George William Curtis° 5 described in the "Potiphar Papers." The black hair-cloth furniture in the dining-room scratched the bare legs of the children when they sat on it. The middle room was a library, with tables, chairs, and bookcases of gloomy respectability. It was without windows, and so 10 was available only at night. The front room, the parlor, seemed to us children to be a room of much splendor, but was open for general use only on Sunday evening or on rare occasions when there were parties. The Sunday evening family gathering was the redeeming feature in a 15 day which otherwise we children did not enjoy—chiefly because we were all of us made to wear clean clothes and keep neat. The ornaments of that parlor I remember now, including the gas chandelier decorated with a great quan-

[1] This and the succeeding autobiographical selections are reprinted from *Theodore Roosevelt, An Autobiography*, by permission of Mrs. Roosevelt and the holder of the copyright, the Macmillan Company.

tity of cut-glass prisms. These prisms struck me as possessing peculiar magnificence. One of them fell off one day,
and I hastily grabbed it and stowed it away, passing several
days of furtive delight in the treasure, a delight always
5 alloyed with fear that I would be found out and con-
victed of larceny. There was a Swiss wood-carving rep-
resenting a very big hunter on one side of an exceedingly
small mountain, and a herd of chamois, disproportion-
ately small for the hunter and large for the mountain,
10 just across the ridge. This always fascinated us; but
there was a small chamois kid for which we felt agonies
lest the hunter might come on it and kill it. There was
also a Russian moujik ° drawing a gilt sledge on a piece of
malachite.° Some one mentioned in my hearing that
15 malachite was a valuable marble. This fixed in my mind
that it was valuable exactly as diamonds are valuable.
I accepted that moujik as a priceless work of art, and it
was not until I was well in middle age that it occurred to
me that I was mistaken.
20   The summers we spent in the country, now at one place
now at another. We children of course loved the country
beyond anything. We disliked the city. We were always
wildly eager to get to the country when spring came, and
very sad when in the late fall the family moved back to
25 town. In the country we of course had all kinds of pets—
cats, dogs, rabbits, a coon, and a sorrel Shetland pony
named General Grant. When my younger sister first
heard of the real General Grant,° by the way, she was
much struck by the coincidence that some one should
30 have given him the same name as the pony. (Thirty
years later my own children had *their* pony Grant.) In
the country we children ran barefoot much of the time,

and the seasons went by in a round of uninterrupted and enthralling pleasures—supervising the haying and harvesting, picking apples, hunting frogs successfully and woodchucks unsuccessfully, gathering hickory-nuts and chestnuts for sale to patient parents, building wigwams 5 in the woods, and sometimes playing Indians in too realistic manner by staining ourselves (and incidentally our clothes) in liberal fashion with poke-cherry juice. Thanksgiving was an appreciated festival, but it in no way came up to Christmas. Christmas was an occasion of literally 10 delirious joy. In the evening we hung up our stockings— or rather the biggest stockings we could borrow from the grown-ups—and before dawn we trooped in to open them while sitting on father's and mother's bed; and the bigger presents were arranged, those for each child on its own 15 table, in the drawing-room, the doors to which were thrown open after breakfast. I never knew any one else have what seemed to me such attractive Christmases, and in the next generation I tried to reproduce them exactly for my own children.   20

My father, Theodore Roosevelt,° was the best man I ever knew. He combined strength and courage with gentleness, tenderness, and great unselfishness. He would not tolerate in us children selfishness or cruelty, idleness, cowardice, or untruthfulness. As we grew older he made 25 us understand that the same standard of clean living was demanded for the boys as for the girls; that what was wrong in a woman could not be right in a man. With great love and patience, and the most understanding sympathy and consideration, he combined insistence on 30 discipline. He never physically punished me but once, but he was the only man of whom I was ever really afraid.

I do not mean that it was a wrong fear, for he was entirely just, and we children adored him. We used to wait in the evening until we could hear his key rattling in the latch of the front hall, and then rush out to greet him; and we 5 would troop into his room while he was dressing, to stay there as long as we were permitted, eagerly examining anything which came out of his pockets which could be regarded as an attractive novelty. Every child has fixed in his memory various details which strike it as of grave 10 importance. The trinkets he used to keep in a little box on his dressing-table we children always used to speak of as "treasures." The word, and some of the trinkets themselves, passed on to the next generation. My own children, when small, used to troop into my room while I was dress- 15 ing, and the gradually accumulating trinkets in the "ditty-box"—the gift of an enlisted man in the navy—always excited rapturous joy. On occasions of solemn festivity each child would receive a trinket for his or her "very own." My own children, when very small, by the way, 20 enjoyed one pleasure I do not remember enjoying myself. When I came back from riding, the child who brought the bootjack would itself promptly get into the boots, and clump up and down the room with a delightful feeling of kinship with Jack of the seven-league strides.

25 The punishing incident I have referred to happened when I was four years old. I bit my elder sister's arm. I do not remember biting her arm, but I do remember running down to the yard, perfectly conscious that I had committed a crime. From the yard I went into the kitchen, 30 got some dough from the cook, and crawled under the kitchen table. In a minute or two my father entered from the yard and asked where I was. The warm-hearted

Irish cook had a characteristic contempt for "informers," but although she said nothing she compromised between informing and her conscience by casting a look under the table. My father immediately darted for me under the table. I feebly heaved the dough at him, and, having the 5 advantage of him because I could stand up under the table, got a fair start for the stairs, but was caught halfway up them. The punishment that ensued fitted the crime, and I hope—and believe—that it did me good.

10

My mother, Martha Bulloch,° was a sweet, gracious, beautiful Southern woman, a delightful companion and be-loved by everybody. She was entirely "unreconstructed"° to the day of her death. Her mother, my grandmother, one of the dearest of old ladies, lived with us, and was dis- 15 tinctly over-indulgent to us children, being quite unable to harden her heart towards us even when the occasion demanded it. Towards the close of the Civil War, although a very small boy, I grew to have a partial but alert under-standing of the fact that the family were not one in their 20 views about that conflict, my father being a strong Lincoln Republican; and once, when I felt that I had been wronged by maternal discipline during the day, I attempted a par-tial vengeance by praying with loud fervor for the success of the Union arms, when we all came to say our prayers 25 before my mother in the evening. She was not only a most devoted mother, but was also blessed with a strong sense of humor, and she was too much amused to punish me; but I was warned not to repeat the offense, under penalty of my father's being informed—he being the dispenser of 30 serious punishment. Morning prayers were with my father. We used to stand at the foot of the stairs, and when father

came down we called out, "I speak for you and the cubby-
hole too!" There were three of us young children, and
we used to sit with father on the sofa while he conducted
morning prayers. The place between father and the arm
5 of the sofa we called the "cubby-hole." The child who
got that place we regarded as especially favored both in
comfort and somehow or other in rank and title. The two
who were left to sit on the much wider expanse of sofa on
the other side of father were outsiders for the time being.
10   My Aunt Anna, my mother's sister, lived with us. She
was as devoted to us children as was my mother herself,
and we were equally devoted to her in return. She taught
us our lessons while we were little. She and my mother
used to entertain us by the hour with tales of life on the
15 Georgia plantations; of hunting fox, deer, and wildcat;
of the long-tailed driving horses, Boone and Crockett,°
and of the riding horses, one of which was named Buena
Vista° in a fit of patriotic exaltation during the Mexican
War; and of the queer goings on in the Negro quarters.
20 She knew all the "Br'er Rabbit"° stories, and I was
brought up on them. One of my uncles, Robert Roosevelt,
was much struck with them, and took them down from
her dictation, publishing them in "Harper's"° where
they fell flat. This was a good many years before a genius°
25 arose who in "Uncle Remus" made the stories immortal.

I was a sickly, delicate boy, suffered much from asthma,
and frequently had to be taken away on trips to find a
place where I could breathe. One of my memories is of
30 my father walking up and down the room with me in his
arms at night when I was a very small person, and of sitting up in bed gasping, with my father and mother trying

to help me. I went very little to school. I never went to
the public schools, as my own children later did, both at
the "Cove school" at Oyster Bay and at the "Ford school"
in Washington. For a few months I attended Professor
McMullen's school in Twentieth Street near the house 5
where I was born, but most of the time I had tutors. As I
have already said, my aunt taught me when I was small.
At one time we had a French governess, a loved and valued
"mam'selle," in the household.

10

While still a small boy I began to take interest in natural
history.° I remember distinctly the first day that I started
on my career as zoölogist. I was walking up Broadway,
and as I passed the market to which I used sometimes to
be sent before breakfast to get strawberries I suddenly 15
saw a dead seal laid out on a slab of wood. That seal filled
me with every possible feeling of romance and adventure.
I asked where it was killed, and was informed in the harbor.
I had already begun to read some of Mayne Reid's books °
and other boys' books of adventure, and I felt that this 20
seal brought all these adventures in realistic fashion before me. As long as that seal remained there I haunted
the neighborhood of the market day after day. I measured
it, and I recall that, not having a tape measure, I had
to do my best to get its girth with a folding pocket 25
foot-rule, a difficult undertaking. I carefully made
a record of the utterly useless measurements, and at
once began to write a natural history of my own, on
the strength of that seal. This, and subsequent natural
histories, were written down in blank books in simplified 30
spelling wholly unpremeditated and unscientific. I had
vague aspirations of in some way or another owning and

preserving that seal, but they never got beyond the purely
formless stage. I think, however, I did get the seal's
skull, and with two of my cousins promptly started what
we ambitiously called the "Roosevelt Museum of Na-
5 tural History." The collections were at first kept in my
room, until a rebellion on the part of the chambermaid
received the approval of the higher authorities of the
household and the collection was moved up to a kind of
bookcase in the back hall upstairs. It was the ordinary
10 small boy's collection of curios, quite incongruous and
entirely valueless except from the standpoint of the boy
himself. My father and mother encouraged me warmly
in this, as they always did in anything that would give
me wholesome pleasure or help to develop me.
15 The adventure of the seal and the novels of Mayne
Reid together strengthened my instinctive interest in
natural history. I was too young to understand much
of Mayne Reid, excepting the adventure part and
the natural history part—these enthralled me. But of
20 course my reading was not wholly confined to natural
history. There was very little effort made to compel
me to read books, my mother and father having the
good sense not to try to get me to read anything I did
not like, unless it was in the way of study. I was given
25 the chance to read books that they thought I ought
to read, but if I did not like them I was then given some
other good book that I did like.

Quite unknown to myself, I was, while a boy, under
30 a hopeless disadvantage in studying nature. I was very
near-sighted, so that the only things I could study were
those I ran against or stumbled over. When I was about

thirteen I was allowed to take lessons in taxidermy from a Mr. Bell, a tall, clean-shaven, white-haired old gentleman, as straight as an Indian, who had been a companion of Audubon's.° He had a musty little shop, somewhat on the order of Mr. Venus's shop° in "Our Mutual Friend," a 5 little shop in which he had done very valuable work for science. This "vocational study," as I suppose it would be called by modern educators, spurred and directed my interest in collecting specimens for mounting and preservation. It was this summer that I got my first gun, 10 and it puzzled me to find that my companions seemed to see things to shoot at which I could not see at all. One day they read aloud an advertisement in huge letters on a distant billboard, and I then realized that something was the matter, for not only was I unable to read the sign 15 but I could not even see the letters. I spoke of this to my father, and soon afterwards got my first pair of spectacles, which literally opened an entirely new world to me. I had no idea how beautiful the world was until I got those spectacles. I had been a clumsy and awkward 20 little boy, and while much of my clumsiness and awkwardness was doubtless due to general characteristics, a good deal of it was due to the fact that I could not see and yet was wholly ignorant that I was not seeing. The recollection of this experience gives me a keen sympathy with those 25 who are trying in our public schools and elsewhere to remove the physical causes of deficiency in children, who are often unjustly blamed for being obstinate or unambitious, or mentally stupid.

This same summer, too, I obtained various new books 30 on mammals and birds, including the publications of Spencer Baird°, for instance, and made an industrious book-

study of the subject. I did not accomplish much in outdoor study because I did not get spectacles until late in
the fall, a short time before I started with the rest of the
family for a second trip to Europe.° We were living at
5 Dobbs Ferry, on the Hudson. My gun was a breech-
loading, pin-fire double-barrel, of French manufacture. It
was an excellent gun for a clumsy and often absent-minded
boy. There was no spring to open it, and if the mechanism became rusty it could be opened with a brick with-
10 out serious damage. When the cartridges stuck they
could be removed in the same fashion. If they were
loaded, however, the result was not always happy, and I
tattooed myself with partially unburned grains of powder
more than once.

15
In the fall of 1876 I entered Harvard,° graduating in
1880. I thoroughly enjoyed Harvard, and I am sure it
did me good, but only in the general effect, for there was
very little in my actual studies which helped me in after
20 life. More than one of my own sons have already profited by their friendship with certain of their masters in
school or college. I certainly profited by my friendship
with one of my tutors, Mr. Cutler;° and in Harvard I owed
much to the professor of English, Mr. A. S. Hill.° Doubt-
25 less through my own fault, I saw almost nothing of President Eliot° and very little of the professors. I ought to
have gained much more than I did gain from writing the
themes and forensics.° My failure to do so may have
been partly due to my taking no interest in the subjects.
30 Before I left Harvard I was already writing one or two
chapters of a book I afterwards published on the Naval
War of 1812. Those chapters were so dry that they would

have made a dictionary seem light reading by comparison. Still, they represented purpose and serious interest on my part, not the perfunctory effort to do well enough to get a certain mark; and corrections of them by a skilled older man than myself would have impressed me and have 5 commanded my respectful attention. But I was not sufficiently developed to make myself take an intelligent interest in some of the subjects assigned me—the character of the Gracchi,° for instance. A very clever and studious lad would no doubt have done so, but I personally did not 10 grow up to this particular subject until a good many years later. The frigate and sloop actions between the American and British sea-tigers of 1812 were much more within my grasp. I worked drearily at the Gracchi because I had to; my conscientious and much-to-be-pitied professor 15 dragging me through the theme by main strength, with my feet firmly planted in dull and totally idea-proof resistance.

I had at the time no idea of going into public life, and I never studied elocution or practiced debating. This was 20 a loss to me in one way. In another way it was not. Personally I have not the slightest sympathy with debating contests in which each side is arbitrarily assigned a given proposition and told to maintain it without the least reference to whether those maintaining it believe in it or not. I 25 know that under our system this is necessary for lawyers, but I emphatically disbelieve in it as regards general discussion of political, social, and industrial matters. What we need is to turn out of our colleges young men with ardent convictions on the side of the right; not young men who 30 can make a good argument for either right or wrong as their interest bids them. The present method of carrying

on debates on such subjects as "Our Colonial Policy," or
"The Need of a Navy," or "The Proper Position of the
Courts in Constitutional Questions," encourages precisely
the wrong attitude among those who take part in them.
5 There is no effort to instill sincerity and intensity of
conviction. On the contrary, the net result is to make
the contestants feel that their convictions have nothing to
do with their arguments. I am sorry I did not study
elocution in college; but I am exceedingly glad that I did
10 not take part in the type of debate in which stress is laid,
not upon getting a speaker to think rightly, but on getting
him to talk glibly on the side to which he is assigned,
without regard either to what his convictions are or to
what they ought to be.
15 I was a reasonably good student in college, standing just
within the first tenth of my class, if I remember rightly;
although I am not sure whether this means the tenth of
the whole number that entered or of those that graduated.
I was given a Phi Beta Kappa° "key." My chief interests
20 were scientific. When I entered college, I was devoted to
out-of-doors natural history, and my ambition was to be
a scientific man of the Audubon, or Wilson,° or Baird, or
Coues° type—a man like Hart Merriam,° or Frank
Chapman,° or Hornaday,° to-day. My father had from
25 the earliest days instilled into me the knowledge that I was
to work and to make my own way in the world, and I had
always supposed that this meant that I must enter business. But in my freshman year (he died when I was a
sophomore) he told me that if I wished to become a scien-
30 tific man I could do so. He explained that I must be sure
that I really intensely desired to do scientific work, because
if I went into it I must make it a serious career; that he

had made money enough to enable me to take up such a career and do non-remunerative work of value *if I intended to do the very best work there was in me;* but that I must not dream of taking it up as a dilettante. He also gave me a piece of advice that I have always remem- bered, namely, that, if I was not going to earn money, I must even things up by not spending it. As he expressed it, I had to keep the fraction constant, and if I was not able to increase the numerator, then I must reduce the denominator. In other words, if I went into a scientific career, I must definitely abandon all thought of the enjoyment that could accompany a money-making career, and must find my pleasures elsewhere.

After this conversation I fully intended to make science my life work. I did not, for the simple reason that at that time Harvard, and I suppose our other colleges, utterly ignored the possibilities of the faunal naturalist, the outdoor naturalist and observer of nature. They treated biology as purely a science of the laboratory and the microscope, a science whose adherents were to spend their time in the study of minute forms of marine life, or else in section-cutting and the study of the tissues of the higher organisms under the microscope. This attitude was, no doubt, in part due to the fact that in most colleges then there was a not always intelligent copying of what was done in the great German universities. The sound revolt against superficiality of study had been carried to an extreme; thoroughness in minutiæ as the only end of study had been erected into a fetish. There was a total failure to understand the great variety of kinds of work that could be done by naturalists, including what could be done by outdoor naturalists—the kind of work which

Hart Merriam and his assistants in the Biological Survey have carried to such a high degree of perfection as regards North American mammals. In the entirely proper desire to be thorough and to avoid slipshod methods, the tend-
5 ency was to treat as not serious, as unscientific, any kind of work that was not carried on with laborious minuteness in the laboratory. My taste was specialized in a totally different direction, and I had no more desire or ability to be a microscopist and section-cutter than to
10 be a mathematician. Accordingly I abandoned all thought of becoming a scientist. Doubtless this meant that I really did not have the intense devotion to science which I thought I had; for, if I had possessed such devotion, I would have carved out a career for myself some-
15 how without regard to discouragements.

The teaching which I received was genuinely democratic in one way. It was not so democratic in another. I grew into manhood thoroughly imbued with the feeling that a man must be respected for what he made of
20 himself. But I had also, consciously or unconsciously, been taught that socially and industrially pretty much the whole duty of the man lay in thus making the best of himself; that he should be honest in his dealings with others and charitable in the old-fashioned way to the un-
25 fortunate; but that it was no part of his business to join with others in trying to make things better for the many by curbing the abnormal and excessive development of individualism in a few. Now I do not mean that this training was by any means all bad. On the contrary,
30 the insistence upon individual responsibility was, and is, and always will be, a prime necessity. Teaching of

the kind I absorbed from both my text-books and my surroundings is a healthy anti-scorbutic to the sentimentality which by complacently excusing the individual for all his shortcomings would finally hopelessly weaken the spring of moral purpose. It also keeps alive that virile vigor for the lack of which in the average individual no possible perfection of law or of community action can ever atone. But such teaching, if not corrected by other teaching, means acquiescence in a riot of lawless business individualism which would be quite as destructive to real civilization as the lawless military individualism of the Dark Ages.° I left college and entered the big world owing more than I can express to the training I had received, especially in my own home; but with much else also to learn if I were to become really fitted to do my part in the work that lay ahead for the generation of Americans to which I belonged.

THE VIGOR OF LIFE

HAVING been a sickly boy, with no natural bodily prowess, and having lived much at home, I was at first quite unable to hold my own when thrown into contact with other boys of rougher antecedents. I was nervous and
5 timid. Yet from reading of the people I admired—ranging from the soldiers of Valley Forge,° and Morgan's riflemen,° to the heroes of my favorite stories—and from hearing of the feats performed by my Southern forefathers and kinsfolk, and from knowing my father, I
10 felt a great admiration for men who were fearless and who could hold their own in the world, and I had a great desire to be like them. Until I was nearly fourteen I let this desire take no more definite shape than day-dreams. Then an incident happened that did me real good. Hav-
15 ing an attack of asthma, I was sent off by myself to Moosehead Lake.° On the stage-coach ride thither I encountered a couple of other boys who were about my own age, but very much more competent and also much more mischievous. I have no doubt they were good-
20 hearted boys, but they were boys! They found that I was a foreordained and predestined victim, and industriously proceeded to make life miserable for me. The worst feature was that when I finally tried to fight them I discovered that either one singly could not only handle
25 me with easy contempt, but handle me so as not to hurt me much and yet to prevent my doing any damage whatever in return.

The experience taught me what probably no amount of good advice could have taught me. I made up my mind

16

that I must try to learn so that I would not again be put in such a helpless position, and having become quickly and bitterly conscious that I did not have the natural prowess to hold my own, I decided that I would try to supply its place by training. Accordingly, with my 5 father's hearty approval, I started to learn to box. I was a painfully slow and awkward pupil, and certainly worked two or three years before I made any perceptible improvement whatever. My first boxing master was John Long, an ex-prize-fighter. I can see his rooms now, with colored 10 pictures of the fights between Tom Hyer and Yankee Sullivan, and Heenan° and Sayers, and other great events in the annals of the squared circle. On one occasion, to excite interest among his patrons, he held a series of "championship" matches for the different weights, the prizes 15 being, at least in my own class, pewter mugs of a value, I should suppose, approximating fifty cents. Neither he nor I had any idea that I could do anything, but I was entered in the lightweight contest, in which it happened that I was pitted in succession against a couple of reedy striplings 20 who were even worse than I was. Equally to their surprise and to my own, and to John Long's, I won, and the pewter mug became one of my most prized possessions. I kept it, and alluded to it, and I fear bragged about it, for a number of years, and I only wish I knew where it 25 was now. Years later I read an account of a little man who once in a fifth-rate handicap race won a worthless pewter medal and joyed in it ever after. Well, as soon as I read that story I felt that that little man and I were brothers.
30

This was, as far as I remember, the only one of my exceedingly rare athletic triumphs which would be worth .

relating. I did a good deal of boxing and wrestling in
Harvard, but never attained to the first rank in either,
even at my own weight. Once, in the big contests in the
Gym, I got either into the finals or semi-finals, I forget
5 which; but aside from this the chief part I played was to
act as trial horse for some friend or classmate who did
have a chance of distinguishing himself in the championship contests.

I was fond of horseback-riding, but I took to it slowly
10 and with difficulty, exactly as with boxing. It was a
long time before I became even a respectable rider,
and I never got much higher. I mean by this that I
never became a first-flight man in the hunting field, and
never even approached the bronco-busting class in the
15 West. Any man, if he chooses, can gradually school
himself to the requisite nerve, and gradually learn the
requisite seat and hands, that will enable him to do re-
spectably across country, or to perform the average work
on a ranch. Of my ranch experiences I shall speak later.

20   I was fond of walking and climbing. As a lad I used to
go to the north woods, in Maine, both in fall and winter.
There I made life friends of two men, Will Dow and
Bill Sewall: I canoed with them, and tramped through
the woods with them, visiting the winter logging camps
25 on snow-shoes. Afterward they were with me in the
West. Will Dow is dead. Bill Sewall was collector of
customs under me, on the Aroostook° border. Except
when hunting I never did any mountaineering save for
a couple of conventional trips up the Matterhorn° and
30 the Jungfrau° on one occasion when I was in Switzerland.

I never did much with the shotgun, but I practiced a

good deal with the rifle. I had a rifle range at Sagamore Hill,° where I often took friends to shoot. Once
or twice when I was visited by parties of released Boer
prisoners, after the close of the South African War,°
they and I held shooting matches together. The best 5
man with both pistol and rifle who ever shot there was
Stewart Edward White.°

My own experience as regards marksmanship was
much the same as my experience as regards horsemanship. There are men whose eye and hand are so quick 10
and so sure that they achieve a perfection of marksmanship to which no practice will enable ordinary men to
attain. There are other men who cannot learn to shoot
with any accuracy at all. In between come the mass of
men of ordinary abilities who, if they choose resolutely 15
to practice, can by sheer industry and judgment make
themselves fair rifle shots. The men who show this
requisite industry and judgment can without special
difficulty raise themselves to the second class of respectable rifle shots; and it is to this class that I belong. 20
But to have reached this point of marksmanship with the
rifle at a target by no means implies ability to hit game in
the field, especially dangerous game. All kinds of other
qualities, moral and physical, enter into being a good
hunter, and especially a good hunter after dangerous 25
game, just as all kinds of other qualities in addition to
skill with the rifle enter into being a good soldier. With
dangerous game, after a fair degree of efficiency with the
rifle has been attained, the prime requisites are cool
judgment and that kind of nerve which consists in avoid- 30
ing being rattled. Any beginner is apt to have "buck

fever," ° and therefore no beginner should go at dangerous
game.

I have shot only kinds of animals which could fairly
be called dangerous game—that is, the lion, elephant,
5 rhinoceros and buffalo in Africa, and the big grizzly bear
a quarter of a century ago in the Rockies. Taking into
account not only my own personal experience, but the
experiences of many veteran hunters, I regard all the four
African animals, but especially the lion, elephant, and
10 buffalo, as much more dangerous than the grizzly. As
it happened, however, the only narrow escape I personally ever had was from a grizzly, and in Africa the animal
killed closest to me as it was charging was a rhinoceros—
all of which goes to show that a man must not general-
15 ize too broadly from his own personal experiences. On
the whole, I think the lion the most dangerous of all these
five animals; that is, I think that, if fairly hunted, there is
a larger percentage of hunters killed or mauled for a
given number of lions killed than for a given number
20 of any one of the other animals. Yet I personally had
no difficulties with lions. I twice killed lions which
were at bay and just starting to charge, and I killed a
heavy-maned male while it was in full charge. But in
each instance I had plenty of leeway, the animal being
25 so far off that even if my bullet had not been fatal I
should have had time for a couple of more shots. The
African buffalo is undoubtedly a dangerous beast, but
it happened that the few that I shot did not charge. A
bull elephant, a vicious "rogue," which had been killing
30 people in the native villages, did charge before being shot at.
My son Kermit and I stopped it at forty yards. Another

bull elephant, also unwounded, which charged, nearly got me, as I had just fired both cartridges from my heavy double-barreled rifle in killing the bull I was after—the first wild elephant I had ever seen. The second bull came through the thick brush to my left like a steam plow 5 through a light snowdrift, everything snapping before his rush, and was so near that he could have hit me with his trunk. I slipped past him behind a tree. People have asked me how I felt on this occasion. My answer has always been that I suppose I felt as most men of 10 like experience feel on such occasions. At such a moment a hunter is so very busy that he has no time to get frightened. He wants to get in his cartridges and try another shot.

Rhinòceros are truculent, blustering beasts, much 15 the most stupid of all the dangerous game I know. Generally their attitude is one of mere stupidity and bluff. But on occasions they do charge wickedly, both when wounded and when entirely unprovoked. The first I ever shot I mortally wounded at a few rods' distance, and it 20 charged with the utmost determination, whereat I and my companion both fired, and more by good luck than anything else brought it to the ground just thirteen paces from where we stood. Another rhinoceros may or may not have been meaning to charge me; I have never 25 been certain which. It heard us and came at us through rather thick brush, snorting and tossing its head. I am by no means sure that it had fixedly hostile intentions, and indeed with my present experience I think it likely that if I had not fired it would have flinched at 30 the last moment and either retreated or gone by me. But I am not a rhinoceros mind reader, and its actions were

such as to warrant my regarding it as a suspicious character. I stopped it with a couple of bullets, and then
followed it up and killed it. The skins of all these animals
which I thus killed are in the National Museum at Wash-
5 ington.

When obliged to live in cities, I for a long time found
that boxing and wrestling enabled me to get a good deal
of exercise in condensed and attractive form. I was
reluctantly obliged to abandon both as I grew older.
10 I dropped the wrestling earliest. When I became Governor,° the champion middleweight wrestler of America
happened to be in Albany, and I got him to come round
three or four afternoons a week. Incidentally I may mention that his presence caused me a difficulty with the
15 Comptroller, who refused to audit a bill I put in for a
wrestling-mat, explaining that I could have a billiard-
table, billiards being recognized as a proper Guber-
natorial amusement, but that a wrestling-mat symbolized something unusual and unheard of and could not
20 be permitted. The middleweight champion was of
course so much better than I was that he could not only
take care of himself but of me too and see that I was
not hurt—for wrestling is a much more violent amusement than boxing. But after a couple of months he had
25 to go away, and he left as a substitute a good-humored,
stalwart professional oarsman. The oarsman turned out
to know very little about wrestling. He could not even
take care of himself, not to speak of me. By the end of our
second afternoon one of his long ribs had been caved in and
30 two of my short ribs badly damaged, and my left shoulder-
blade so nearly shoved out of place that it creaked. He

was nearly as pleased as I when I told him I thought we would "vote the war a failure" and abandon wrestling. After that I took up boxing again. While President I used to box with some of the aides, as well as play single-stick° with General Wood.° After a few years I had to 5 abandon boxing as well as wrestling, for in one bout a young captain of artillery cross-countered me on the eye, and the blow smashed the little blood-vessels. Fortunately it was my left eye, but the sight has been dim ever since, and if it had been the right eye, I should have 10 been entirely unable to shoot. Accordingly I thought it better to acknowledge that I had become an elderly man and would have to stop boxing. I then took up jiu-jitsu° for a year or two.

I have mentioned all these experiences, and I could 15 mention scores of others, because out of them grew my philosophy—perhaps they were in part caused by my philosophy—of bodily vigor as a method of getting that vigor of soul without which vigor of the body counts for nothing. The dweller in cities has less chance than the 20 dweller in the country to keep his body sound and vigorous. But he can do so, if only he will take the trouble. Any young lawyer, shopkeeper, or clerk, or shop-assistant, can keep himself in good condition if he tries. Some of the best men who have ever served under me in the 25 National Guard and in my regiment were former clerks or floor-walkers. Why, Johnny Hayes,° the Marathon victor, and at one time world champion, one of my valued friends and supporters, was a floor-walker in Bloomingdale's big department store. Surely with Johnny 30 Hayes as an example, any young man in a city can

hope to make his body all that a vigorous man's body
should be.

I once made a speech to which I gave the title "The
Strenuous Life."°   Afterwards I published a volume of
5 essays with this for a title.   There were two transla-
tions of it which always especially pleased me.   One was
by a Japanese soldier who knew English well, and who
had carried the essay all through the Manchurian° campaign, and later translated it for the benefit of his country-
10 men.   The other was by an Italian lady, whose brother,
an officer in the Italian army who had died on duty in a
foreign land, had also greatly liked the article and carried
it round with him.   In translating the title the lady
rendered it in Italian as "Vigor di Vita."   I thought
15 this translation a great improvement on the original,
and have always wished that I had myself used "The
Vigor of Life" as a heading to indicate what I was
trying to preach, instead of the heading I actually did
use.

20   There are two kinds of success, or rather two kinds of
ability displayed in the achievement of success.   There
is, first, the success either in big things or small things
which comes to the man who has in him the natural
power to do what no one else can do, and what no
25 amount of training, no perseverance or will power, will
enable any ordinary man to do.   This success, of course,
like every other kind of success, may be on a very big
scale or on a small scale.   The quality which the man
possesses may be that which enables him to run a
30 hundred yards in nine and three-fifths seconds, or to
play ten separate games of chess at the same time
blindfolded, or to add five columns of figures at once

without effort, or to write the "Ode to a Grecian
Urn,"° or to deliver the Gettysburg speech,° or to
show the ability of Frederick° at Leuthen or Nelson°
at Trafalgar. No amount of training of body or mind
would enable any good ordinary man to perform any one 5
of these feats. Of course the proper performance of each
implies much previous study or training, but in no one
of them is success to be attained save by the altogether
exceptional man who has in him the something additional
which the ordinary man does not have.   10
    This is the most striking kind of success, and it can be
attained only by the man who has in him the quality
which separates him in kind no less than in degree from
his fellows. But much the commoner type of success in
every walk of life and in every species of effort is that 15
which comes to the man who differs from his fellows not
by the kind of quality which he possesses but by the
degree of development which he has given that quality.
This kind of success is open to a large number of persons,
if only they seriously determine to achieve it. It is the 20
kind of success which is open to the average man of
sound body and fair mind, who has no remarkable mental or physical attributes, but who gets just as much as
possible in the way of work out of the aptitudes that he
does possess. It is the only kind of success that is open 25
to most of us. Yet some of the greatest successes in history have been those of this second class—when I call
it second class I am not running it down in the least, I
am merely pointing out that it differs in kind from the
first class. To the average man it is probably more use- 30
ful to study this second type of success than to study the
first. From the study of the first he can learn inspira-

tion, he can get uplift and lofty enthusiasm. From the study of the second he can, if he chooses, find out how to win a similiar success himself.

I need hardly say that all the successes I have ever won 5 have been of the second type. I never won anything without hard labor and the exercise of my best judgment and careful planning and working long in advance. Having been a rather sickly and awkward boy, I was as a young man at first both nervous and distrustful of my 10 own prowess. I had to train myself painfully and laboriously not merely as regards my body but as regards my soul and spirit.

When a boy I read a passage in one of Marryat's books° which always impressed me. In this passage the 15 captain of some small British man-of-war is explaining to the hero how to acquire the quality of fearlessness. He says that at the outset almost every man is frightened when he goes into action, but that the course to follow is for the man to keep such a grip on himself that 20 he can act just as if he was not frightened. After this is kept up long enough it changes from pretense to reality, and the man does in very fact become fearless by sheer dint of practicing fearlessness when he does not feel it. (I am using my own language, not Marryat's.) This 25 was the theory upon which I went. There were all kinds of things of which I was afraid at first, ranging from grizzly bears to "mean" horses and gun-fighters; but by acting as if I was not afraid I gradually ceased to be afraid. Most men can have the same experience if 30 they choose. They will first learn to bear themselves well in trials which they anticipate and school themselves in advance to meet. After a while the habit will grow on them, and they will behave well in sudden and unexpected emergencies which come upon them unawares.

It is of course much pleasanter if one is naturally fearless, and I envy and respect the men who are naturally fearless. But it is a good thing to remember that 5 the man who does not enjoy this advantage can nevertheless stand beside the man who does, and can do his duty with the like efficiency, *if he chooses to*. Of course he must not let his desire take the form merely of a daydream. Let him dream about being a fearless man, 10 and the more he dreams the better he will be, always provided he does his best to realize the dream in practice. He can do his part honorably and well provided only he sets fearlessness before himself as an ideal, schools himself to think of danger merely as something to be 15 faced and overcome, and regards life itself as he should regard it, not as something to be thrown away, but as a pawn to be promptly hazarded whenever the hazard is warranted by the larger interests of the great game in which we are all engaged.   20

ENTERING POLITICS °

WHEN I left Harvard, I took up the study of law. If I had been sufficiently fortunate to come under Professor Thayer,° of the Harvard Law School, it may well be that I would have realized that the lawyer can do a great
5 work for justice and against legalism.

But, doubtless chiefly through my own fault, some of the teaching of the law books and of the class-room seemed to me to be against justice. The *caveat emptor*° side of the law, like the *caveat emptor* side of business, seemed
10 to me repellent; it did not make for social fair dealing. The "let the buyer beware" maxim, when translated into actual practice, whether in law or business, tends to translate itself further into the seller making his profit at the expense of the buyer, instead of by a bargain
15 which shall be to the profit of both. It did not seem to me that the law was framed to discourage as it should sharp practice, and all other kinds of bargains except those which are fair and of benefit to both sides. I was young; there was much in the judgment which I then
20 formed on this matter which I should now revise; but, then as now, many of the big corporation lawyers, to whom the ordinary members of the bar then as now looked up, held certain standards which were difficult to recognize as compatible with the idealism I suppose every
25 high-minded young man is apt to feel. If I had been obliged to earn every cent I spent, I should have gone whole-heartedly into the business of making both ends meet, and should have taken up the law or any other respectable occupation—for I then held, and now hold, the be-

28

lief that a man's first duty is to pull his own weight and to take care of those dependent upon him; and I then believed, and now believe, that the greatest privilege and greatest duty for any man is to be happily married, and that no other form of success or service, for either man or 5 woman, can be wisely accepted as a substitute or alternative. But it happened that I had been left enough money by my father not to make it necessary for me to think solely of earning bread for myself and family. I had enough to get bread. What I had to do, if I wanted butter 10 and jam, was to provide the butter and jam, but to count their cost as compared with other things. In other words, I made up my mind that, while I must earn money, I could afford to make earning money the secondary instead of the primary object of my career. If I had had no 15 money at all, then my first duty would have been to earn it in any honest fashion. As I had some money, I felt that my need for more money was to be treated as a secondary need, and that while it was my business to make more money where I legitimately and properly 20 could, yet that it was also my business to treat other kinds of work as more important than money-making.

Almost immediately after leaving Harvard in 1880 I began to take an interest in politics. I did not then believe, and I do not now believe, that any man should 25 ever attempt to make politics his only career. It is a dreadful misfortune for a man to grow to feel that his whole livelihood and whole happiness depend upon his staying in office. Such a feeling prevents him from being of real service to the people while in office, and always 30 puts him under the heaviest strain of pressure to barter his convictions for the sake of holding office. A man

should have some other occupation—I had several other
occupations—to which he can resort if at any time he
is thrown out of office, or at any time he finds it necessary
to choose a course which will probably result in his being
5 thrown out, unless he is willing to stay in at cost to his
conscience.

I was elected to the Legislature ° in the fall of 1881 and
found myself the youngest man in that body. I was
re-elected the two following years. Like all young men
10 and inexperienced members, I had considerable difficulty in teaching myself to speak. I profited much by
the advice of a hard-headed old countryman—who was
unconsciously paraphrasing the Duke of Wellington,°
who was himself doubtless paraphrasing somebody else.
15 The advice ran: "Don't speak until you are sure you
have something to say, and know just what it is; then
say it, and sit down."
My first days in the Legislature were much like those of
a boy in a strange school. My fellow-legislators and I eyed
20 one another with mutual distrust. Each of us chose his
seat, each began by following the lead of some veteran in
the first routine matters, and then, in a week or two, we
began to drift into groups according to our several af-
finities. The Legislature was Democratic. I was a
25 Republican from the "silk stocking" district, the wealthiest district in New York, and I was put, as one of the
minority members, on the Committee of Cities. It was
a coveted position. I did not make any effort to get
on, and, as far as I know, was put there merely because
30 it was felt to be in accordance with the fitness of
things.

My closest friend for the three years I was there was
Billy O'Neill, from the Adirondacks. He kept a small
crossroads store. He was a young man, although a few
years older than I was, and, like myself, had won his
position without regard to the machine. He had thought 5
he would like to be Assemblyman, so he had taken
his buggy and had driven around Franklin County
visiting everybody, had upset the local ring, and came
to the Legislature as his own master. There is surely
something in American traditions that does tend to- 10
ward real democracy in spite of our faults and shortcomings. In most other countries two men of as different antecedents, ancestry, and surroundings as Billy
O'Neill and I would have had far more difficulty in coming
together. I came from the biggest city in America and 15
from the wealthiest ward of that city, and he from a backwoods county where he kept a store at a crossroads. In all
the unimportant things we seemed far apart. But in
all the important things we were close together. We
looked at all questions from substantially the same 20
view-point, and we stood shoulder to shoulder in every
legislative fight during those three years. He abhorred
demagogy just as he abhorred corruption. He had
thought much on political problems; he admired Alexander Hamilton° as much as I did, being a strong be- 25
liever in a powerful National government; and we both
of us differed from Alexander Hamilton in being stout
adherents of Abraham Lincoln's views wherever the
rights of the people were concerned. Any man who has
met with success, if he will be frank with himself, must 30
admit that there has been a big element of fortune in
the success. Fortune favored me, whereas her hand was

heavy against Billy O'Neill. All his life he had to strive hard to wring his bread from harsh surroundings and a reluctant fate; if fate had been but a little kinder, I believe he would have had a great political career; and he 5 would have done good service for the country in any position in which he might have been put.

In the Legislature the problems with which I dealt were mainly problems of honesty and decency and of legislative and adminisistrative efficiency. They rep-10 resented the effort, the wise, the vitally necessary effort, to get efficient and honest government. But as yet I understood little of the effort which was already beginning, for the most part under very bad leadership, to secure a more genuine social and industrial justice. Nor 15 was I especially to blame for this. The good citizens I then knew best, even when themselves men of limited means—men like my colleague Billy O'Neill, and my backwoods friends Sewall and Dow—were no more awake than I was to the changing needs the changing 20 times were bringing. Their outlook was as narrow as my own, and, within its limits, as fundamentally sound. I wish to dwell on the soundness of our outlook on life, even though as yet it was not broad enough. We were no respecters of persons. Where our vision was devel-25 oped to a degree that enabled us to see crookedness, we opposed it whether in great or small. As a matter of fact, we found that it needed much more courage to stand up *openly* against labor men when they were wrong than against capitalists when they were wrong. The sins 30 against labor are usually committed, and the improper services to capitalists are usually rendered, behind closed

doors. Very often the man with the moral courage to speak
in the open against labor when it is wrong is the only man
anxious to do effective work for labor when labor is
right.

The only kinds of courage and honesty which are 5
permanently useful to good institutions anywhere are
those shown by men who decide all cases with impartial
justice on grounds of conduct and not on grounds of class.
We found that in the long run the men who in public
blatantly insisted that labor was never wrong were the 10
very men who in private could not be trusted to stand
for labor when it was right. We grew heartily to distrust the reformer who never denounced wickedness
unless it was embodied in a rich man. Human nature
does not change; and that type of "reformer" is as noxious 15
now as he ever was. The loud-mouthed upholder of
popular rights who attacks wickedness only when it is
allied with wealth, and who never publicly assails any
misdeed, no matter how flagrant, if committed nominally in the interest of labor, has either a warped mind 20
or a tainted soul, and should be trusted by no honest man.
It was largely the indignant and contemptuous dislike
aroused in our minds by the demagogues of this class
which then prevented those of us whose instincts at
bottom were sound from going as far as we ought to have 25
gone along the lines of governmental control of corporations and governmental interference on behalf of labor.

Traps were set for more than one of us, and if we had
walked into these traps our public careers would have
ended, at least so far as following them under the condi- 30
tions which alone make it worth while to be in public life at

all. A man can of course hold public office, and many a man does hold public office, and lead a public career of a sort, even if there are other men who possess secrets about him which he cannot afford to have divulged. But no man can 5 lead a public career really worth leading, no man can act with rugged independence in serious crises, nor strike at great abuses, nor afford to make powerful and unscrupulous foes, if he is himself vulnerable in his private character. Nor will clean conduct by itself enable a man to 10 render good service. I have always been fond of Josh Billings's° remark that "it is much easier to be a harmless dove than a wise serpent." There are plenty of decent legislators, and plenty of able legislators; but the blamelessness and the fighting edge are not always com- 15 bined. Both qualities are necessary for the man who is to wage active battle against the powers that prey. He must be clean of life, so that he can laugh when his public or his private record is searched; and yet being clean of life will not avail him if he is either foolish or timid. He 20 must walk warily and fearlessly, and while he should never brawl if he can avoid it, he must be ready to hit hard if the need arises. Let him remember, by the way, that the unforgivable crime is soft hitting. Do not hit at all if it can be avoided; but *never* hit softly.

25 Like most young men in politics, I went through various oscillations of feeling before I "found myself." At one period I became so impressed with the virtue of complete independence that I proceeded to act on each case purely as I personally viewed it, without paying any 30 heed to the principles and prejudices of others. The result was that I speedily, and deservedly, lost all power of accomplishing anything at all; and I thereby learned

the invaluable lesson that in the practical activities of
life no man can render the highest service unless he can
act in combination with his fellows, which means a certain amount of give-and-take between him and them.
Again, I at one period began to believe that I had a 5
future before me, and that it behooved me to be very far-
sighted and scan each action carefully with a view to its
possible effect on that future. This speedily made me
useless to the public and an object of aversion to myself;
and I then made up my mind that I would try not to 10
think of the future at all, but would proceed on the
assumption that each office I held would be the last I
ever should hold, and that I would confine myself to
trying to do my work as well as possible while I held
that office. I found that for me personally this was the 15
only way in which I could either enjoy myself or render
good service to the country, and I never afterwards de-
viated from this plan.

During my three years' service in the Legislature I
worked on a very simple philosophy of government. It 20
was that personal character and initiative are the prime
requisites in political and social life. It was not only a
good but an absolutely indispensable theory as far as it
went; but it was defective in that it did not sufficiently
allow for the need of collective action. I shall never 25
forget the men with whom I worked hand in hand in
these legislative struggles, not only my fellow-legislators,
but some of the newspaper reporters, such as Spinney
and Cunningham; and then in addition the men in the
various districts who helped us. We had made up our 30
minds that we must not fight fire with fire, that on the
contrary the way to win out was to equal our foes in prac-

tical efficiency and yet to stand at the opposite plane from
them in applied morality.

It was not always easy to keep the just middle, especially when it happened that on one side there were
5 corrupt and unscrupulous demagogues, and on the other
side corrupt and unscrupulous reactionaries. Our effort
was to hold the scales even between both. We tried to
stand with the cause of righteousness even though its
advocates were anything but righteous. We endeavored
10 to cut out the abuses of property, even though good men
of property were misled into upholding those abuses. We
refused to be frightened into sanctioning improper assaults upon property, although we knew that the champions
of property themselves did things that were wicked and
15 corrupt. We were as yet by no means as thoroughly
awake as we ought to have been to the need of controlling
big business and to the damage done by the combination
of politics with big business. In this matter I was not
behind the rest of my friends; indeed, I was ahead of
20 them, for no serious leader in political life then appreciated the prime need of grappling with these questions.
One partial reason—not an excuse or a justification, but
a partial reason—for my slowness in grasping the importance of action in these matters was the corrupt and
25 unattractive nature of so many of the men who championed
popular reforms, their insincerity, and the folly of so
many of the actions which they advocated. Even at
that date I had neither sympathy with nor admiration
for the man who was merely a money king, and I did
30 not regard the "money touch," when divorced from
other qualities, as entitling a man to either respect or
consideration. As recited above, we did on more than

one occasion fight battles, in which we neither took nor
gave quarter, against the most prominent and powerful
financiers and financial interests of the day. But most of
the fights in which we were engaged were for pure honesty and decency, and they were more apt to be against 5
that form of corruption which found its expression in
demagogy than against that form of corruption which
defended or advocated privilege.

To play the demagogue for purposes of self-interest is
a cardinal sin against the people in a democracy, exactly 10
as to play the courtier for such purposes is a cardinal sin
against the people under other forms of government.
A man who stays long in our American political life, if
he has in his soul the generous desire to do effective
service for great causes, inevitably grows to regard him- 15
self merely as one of many instruments, all of which it
may be necessary to use, one at one time, one at another, in
achieving the triumph of those causes; and whenever the
usefulness of any one has been exhausted it is to be thrown
aside. If such a man is wise, he will gladly do the thing 20
that is next, when the time and the need come together,
without asking what the future holds for him. Let the
half-god play his part well and manfully, and then be
content to draw aside when the god appears. Nor
should he feel vain regrets that to another it is given to 25
render greater services and reap a greater reward. Let it
be enough for him that he too has served, and that by
doing well he has prepared the way for the other man
who can do better.

IN COWBOY LAND

THOUGH I had previously made a trip into the then Territory of Dakota,° beyond the Red River, it was not until 1883 that I went to the Little Missouri, and there took hold of two cattle ranches, the Chimney Butte and the 5 Elkhorn.

It was still the Wild West in those days, the Far West, the West of Owen Wister's stories° and Frederic Remington's drawings,° the West of the Indian and the buffalo-hunter, the soldier and the cow-puncher. That 10 land of the West has gone now, "gone, gone with the lost Atlantis,°" gone to the isle of ghosts and of strange dead memories. It was a land of vast silent spaces, of lonely rivers, and of plains where the wild game stared at the passing horseman. It was a land of scattered ranches, 15 of herds of long-horned cattle, and of reckless riders who unmoved looked into the eyes of life or of death. In that land we led a free and hardy life, with horse and rifle. We worked under the scorching midsummer sun, when the wide plains shimmered and wavered in the heat; and we 20 knew the freezing misery of riding night guard round the cattle in the late fall round-up. In the soft springtime the stars were glorious in our eyes each night before we fell asleep; and in the winter we rode through blinding blizzards, when the driven snow-dust burnt our faces. 25 There were monotonous days, as we guided the trail cattle or the beef herds, hour after hour, at the slowest of walks; and minutes or hours teeming with excitement as we stopped stampedes or swam the herds across rivers treacherous with quicksands or brimmed with running ice. We knew toil and hardship and hunger and thirst; and we saw men die violent deaths as they worked among the horses and cattle, or fought in evil feuds with one another; but we felt the beat of hardy life in our veins, and ours was the glory of work and the joy of living.

It was right and necessary that this life should pass, for the safety of our country lies in its being made the country of the small home-maker. The great un-fenced ranches, in the days of "free grass," necessarily represented a temporary stage in our history. The large migratory flocks of sheep, each guarded by the hired shepherds of absentee owners, were the first enemies of the cattle-men; and owing to the way they ate out the grass and destroyed all other vegetation, these roving sheep bands represented little of permanent good to the country. But the homesteaders, the permanent settlers, the men who took up each his own farm on which he lived and brought up his family, these represented from the National standpoint the most desirable of all possible users of, and dwellers on, the soil. Their advent meant the breaking up of the big ranches; and the change was a National gain, although to some of us an individual loss.

I reached the Little Missouri on a Northern Pacific train about three in the morning of a cool September day in 1883. Aside from the station, the only building was a ramshackle structure called the Pyramid Park Hotel. I dragged my duffle-bag³ thither, and hammered at the door until the frowsy proprietor appeared, muttering oaths. He ushered me upstairs, where I was given one of the fourteen beds in the room which by itself constituted the entire upper floor. Next day I walked over to the

abandoned army post, and, after some hours among the
gray log shacks, a ranchman who had driven into the
station agreed to take me out to his ranch, the Chimney
Butte ranch, where he was living with his brother and
5 their partner.

The ranch was a log structure with a dirt roof, a
corral for horses near by, and a chicken-house jabbed
against the rear of the ranch house. Inside there was
only one room, and a table, three or four chairs, a cooking-
10 stove, and three bunks. The owners were Sylvane and
Joe Ferris and William J. Merrifield. . . . There was
a fourth man, George Meyer, who also worked for
me later. That evening we all played old sledge° round
the table, and at one period the game was interrupted
15 by a frightful squawking outside which told us that a
bobcat had made a raid on the chicken-house.

After a buffalo hunt with my original friend, Joe Ferris,
I entered into partnership with Merrifield and Sylvane
Ferris, and we started a cow ranch, with the maltese
20 cross brand—always known as "maltee cross," by the
way, as the general impression along the Little Missouri
was that "maltese" must be a plural. . . . They were
among my most constant companions for the few years
next succeeding the evening when the bobcat interrupted
25 the game of old sledge. I lived and worked with them
on the ranch, and with them and many others like them
on the round-up; and I brought out from Maine, in order
to start the Elkhorn ranch lower down the river, my two
backwoods friends Sewall and Dow. My brands for
30 the lower ranch were the elkhorn and triangle.

I do not believe there ever was any life more attractive
to a vigorous young fellow than life on a cattle ranch in

those days. It was a fine, healthy life, too; it taught a
man self-reliance, hardihood, and the value of instant
decision—in short, the virtues that ought to come from
life in the open country. I enjoyed the life to the full.
After the first year I built on the Elkhorn ranch a long, 5
low ranch house of hewn logs, with a veranda, and with,
in addition to the other rooms, a bedroom for myself,
and a sitting-room with a big fire-place. I got out a
rocking-chair—I am very fond of rocking-chairs—and
enough books to fill two or three shelves, and a rubber 10
bath-tub so that I could get a bath. And then I do not
see how any one could have lived more comfortably. We
had buffalo robes and bearskins of our own killing. We
always kept the house clean—using the word in a rather
large sense. There were at least two rooms that were 15
always warm, even in the bitterest weather; and we had
plenty to eat. Commonly the mainstay of every meal
was game of our own killing, usually antelope or deer,
sometimes grouse or ducks, and occasionally, in the earlier
days, buffalo or elk. We also had flour and bacon, sugar, 20
salt, and canned tomatoes. And later, when some of
the men married and brought out their wives, we had all
kinds of good things, such as jams and jellies made from
the wild plums and the buffalo berries, and potatoes from
the forlorn little garden patch. Moreover, we had milk. 25
Most ranchmen at that time never had milk. I knew
more than one ranch with ten thousand head of cattle
where there was not a cow that could be milked. We made
up our minds that we would be more enterprising. Accordingly, we started to domesticate some of the cows. Our 30
first effort was not successful, chiefly because we did
not devote the needed time and patience to the matter.

And we found that to race a cow two miles at full speed on horseback, then rope her, throw her, and turn her upside down to milk her, while exhilarating as a pastime, was not productive of results. Gradually we accumulated
5 tame .cows, and, after we had thinned out the bobcats and coyotes, more chickens.

The ranch house stood on the brink of a low bluff overlooking the broad, shallow bed of the Little Missouri, through which at most seasons there ran only a trickle
10 of water, while in times of freshet it was filled brimful with the boiling, foaming, muddy torrent. There was no neighbor for ten or fifteen miles on either side of me. The river twisted down in long curves between narrow bottoms bordered by sheer cliff walls, for the Bad Lands,
15 a chaos of peaks, plateaus, and ridges, rose abruptly from the edges of the level tree-clad, or grassy, alluvial meadows. In front of the ranch-house veranda was a row of cotton-wood trees with gray-green leaves which quivered all day long if there was a breath of air. From these trees came the
20 faraway, melancholy cooing of mourning doves, and little owls perched in them and called tremulously at night. In the long summer afternoons we would sometimes sit on the piazza, when there was no work to be done, for an hour or two at a time, watching the cattle on the sand-bars, and
25 the sharply channeled and strangly carved amphitheater of cliffs across the bottom opposite; while the vultures wheeled overhead, their black shadows gliding across the glaring white of the dry river-bed. Sometimes from the ranch we saw deer, and once when we needed meat I
30 shot one across the river as I stood on the piazza. In the winter, in the days of iron cold, when everything was white under the snow, the river lay in its bed fixed and

immovable as a bar of bent steel, and then at night wolves and lynxes traveled up and down it as if it had been a highway passing in front of the ranch house. Often in the late fall or early winter, after a hard day's hunting, or when returning from one of the winter line camps, we 5 did not reach the ranch until hours after sunset; and after the weary tramping in the cold it was keen pleasure to catch the first red gleam of the fire-lit windows across the snowy wastes.

The Elkhorn ranch house was built mainly by Sewall 10 and Dow, who, like most men from the Maine woods, were mighty with the ax. I could chop fairly well for an amateur, but I could not do one-third the work they could. One day when we were cutting down the cotton-wood trees, to begin our building operations, I heard 15 some one ask Dow what the total cut had been, and Dow not realizing that I was within hearing, answered: "Well, Bill cut down fifty-three, I cut forty-nine, and the boss he beavered down seventeen." Those who have seen the stump of a tree which has been gnawed down by a beaver 20 will understand the exact force of the comparison.

In those days on a cow ranch the men were apt to be away on the various round-ups at least half the time. It was interesting and exciting work, and except for the lack of sleep on the spring and summer round-ups it was not ex- 25 hausting work; compared to lumbering or mining or black-smithing, to sit in the saddle is an easy form of labor. The ponies were of course grass-fed and unshod. Each man had his own string of nine or ten. One pony would be used for the morning work, one for the afternoon, and neither 30 would again be used for the next three days. A separate pony was kept for night riding.

I never became a good roper, nor more than an average
rider, according to ranch standards. Of course a man on
a ranch has to ride a good many bad horses, and is bound
to encounter a certain number of accidents, and of these
5 I had my share, at one time cracking a rib, and on another
occasion the point of my shoulder. We were hundreds of
miles from a doctor, and each time, as I was on the round-
up, I had to get through my work for the next few weeks as
best I could, until the injury healed of itself. When I had
10 the opportunity, I broke my own horses, doing it gently
and gradually and spending much time over it, and choosing the horses that seemed gentle to begin with. With
these horses I never had any difficulty. But frequently
there was neither time nor opportunity to handle our,
15 mounts so elaborately. We might get a band of horses,
each having been bridled and saddled two or three times,
but none of them having been broken beyond the extent
implied in this bridling and saddling. Then each of us in
succession would choose a horse (for his string), I as owner
20 of the ranch being given the first choice on each round, so
to speak. The first time I was ever on a round-up Sylvane
Ferris, Merrifield, Meyer, and I each chose his string in
this fashion. Three or four of the animals I got were not
easy to ride. The effort both to ride them and to look as
25 if I enjoyed doing so, on some cool morning when my grin-
ning cowboy friends had gathered round "to see whether
the high-headed bay could buck the boss off," doubtless
was of benefit to me, but lacked much of being enjoyable.
The time I smashed my rib I was bucked off on a stone.
30 The time I hurt the point of my shoulder I was riding a
big, sulky horse named Ben Butler, which went over backwards with me. When we got up it still refused to go any-

where; so, while I sat it, Sylvane Ferris and George Meyer got their ropes on its neck and dragged it a few hundred yards, choking but stubborn, all four feet firmly planted and plowing the ground. When they released the ropes it lay down and wouldn't get up. The round-up had started; 5 so Sylvane gave me his horse, Baldy, which sometimes bucked but never went over backwards, and he got onto the now re-arisen Ben Butler. To my discomfiture Ben started quietly beside us, while Sylvane remarked, "Why, there's nothing the matter with this horse; he's a plumb gentle 10 horse." Then Ben fell slightly behind and I heard Sylvane again, "That's all right! Come along! Here, you! Go on, you! Hi, hi, fellows, help me out! he's lying on me!" Sure enough, he was; and when we dragged Sylvane from under him the first thing the rescued Sylvane did was to execute 15 a war-dance, spurs and all, on the iniquitous Ben. We could do nothing with him that day; subsequently we got him so that we could ride him; but he never became a nice saddle-horse.

20

On several occasions we had to fight fire. In the geography books of my youth prairie fires were always portrayed as taking place in long grass, and all living things ran before them. On the northern cattle plains the grass was never long enough to be a source of danger to man or beast. 25 The fires were nothing like the forest fires in the Northern woods. But they destroyed large quantities of feed, and we had to stop them where possible. The process we usually followed was to kill a steer, split it in two length-wise, and then have two riders drag each half-steer, the rope 30 of one running from his saddle-horn to the front leg, and that of the other to the hind leg. One of the men would

spur his horse over or through the line of fire, and the two would then ride forward, dragging the steer bloody side downward along the line of flame, men following on foot with slickers or wet horse-blankets to beat out any flick-
5 ering blaze that was still left. It was exciting work, for the fire and the twitching and plucking of the ox carcass over the uneven ground maddened the fierce little horses so that it was necessary to do some riding in order to keep them to their work. After a while it also became very exhausting,
10 the thirst and fatigue being great, as, with parched lips and blackened from head to foot, we toiled at our task.

In the old days in the ranch country we depended upon game for fresh meat. Nobody liked to kill a beef, and although now and then a maverick° yearling might be killed
15 on the round-up, most of us looked askance at the deed, because if the practice of beef-killing was ever allowed to start, the rustlers—the horse thieves and cattle thieves— would be sure to seize on it as an excuse for general slaughter. Getting meat for the ranch usually devolved upon
20 me. I almost always carried a rifle when I rode, either in a scabbard under my thigh, or across the pommel. Often I would pick up a deer or antelope while about my regular work, when visiting a line camp or riding after the cattle. At other times I would make a day's trip after them. In the
25 fall we sometimes took a wagon and made a week's hunt, returning with eight or ten deer carcasses, and perhaps an elk or a mountain sheep as well. I never became more than a fair hunter, and at times I had most exasperating experiences, either failing to see game which I ought to have
30 seen, or committing some blunder in the stalk, or failing to kill when I fired. Looking back, I am inclined to say that

if I had any good quality as a hunter it was that of perseverance. "It is dogged that does it" in hunting as in in many other things. Unless in wholly exceptional cases, when we were very hungry, I never killed anything but bucks. 5

Occasionally I made long trips away from the ranch and among the Rocky Mountains with my ranch foreman Merrifield; or in later years with Tazewell Woody, John Willis, or John Goff. We hunted bears, both the black and the grizzly, cougars and wolves, and moose, 10 wapiti, and white goat. On one of these trips I killed a bison bull, and I also killed a bison bull on the Little Missouri some fifty miles south of my ranch on a trip which Joe Ferris and I took together. It was rather a rough trip. Each of us carried only his slicker behind 15 him on the saddle, with some flour and bacon done up in it. We met with all kinds of misadventures. Finally one night, when we were sleeping by a slimy little prairie pool where there was not a stick of wood, we had to tie the horses to the horns of our saddles; and 20 then we went to sleep with our heads on the saddles. In the middle of the night something stampeded the horses, and away they went, with the saddles after them. As we jumped to our feet Joe eyed me with an evident suspicion that I was the Jonah of the party, and said: "O 25 Lord! *I've* never done anything to deserve this. Did *you* ever do anything to deserve this?"

I owe more than I can ever express to the West, which of course means to the men and women I met in the West. 30 There were a few people of bad type in my neighborhood—that would be true of every group of men, even in a theological seminary—but I could not speak with too great affection and respect of the great majority of my friends, the hard-working men and women who dwelt for a space of perhaps a hundred and fifty miles along the Little Missouri. I was always as welcome at their houses as they were at mine. Everybody worked, everybody was willing to help everybody else, and yet nobody asked any favors. The same thing was true of the people whom I got to know fifty miles east and fifty miles west of my own range, and of the men I met on the round-ups. They soon accepted me as a friend and fellow-worker who stood on an equal footing with them, and I believe that most of them have kept their feeling for me ever since. No guests were ever more welcome at the White House than these old friends of the cattle ranches and the cow camps—the men with whom I had ridden the long circle and eaten at the tail-board of a chuck-wagon—whenever they turned up at Washington during my Presidency. I remember one of them who appeared at Washington one day just before lunch, a huge, powerful man who, when I knew him, had been distinctly a fighting character. It happened that on that day another old friend, the British Ambassador, Mr. Bryce,° was among those coming to lunch. Just before we went in I turned to my cowpuncher friend and said to him with great solemnity, "Remember, Jim, that if you shot at the feet of the British Ambassador to make him dance, it would be likely to cause international complications;" to which Jim responded with unaffected horror, "Why, Colonel, I shouldn't think of it, I shouldn't think of it!"

Not only did the men and the women whom I met in the cow country quite unconsciously help me, by the insight which working and living with them enabled me to get into the mind and soul of the average American of the right type, but they helped me in another way. I made up my mind that they were men of just the kind whom it would be well to have with me if ever it became neces- 5 sary to go to war. When the Spanish War came, I gave this thought practical realization.

Fortunately, Wister and Remington, with pen and pencil, have made these men live as long as our literature lives. I have sometimes been asked if Wister's 10 "Virginian" is not overdrawn; why, one of the men I have mentioned in this chapter was in all essentials the Virginian in real life, not only in his force but in his charm. Half of the men I worked with or played with and half of the men who soldiered with me afterwards in my 15 regiment might have walked out of Wister's stories or Remington's pictures.

There were bad characters in the Western country at that time, of course, and under the conditions of life they were probably more dangerous than they would 20 have been elsewhere. I hardly ever had any difficulty, however. I never went into a saloon, and in the little hotels I kept out of the bar-room unless, as sometimes happened, the bar-room was the only room on the lower floor except the dining-room. I always endeavored to 25 keep out of a quarrel until self-respect forbade my making any further effort to avoid it, and I very rarely had even the semblance of trouble.

Of course amusing incidents occurred now and then. Usually these took place when I was hunting lost horses, 30 for in hunting lost horses I was ordinarily alone, and occasionally had to travel a hundred or a hundred and fifty

miles away from my own country. On one such occasion I reached a little cow town long after dark, stabled my horse in an empty outbuilding, and when I reached the hotel was informed in response to my request for a bed that
5 I could have the last one left, as there was only one other man in it. The room to which I was shown contained two double beds; one contained two men fast asleep, and the other only one man, also asleep. This man proved to be a friend, one of the Bill Joneses whom I have previously men-
10 tioned. I undressed according to the fashion of the day and place, that is, I put my trousers, boots, shaps, and gun down beside the bed, and turned in. A couple of hours later I was awakened by the door being thrown open and a lantern flashed in my face, the light gleaming on the
15 muzzle of a cocked .45. Another man said to the lantern-bearer, "It ain't him;" the next moment my bedfellow was covered with two guns, and addressed, "Now, Bill, don't make a fuss, but come along quiet." "I'm not think-ing of making a fuss," said Bill. "That's right," was the
20 answer; "we're your friends; we don't want to hurt you; we just want you to come along, you know why." And Bill pulled on his trousers and boots and walked out with them. Up to this time there had not been a sound from the other bed. Now a match was scratched, a candle lit,
25 and one of the men in the other bed looked round the room. At this point I committed the breach of etiquette of asking questions. "I wonder why they took Bill," I said. There was no answer, and I repeated "I wonder why they took Bill." "Well," said the man with the candle, dryly,
30 "I reckon they wanted him," and with that he blew out the candle and conversation ceased. Later I discovered that Bill in a fit of playfulness had held up the Northern

Pacific train at a near-by station by shooting at the feet of the conductor to make him dance. This was purely a joke on Bill's part, but the Northern Pacific people possessed a less robust sense of humor, and on their complaint the United States Marshal was sent after Bill, on the 5 ground that by delaying the train he had interfered with the mails.

The only time I ever had serious trouble was at an even more primitive little hotel than the one in question. It was also on an occasion when I was out after lost horses. 10 Below the hotel had merely a bar-room, a dining-room, and a lean-to kitchen; above was a loft with fifteen or twenty beds in it. It was late in the evening when I reached the place. I heard one or two shots in the barroom as I came up, and I disliked going in. But there 15 was nowhere else to go, and it was a cold night. Inside the room were several men, who, including the bartender, were wearing the kind of smile worn by men who are making believe to like what they don't like. A shabby individual in a broad hat with a cocked gun in each hand 20 was walking up and down the floor talking with strident profanity. He had evidently been shooting at the clock, which had two or three holes in its face.

He was not a "bad man" of the really dangerous type, the true man-killer type, but he was an objectionable 25 creature, a would-be bad man, a bully who for the moment was having things all his own way. As soon as he saw me he hailed me as "Four eyes," in reference to my spectacles, and said, "Four eyes is going to treat." I joined in the laugh and got behind the stove and sat down, 30 thinking to escape notice. He followed me, however, and though I tried to pass it off as a jest this merely made him

more offensive, and he stood leaning over me, a gun in each hand, using very foul language. He was foolish to stand so near, and, moreover, his heels were close together, so that his position was unstable. Accordingly, in response
5 to his reiterated command that I should set up the drinks, I said, "Well, if I've got to, I've got to," and rose, looking past him.

As I rose, I struck quick and hard with my right just to one side of the point of his jaw, hitting with my left
10 as I straightened out, and then again with my right. He fired the guns, but I do not know whether this was merely a convulsive action of his hands or whether he was trying to shoot at me. When he went down he struck the corner of the bar with his head. It was not a case in which one could
15 afford to take chances, and if he had moved I was about to drop on his ribs with my knees; but he was senseless. I took away his guns, and the other people in the room, who were now loud in their denunciation of him, hustled him out and put him in a shed. I got dinner as soon as
20 possible, sitting in a corner of the dining-room away from the windows, and then went upstairs to bed where it was dark so that there would be no chance of any one shooting at me from the outside. However, nothing happened. When my assailant came to, he went down to the station
25 and left on a freight.

There was one bit of frontier philosophy which I should like to see imitated in more advanced communities. Certain crimes of revolting baseness and cruelty were never
30 forgiven. But in the case of ordinary offenses, the man who had served his term and who then tried to make good was given a fair chance; and of course this was equally

true of the women. Every one who has studied the subject at all is only too well aware that the world offsets the
readiness with which it condones a crime for which a man
escapes punishment, by its unforgiving relentlessness to
the often far less guilty man who *is* punished, and who 5
therefore has made his atonement. On the frontier, if the
man honestly tried to behave himself there was generally
a disposition to give him fair play and a decent show. Several of the men I knew and whom I particularly liked came
in this class. There was one such man in my regiment, a 10
man who had served a term for robbery under arms, and
who had atoned for it by many years of fine performance
of duty. I put him in a high official position, and no man
under me rendered better service to the State, nor was
there any man whom, as soldier, as civil officer, as citizen, 15
and as friend, I valued and respected—and now value and
respect—more.

Now I suppose some good people will gather from this
that I favor men who commit crimes. I certainly do not
favor them. I have not a particle of sympathy with the sen- 20
timentality—as I deem it, the mawkishness—which over-
flows with foolish pity for the criminal and cares not at
all for the victim of the criminal. I am glad to see wrong-
doers punished. The punishment is an absolute necessity
from the standpoint of society; and I put the reformation 25
of the criminal second to the welfare of society. But I
do desire to see the man or woman who has paid the penalty and who wishes to reform given a helping hand—
surely every one of us who knows his own heart must know
that he too may stumble, and should be anxious to help his 30
brother or sister who has stumbled. When the criminal
has been punished, if he then shows a sincere desire to lead

a decent and upright life, he should be given the chance, he should be helped and not hindered; and if he makes good, he should receive that respect from others which so often aids in creating self-respect—the most invaluable 5 of all possessions.

THE ROUGHRIDERS

In the spring of 1897 President McKinley appointed me Assistant Secretary of the Navy. I owed the appointment chiefly to the efforts of Senator H. C. Lodge,° of Massachusetts, who doubtless was actuated chiefly by his long and close friendship for me, but also—I like to be-5 lieve—by his keen interest in the Navy.° The first book I had ever published, fifteen years previously, was "The History of the Naval War of 1812;" and I have always taken the interest in the Navy which every good American ought to take. At the time I wrote the book, in the 10 early eighties, the navy had reached its nadir, and we were then utterly incompetent to fight Spain or any other power that had a navy at all. Shortly afterwards we began timidly and hesitatingly to build up a fleet. It is amusing to recall the roundabout steps we took to accom-15 plish our purpose. In the reaction after the colossal struggle of the Civil War our strongest and most capable men had thrown their whole energy into business, into money-making, into the development, and above all the exploitation and exhaustion at the most rapid rate pos-20 sible, of our natural resources—mines, forests, soil, and rivers. These men were not weak men, but they permitted themselves to grow shortsighted and selfish; and while many of them down at the bottom possessed the fundamental virtues, including the fighting virtues, others 25 were purely of the glorified huckster or glorified pawnbroker type—which when developed to the exclusion of everything else makes about as poor a national type as the world has seen. This unadulterated huckster or pawnbroker type is rarely keenly sympathetic in matters of social and industrial justice, and is usually physically timid and likes to cover an unworthy fear of the most just war under high-sounding names.

5 It was reinforced by the large mollycoddle vote—the people who are soft physically and morally, or who have a twist in them which makes them acidly cantankerous and unpleasant as long as they can be so with safety to their bodies. In addition there are the good people with 10 no imagination and no foresight, who think war will not come, but that if it does come armies and navies can be improvised—a very large element, typified by a Senator I knew personally who, in a public speech, in answer to a question as to what we would do if America were sud-15 denly assailed by a first-class military power, answered that "we would build a battle-ship in every creek." Then, among the wise and high-minded people who in self-respecting and genuine fashion strive earnestly for peace, for there are the foolish fanatics always to be found 20 in such a movement and always discrediting it—the men who form the lunatic fringe in all reform movements.

All these elements taken together made a body of public opinion so important during the decades immediately 25 succeeding the Civil War as to put a stop to any serious effort to keep the Nation in a condition of reasonable military prepardness. The representatives of this opinion then voted just as they now do when they vote against battleships or against fortifying the Panama Canal. It would 30 have been bad enough if we had been content to be weak, and, in view of our weakness, not to bluster. But we were not content with such a policy. We wished to enjoy . the incompatible luxuries of an unbridled tongue and an unready hand. There was a very large element which was ignorant of our military weakness, or, naturally enough, unable to understand it; and another large element which liked to please its own vanity by 5 listening to offensive talk about foreign nations. Accordingly, too many of our politicians, especially in Congress found that the cheap and easy thing to do was to please the foolish peace people by keeping us weak, and to please the foolish violent people by passing denuncia- 10 tory resolutions about international matters—resolutions which would have been improper even if we had been strong. Their idea was to please both the mollycoddle vote and the vote of the international tail-twisters by uphold- ing, with pretended ardor and mean intelligence, a Na- 15 tional policy of peace with insult.

I abhor unjust war. I abhor injustice and bullying by the strong at the expense of the weak, whether among nationals or individuals. I abhor violence and bloodshed. I believe that war should never be resorted to when, or so 20 long as, it is possible honorably to avoid it. I respect all men and women who from high motives and with sanity and self-respect do all they can to avert war. I advocate preparation for war in order to avert war; and I should never advocate war unless it were the only alternative 25 to dishonor. I describe the folly of which so many of our people were formerly guilty, in order that we may in our own day be on our guard against similar folly.

We did not at the time of which I write take our for- eign duties seriously, and as we combined bluster in speech 30 with refusal to make any preparation whatsoever for action, we were not taken seriously in return. Gradually a slight change for the better occurred, the writings of Captain Mahan° playing no small part therein. We built some modern cruisers to start with; the people who felt that battle-ships were wicked compromising with their misguided consciences by saying that the cruisers could be used "to protect our commerce"—which they could not be, unless they had battle-ships to back them. Then we attempted to build more powerful fighting vessels, and as there was a section of the public which regarded battle-ships as possessing a name immorally suggestive of violence, we compromised by calling the new ships armored cruisers, and making them combine with exquisite nicety all the defects and none of the virtues of both types. Then we got to the point of building battle-ships. But there still remained a public opinion, as old as the time of Jefferson,° which thought that in the event of war all our problem ought to be one of coast defense, that we should do nothing except repel attack; an attitude about as sensible as that of a prize-fighter who expected to win by merely parrying instead of hitting. To meet the susceptibilities of this large class of well-meaning people, we provided for the battle-ships under the name of "coast defense battle-ships;" meaning thereby that we did not make them quite as seaworthy as they ought to have been, or with quite as much coal capacity as they ought to have had. Then we decided to build real battle-ships. But there still remained a lingering remnant of public opinion that clung to the coast defense theory, and we met this in beautiful fashion by providing for "seagoing coast defense battle-ships"— the fact that the name was a contradiction in terms being of very small consequence compared to the fact that we did thereby get real battle-ships.

Our men had to be trained to handle the ships singly and in fleet formation, and they had to be trained to use the new weapons of precision with which the ships were armed. Not a few of the older officers, kept in the service under our foolish rule of pure seniority promotion, were 5 not competent for the task; but a proportion of the older officers were excellent, and this was true of almost all the younger officers. They were naturally first-class men, trained in the admirable naval school at Annapolis. They were overjoyed that at last they were given proper 10 instruments to work with, and they speedily grew to handle these ships individually in the best fashion. They were fast learning to handle them in squadron and fleet formation; but when the war with Spain broke out, they had as yet hardly grasped the principles of modern 15 scientific naval gunnery.

Soon after I began work as Assistant Secretary of the Navy I became convinced that the war would come. The revolt in Cuba had dragged its weary length until conditions in the island had become so dreadful as to 20 be a standing disgrace to us for permitting them to exist. There is much that I sincerely admire about the Spanish character; and there are few men for whom I have felt greater respect than for certain gentlemen of Spain whom I have known. But Spain attempted to govern her colonies 25 on archaic principles which rendered her control of them incompatible with the advance of humanity and intolerable to the conscience of mankind. In 1898 the so-called war in Cuba had dragged along for years with unspeakable horror, degradation, and misery. It was not 30 "war" at all, but murderous oppression. Cuba was devastated.

When the Maine° was blown up in Havana Harbor, war became inevitable. A number of the peace-at-any-price men of course promptly assumed the position that she had blown herself up; but investigation showed that the 5 explosion was from outside. And, in any event, it would have been impossible to prevent war.

Among my friends was the then Army Surgeon Leonard Wood. He was a surgeon. Not having an income, he had to earn his own living. He had gone through the 10 Harvard Medical School, and had then joined the army in the Southwest as a contract doctor. He had every physical, moral, and mental quality which fitted him for a soldier's life and for the exercise of command. In the inconceivably wearing and harassing campaigns against 15 the Apaches° he had served nominally as a surgeon, really in command of troops, on more than one expedition. He was as anxious as I was that if there were war we should both have our part in it. I had always felt that if there were a serious war I wished to be in a position 20 to explain to my children why I did take part in it, and not why I did not take part in it. Moreover, I had very deeply felt that it was our duty to free Cuba, and I had publicly expressed this feeling; and when a man takes such a position, he ought to be willing to make 25 his words good by his deeds unless there is some very strong reason to the contrary. He should pay with his body.

As soon as war was upon us, Wood and I began to try for a chance to go to the front. Congress had authorized 30 the raising of three National Volunteer Cavalry regiments wholly apart from the State contingents. Secretary

Alger° of the War Department was fond of me personally,
and Wood was his family doctor. Alger had been a gallant soldier in the Civil War, and was almost the only
member of the Administration who felt all along that
we would have to go to war with Spain over Cuba. He 5
liked my attitude in the matter, and because of his remembrance of his own experiences he sympathized with my
desire to go to the front. Accordingly he offered me the
command of one of the regiments. I told him that after
six weeks' service in the field I would feel competent to 10
handle the regiment, but that I would not know how to
equip it or how to get it into the first action; but that
Wood was entirely competent at once to take command,
and that if he would make Wood colonel I would accept
the lieutenant-colonelcy. General Alger thought this 15
an act of foolish self-abnegation on my part—instead
of its being, what it was, the wisest act I could have performed. He told me to accept the colonelcy, and that
he would make Wood lieutenant-colonel, and that Wood
would do the work anyway; but I answered that I did 20
not wish to rise on any man's shoulders; that I hoped
to be given every chance that my deeds and abilities
warranted; but that I did not wish what I did not earn,
and that above all I did not wish to hold any position
where any one else did the work. He laughed at me a 25
little and said I was foolish, but I do not think he really
minded, and he promised to do as I wished. True to
his word, he secured the appointment of Wood as colonel
and of myself as lieutenant-colonel of the First United
States Volunteer Cavalry. This was soon nicknamed, 30
both by the public and by the rest of the army, the Rough
Riders, doubtless because the bulk of the men were from

the Southwestern ranch country and were skilled in the wild horsemanship of the great plains.

Wood instantly began the work of raising the regiment. He first assembled several old non-commissioned officers of experience, put them in office, and gave them blanks for requisitions for the full equipment of a cavalry regiment. He selected San Antonio° as the gathering-place, as it was in a good horse country, near the Gulf, from some port on which we would have to embark, and near an
10 old arsenal and an old army post from which we got a good deal of stuff—some of it practically condemmed, but which we found serviceable at a pinch, and much better than nothing. He organized a horse board in Texas, and began purchasing all horses that were not too big and were sound.
15 A day or two after he was commisioned he wrote out in the office of the Secretary of War, under his authority, telegrams to the Governors of Arizona, New Mexico, Oklahoma, and Indian Territory, in substance as follows:
" The President desires to raise — volunteers in your
20 Territory to form part of a regiment of mounted rifleman to be commanded by Leonard Wood, Colonel; Theodore Roosevelt, Lieutenant-Colonel. He desires that the men selected should be young, sound, good shots and good riders, and that you expedite by all means in your power
25 the enrollment of these men.

" (Signed) R. A. Alger, Secretary of War."

As soon as he had attended to a few more odds and ends he left Washington, and the day after his arrival in San Antonio the troops began to arrive.

30 The regiment assembled at San Antonio. When I reached there, the men, rifles, and horses, which were the

essentials, were coming in fast, and the saddles, blankets, and the like were also accumulating. Thanks to Wood's exertions, when we reached Tampa° we were rather better equipped than most of the regular regiments. We adhered strictly to field equipment, allowing no luxuries 5 or anything else unnecessary, and so we were able to move off the field when ordered, with our own transportation, leaving nothing behind.

I suppose every man tends to brag about his regiment; but it does seem to me that there never was a regiment 10 better worth bragging about than ours. Wood was an exceptional commander, of great power, with a remarkable gift for organization. The rank and file were as fine natural fighting men as ever carried a rifle or rode a horse in any country or any age. We had a number of first- 15 class young fellows from the East, most of them from colleges like Harvard, Yale, and Princeton; but the great majority of the men were Southwesterners, from the then Territories of Oklahoma, Indian Territory, Arizona, and New Mexico. They were accustomed to the use 20 of firearms, accustomed to taking care of themselves in the open; they were intelligent and self-reliant; they possessed hardihood and endurance and physical prowess; and, above all, they had the fighting edge, the cool and resolute fighting temper. They went into the war with 25 full knowledge, having deliberately counted the cost. In the great majority of cases each man was chiefly anxious to find out what he should do to make the regiment a success. They bought, first and last, about 800 copies of the cavalry drill regulations and studied them industri- 30 ously. Such men were practically soldiers to start with, in all the essentials. It is small wonder that with them as

material to work upon the regiment was raised, armed,
equipped, drilled, sent on trains to Tampa, embarked, dis-
embarked, and put through two victorious offensive—not
defensive—fights in which a third of the officers and one-
5 fifth of the men were killed or wounded, all within sixty
days. It is a good record,° and it speaks well for the men
of the regiment; and it speaks well for Wood.

THE PRESIDENCY

On September 6, 1901, President McKinley° was shot by an Anarchist in the city of Buffalo. I went to Buffalo at once. The President's condition seemed to be improving, and after a day or two we were told that he was practically out of danger. I then joined my family, who 5 were in the Adirondacks, near the foot of Mount Tahawus. A day or two afterwards we took a long tramp through the forest, and in the afternoon I climbed Mount Tahawus.

After reaching the top I had descended a few hundred feet to a shelf of land where there was a little lake, when I 10 saw a guide coming out of the woods on our trail from below. I felt at once that he had bad news, and, sure enough, he handed me a telegram saying that the President's condition was much worse and that I must come to Buffalo immediately. It was late in the afternoon, and darkness 15 had fallen by the time I reached the club-house where we were staying. It was some time afterwards before I could get a wagon to drive me out to the nearest railway station, North Creek, some forty or fifty miles distant. The roads were the ordinary wilderness roads and the night was dark. 20 But we changed horses two or three times—when I say "we" I mean the driver and I, as there was no one else with us—and reached the station just at dawn, to learn from Mr. Loeb,° who had a special train waiting, that the President was dead. That evening I took the oath of 25 office, in the house of Ansley Wilcox, at Buffalo.

I at once announced that I would continue unchanged McKinley's policies for the honor and prosperity of the

country, and asked all the members of the Cabinet to
stay.   There were no changes made among them save
as changes were made among their successors whom
I myself appointed.   I continued Mr. McKinley's policies,
5 changing and developing them and adding new policies
only as the questions before the public changed and
as the needs of the public developed. Some of my
friends shook their heads over this, telling me that the
men I retained would not be "loyal to me," and that I
10 would seem as if I were "a pale copy of McKinley."   I
told them that I was not nervous on this score, and that
if the men I retained were loyal to their work they would
be giving me the loyalty for which I most cared; and that
if they were not, I would change them anyhow; and that
15 as for being "a pale copy of McKinley," I was not primarily concerned with either following or not following in
his footsteps, but in facing the new problems that arose;
and that if I were competent I would find ample opportunity to show my competence by my deeds° without
20 worrying myself as to how to convince people of the fact.

OUTDOORS AND INDOORS

THERE are men who love out-of-doors who yet never open a book; and other men who love books but to whom the great book of nature is a sealed volume, and the lines written therein blurred and illegible. Nevertheless, among those men whom I have known, the love of books 5 and the love of outdoors, in their highest expressions, have usually gone hand in hand. It is an affectation for the man who is praising outdoors to sneer at books. Usually the keenest appreciation of what is seen in nature is to be found in those who have also profited by the 10 hoarded and recorded wisdom of their fellow-men. Love of outdoor life, love of simple and hardy pastimes, can be gratified by men and women who do not possess large means, and who work hard; and so can love of good books— not of good bindings and of first editions, excellent enough 15 in their way but sheer luxuries—I mean love of reading books, owning them if possible of course, but, if that is not possible, getting them from a circulating library.

Sagamore Hill takes its name from the old Sagamore Mohannis, who, as chief of his little tribe, signed away his 20 rights to the land two centuries and a half ago. The house stands right on the top of the hill, separated by fields and belts of woodland from all other houses, and looks out over the bay and the Sound. We see the sun go down beyond long reaches of land and of water. Many 25 birds dwell in the trees round the house or in the pastures and the woods near by, and of course in winter gulls, loons, and wild fowl frequent the waters of the bay and the Sound. We love all the seasons: the snows and bare woods

67

of winter; the rush of growing things and the blossom-spray of spring; the yellow grain, the ripening fruits and tasseled corn, and the deep, leafy shades that are heralded by "the green dance of summer;" and the sharp fall winds
5 that tear the brilliant banners with which the trees greet the dying year.

The Sound is always lovely. In the summer nights we watch it from the piazza, and see the lights of the tall Fall River boats as they steam steadily by. Now and then we
10 spend a day on it, the two of us together in the light rowing skiff, or perhaps with one of the boys to pull an extra pair of oars; we land for lunch at noon under wind-beaten oaks on the edge of a low bluff, or among the wild plum bushes on a spit of white sand, while the sails of the coast-
15 ing schooners gleam in the sunlight, and the tolling of the bell-buoy comes landward across the waters.

Long Island is not as rich in flowers as the valley of the Hudson. Yet there are many. Early in April there is one hillside near us which glows like a tender flame with
20 the white of the bloodroot. About the same time we find the shy mayflower, the trailing arbutus; and although we rarely pick wild flowers, one member of the household always plucks a little bunch of mayflowers to send to a friend working in Panama, whose soul hungers for the
25 Northern spring. Then there are shad-blow and delicate anemones, about the time of the cherry blossoms; the brief glory of the apple orchards follows; and then the thronging dog-woods fill the forests with their radiance; and so flowers follow flowers until the springtime splendor
30 closes with the laurel and the evanescent, honey sweet locust bloom. The late summer flowers follow, the flaunting lilies, and cardinal flowers, and marshmallows,

and pale beach rosemary; and the goldenrod and the asters when the afternoons shorten and we again begin to think of fires in the wide fire-places.

Most of the birds in our neighborhood are the ordinary home friends of the house and the barn, the wood lot and the pasture; but now and then the species make queer shifts. The cheery quail, alas! are rarely found near us now; and we no longer hear the whippoorwills at night. But some birds visit us now which formerly did not. When I was a boy neither the black-throated green warbler nor the purple finch nested around us, nor were bobolinks found in our fields. The black-throated green warbler is now one of our commonest summer warblers; there are plenty of purple finches; and, best of all, the bobolinks are far from infrequent. I had written about these new visitors to John Burroughs,° and once when he came out to see me I was able to show them to him.

When I was President, we owned a little house in western Virginia; a delightful house, to us at least, although only a shell of rough boards. We used sometimes to go there in the fall, perhaps at Thanksgiving, and on these occasions we would have quail and rabbits of our own shooting, and once in a while a wild turkey. We also went there in the spring. Of course many of the birds were different from our Long Island friends. There were mocking-birds, the most attractive of all birds, and blue grosbeaks, and cardinals and summer redbirds instead of scarlet tanagers, and those wonderful singers the Bewick's wrens, and Carolina wrens. All these I was able to show John Burroughs when he came to visit us; although, by the way, he did not appreciate as much as we did one set of inmates of the cottage—the flying squirrels. We loved

having the flying squirrels, father and mother and half-
grown young, in their nest among the rafters; and at
night we slept so soundly that we did not in the least mind
the wild gambols of the little fellows through the rooms,
5 even when, as sometimes happened, they would swoop
down to the bed and scuttle across it.

One April I went to Yellowstone Park, when the snow
was still very deep, and I took John Burroughs with me.
I wished to show him the big game of the Park, the wild
10 creatures that have become so astonishingly tame and
tolerant of human presence.   In the Yellowstone the
animals seem always to behave as one wishes them to!
It is always possible to see the sheep and deer and antelope, and also the great herds of elk, which are shyer than
15 the smaller beasts.   In April we found the elk weak after
the short commons and hard living of winter.   Once without much difficulty I regularly rounded up a big band of
them, so that John Burroughs could look at them.   I do
not think, however, that he cared to see them as much as
20 I did.   The birds interested him more, especially a tiny
owl the size of a robin which we saw perched on the top
of a tree in mid-afternoon entirely uninfluenced by the
sun and making a queer noise like a cork being pulled from
a bottle.   I was rather ashamed to find how much better
25 his eyes were than mine in seeing the birds and grasping
their differences.

When wolf-hunting in Texas, and when bear-hunting in
Louisiana and Mississippi, I was not only enthralled by
the sport, but also by the strange new birds and other
30 creatures, and the trees and flowers I had not known before.
By the way, there was one feast at the White House which
stands above all others in my memory—even above the

time when I lured Joel Chandler Harris° thither for a night, a deed in which to triumph, as all who knew that inveterately shy recluse will testify. This was "the bear-hunters' dinner." I had been treated so kindly by my friends on these hunts, and they were such fine fellows, men whom I was so proud to think of as Americans, that I set my heart on having them at a hunters' dinner at the White House. One December I succeeded; there were twenty or thirty of them, all told, as good hunters, as daring riders, as first-class citizens as could be found anywhere; no finer set of guests ever sat at meat in the White House; and among other game on the table was a black bear, itself contributed by one of these same guests.

When I first visited California, it was my good fortune to see the "big trees," the Sequoias,° and then to travel down into the Yosemite with John Muir.° Of course of all people in the world he was the one with whom it was best worth while thus to see the Yosemite. He told me that when Emerson° came to California he tried to get him to come out and camp with him, for that was the only way in which to see at their best the majesty and charm of the Sierras. But at the time Emerson was getting old and could not go. John Muir met me with a couple of packers and two mules to carry our tent, bedding, and food for a three days' trip. The first night was clear, and we lay down in the darkening isles of the great Sequoia grove. The majestic trunks, beautiful in color and in symmetry, rose round us like the pillars of a mightier cathedral than ever was conceived even by the fervor of the Middle Ages. Hermit thrushes sang beautifully in the evening, and again, with a burst of wonderful music, at dawn. I was interested and a little surprised to find

that, unlike John Burroughs, John Muir cared little for
birds or bird songs, and knew little about them.   The
hermit thrushes meant nothing to him, the trees and the
flowers and the cliffs everything.   The only birds he no-
5 ticed or cared for were some that were very conspicuous,
such as the water-ousels—always particular favorites of
mine too.   The second night we camped in a snow-storm,
on the edge of the canyon walls, under the spreading limbs
of a grove of mighty silver firs; and next day we went down
10 into the wonderland of the valley itself.   I shall always be
glad that I was in the Yosemite with John Muir and in the
Yellowstone with John Burroughs.

Our most beautiful singers are the wood thrushes; they
sing not only in the early morning but throughout the
15 long, hot June afternoons.   Sometimes they sing in the
trees immediately around the house, and if the air is still
we can always hear them from among the tall trees at the
foot of the hill. The thrashers sing in the hedgerows beyond
the garden, the catbirds everywhere.   The catbirds have
20 such an attractive song that it is extremely irritating to
know that at any moment they may interrupt it to mew
and squeal.   The bold, cheery music of the robins always
seems typical of the bold, cheery birds themselves.   The
Baltimore orioles nest in the young elms around the house,
25 and the orchard orioles in the apple trees near the garden
and outbuildings.   Among the earliest sounds of spring is
the cheerful, simple, homely song of the song-sparrow; and
in March we also hear the piercing cadence of the meadow-
lark—to us one of the most attractive of all bird calls.   Of
30 late years now and then we hear the rollicking, bubbling
melody of the bobolink in the pastures back of the barn;

and when the full chorus of these and of many other of the
singers of spring is dying down, there are some true hot-
weather songsters, such as the brightly hued indigo bunt-
ings and thistle-finches. Among the finches one of the
most musical and plaintive songs is that of the bush- 5
sparrow—I do not know why the books call it field-
sparrow, for it does not dwell in the open fields like the
vesper-finch, the savannah-sparrow, and the grasshopper-
sparrow, but among the cedars and bayberry bushes and
young locusts in the same places where the prairie war- 10
bler is found. Nor is it only the true songs that delight us.
We love to hear the flickers call, and we readily pardon
any one of their number which, as occasionally happens,
is bold enough to wake us in the early morning by drum-
ming on the shingles of the roof. In our ears the red-winged 15
blackbirds have a very attractive note. We love the
screaming of the red-tailed hawks as they soar high overhead, and even the calls of the night heron that nest in the
tall water maples by one of the wood ponds on our place,
and the little green herons that nest beside the salt marsh. 20
It is hard to tell just how much of the attraction in any
bird-note lies in the music itself and how much in the
associations. This is what makes it so useless to try to
compare the bird songs of one country with those of another.
A man who is worth anything can no more be entirely 25
impartial in speaking of the bird-songs with which from
his earliest childhood he has been familiar than he can be
entirely impartial in speaking of his own family.

At Sagamore Hill we love a great many things—birds
and trees and books, and all things beautiful, and horses 30
and rifles and children and hard work and the joy of life.
We have great fireplaces, and in them the logs roar and

crackle during the long winter evenings. The big piazza
is for the hot, still afternoons of summer.

The books are everywhere. There are as many in the
north room and in the parlor—is drawing-room a more
5 appropriate name than parlor?—as in the library; the gun-
room at the top of the house, which incidentally has the
loveliest view of all, contains more books than any of the
other rooms; and they are particularly delightful books to
browse among, just because they have not much rele-
10 vance to one another, this being one of the reasons why
they are relegated to their present abode. But the books
have overflowed into all the other rooms too.

I could not name any principle upon which the books
have been gathered. Books are almost as individual as
15 friends. There is no earthly use in laying down general
laws about them. Some meet the needs of one person, and
some of another; and each person should beware of the
book-lover's besetting sin, of what Mr. Edgar Allan Poe°
calls "the mad pride of intellectuality," taking the shape
20 of arrogant pity for the man who does not like the same
kind of books. Of course there are books which a man or
woman uses as instruments of a profession—law books,
medical books, cookery books, and the like. I am not
speaking of these, for they are not properly "books" at
25 all; they come in the category of time-tables, telephone
directories, and other useful agencies of civilized life. I am
speaking of books that are meant to be read. Personally,
granted that these books are decent and healthy, the one
test to which I demand that they all submit is that of
30 being interesting. If the book is not interesting to the
reader, then in all but an infinitesimal number of cases it

gives scant benefit to the reader. Of course any reader ought to cultivate his or her taste so that good books will appeal to it, and that trash won't. But after this point has once been reached, the needs of each reader must be met in a fashion that will appeal to those needs. Personally 5 the books by which I have profited infinitely more than by any others have been those in which profit was a by-product of the pleasure; that is, I read them because I enjoyed them, because I liked reading them, and the profit came in as part of the enjoyment. 10

Of course each individual is apt to have some special tastes in which he cannot expect that any but a few friends will share. Now, I am very proud of my big-game library. I suppose there must be many big-game libraries in Continental Europe, and possibly in England more extensive 15 than mine, but I have not happened to come across any such library in this country. Some of the originals go back to the sixteenth century, and there are copies or reproductions of the two or three most famous hunting books of the Middle Ages, such as the Duke of York's 20 translation of Gaston Phœbus,° and the queer book of the Emperor Maximilian.° It is only very occasionally that I meet any one who cares for any of these books. On the other hand, I expect to find many friends who will turn naturally to some of the old or the new books of poetry or 25 romance or history to which we of the household habitually turn. Let me add that ours is in no sense a collector's library. Each book was procured because some one of the family wished to read it. We could never afford to take overmuch thought for the outsides of books; we were 30 too much interested in their insides.

Now and then I am asked as to "what books a statesman should read," and my answer is, poetry and novels—
including short stories under the head of novels. I don't
mean that he should read only novels and modern poetry.
5 If he cannot also enjoy the Hebrew prophets and the
Greek dramatists, he should be sorry. He ought to read
interesting books on history and government, and books
of science and philosophy; and really good books on these
subjects are as enthralling as any fiction ever written in
10 prose or verse. Gibbon° and Macaulay,° Herodotus,°
Thucydides° and Tacitus,° the Heimskringla,° Froissart,°
Joinville° and Villehardouin,° Parkman° and Mahan,°
Mommsen° and Ranke°—why! there are scores and scores
of solid histories, the best in the world, which are as ab-
15 sorbing as the best of all the novels, and of as permanant
value. The same thing is true of Darwin° and Huxley° and
Carlyle° and Emerson,° and parts of Kant,° and of volumes
like Sutherland's° " Growth of the Moral Instinct," or
Acton's° Essays and Lounsbury's° studies—here again I
20 am not trying to class books together, or measure one by
another, or enumerate one in a thousand of those worth
reading, but just to indicate that any man or woman of
some intelligence and some cultivation can in some
line or other of serious thought, scientific or historical or
25 philosophical or economic or governmental, find any number of books which are charming to read, and which in
addition give that for which his or her soul hungers. I do
not for a minute mean that the statesman ought not to
read a great many different books of this character, just
30 as every one else should read them. But, in the final
event, the statesman, and the publicist, and the reformer,
and the agitator for new things, and the upholder of what

is good in old things, all need more than anything else to know human nature, to know the needs of the human soul; and they will find this nature and these needs set forth as nowhere else by the great imaginative writers, whether of prose or of poetry.   5

The room for choice is so limitless that to my mind it seems absurd to try to make catalogues which shall be supposed to appeal to all the best thinkers. This is why I have no sympathy whatever with writing lists of *the* One Hundred Best Books,° or *the* Five-Foot Library.° It 10 is all right for a man to amuse himself by composing *a* list of a hundred very good books; and if he is to go off for a year or so where he cannot get many books, it is an excellent thing to choose a five-foot library of particular books which in that particular year and on that particular 15 trip he would like to read. But there is no such thing as a hundred books that are best for all men, or for the majority of men, or for one man at all times; and there is no such thing as a five-foot library which will satisfy the needs of even one particular man on different occasions extending 20 over a number of years. Milton° is best for one mood and Pope° for another. Because a man likes Whitman° or Browning° or Lowell° he should not feel himself debarred from Tennyson° or Kipling° or Körner° or Heine° or the Bard of the Dimbovitza.° Tolstoy's° novels are good at one 25 time and those of Sienkiewicz° at another; and he is fortunate who can relish "Salammbo"° and "Tom Brown"° and the "Two Admirals"° and "Quentin Durward"° and "Artemus Ward"° and the "Ingoldsby Legends"° and "Pickwick"° and "Vanity Fair."° Why, there 30 are hundreds of books like these, each one of which, if really read, really assimilated, by the person to whom it

happens to appeal, will enable that person quite uncon- '
sciously to furnish himself with much ammunition which
he will find of use in the battle of life.

A book must be interesting to the particular reader at
5 that particular time. But there are tens of thousands of
interesting books, and some of them are sealed to some men
and some are sealed to others; and some stir the soul at
some given point of a man's life and yet convey no message at other times. The reader, the book-lover, must meet
10 his own needs without paying too much attention to what
his neighbors say those needs should be. He must not
hypocritically pretend to like what he does not like. Yet
at the same time he must avoid that most unpleasant of all
the indications of puffed-up vanity which consists in treat-
15 ing mere individual, and perhaps unfortunate, idiosyn-
crasy as a matter of pride. I happen to be devoted to
Macbeth,° whereas I very seldom read Hamlet° (though
I like parts of it). Now I am humbly and sincerely conscious that this is a demerit in me and not in Hamlet; and
20 yet it would not do me any good to pretend that I like
Hamlet as much as Macbeth when, as a matter of fact,
I don't.

Aside from the masters of literature, there are all kinds
of books which one person will find delightful, and which
25 he certainly ought not to surrender just because nobody else
is able to find as much in the beloved volume. There is on
our book-shelves a little pre-Victorian novel or tale called
"The Semi-Attached Couple." It is told with much
humor; it is a story of gentlefolk who are really gentlefolk;
30 and to me it is altogether delightful. But outside the
members of my own family I have never met a human

being who had even heard of it, and I don't suppose I ever shall meet one. I often enjoy a story by some living author so much that I write to tell him so—or to tell her so; and at least half the time I regret my action, because it encourages the writer to believe that the public shares my views, and he then finds that the public doesn't.

Books are all very well in their way, and we love them at Sagamore Hill; but children are better than books. Sagamore Hill is one of three neighboring houses in which small cousins spent very happy years of childhood. In the three houses there were at one time sixteen of these small cousins, all told, and once we ranged them in order of size and took their photograph. There are many kinds of success in life worth having. It is exceedingly interesting and attractive to be a successful business man, or railway man, or farmer, or a successful lawyer or doctor; or a writer, or a President, or a ranchman, or the colonel of a fighting regiment, or to kill grizzly bears and lions. But for unflagging interest and enjoyment, a household of children, if things go reasonably well, certainly makes all other forms of success and achievement lose their importance by comparison.

It may be true that he travels farthest who travels alone; but the goal thus reached is not worth reaching. And as for a life deliberately devoted to pleasure as an end—why, the greatest happiness is the happiness that comes as a by-product of striving to do what must be done, even though sorrow is met in the doing. There is a bit of homely philosophy, quoted by Squire Bill Widener, of Widener's Valley, Virginia, which sums up one's duty in life: "Do what you can, with what you've got, where you are."

The country is the place for children, and if not the country, a city small enough so that one can get out into the country. When our own children were little, we were for several winters in Washington, and each Sunday after-
5 noon the whole family spent in Rock Creek Park, which was then very real country indeed. I would drag one of the children's wagons; and when the very smallest pairs of feet grew tired of trudging bravely after us, or of racing on rapturous side trips after flowers and other treasures,
10 the owners would clamber into the wagon. One of these wagons, by the way, a gorgeous red one, had "Express" painted on it in gilt letters, and was known to the younger children as the "'spress" wagon. They evidently associated the color with the term. Once while we were at
15 Sagamore something happened to the cherished "'spress" wagon, to the distress of the children, and especially of the child who owned it. Their mother and I were just starting for a drive in the buggy, and we promised the bereaved owner that we would visit a store we knew in East Nor-
20 wich, a village a few miles away, and bring back another "'spress" wagon. When we reached the store, we found to our dismay that the wagon which we had seen had been sold. We could not bear to return without the promised gift, for we knew that the brains of small persons are much
25 puzzled when their elders seem to break promises. For-tunately, we saw in the store a delightful little bright-red chair and bright-red table, and these we brought home and handed solemnly over to the expectant recipient, explain-ing that as there unfortunately was not a "'spress" wagon
30 we had brought him back a "'spress" chair and "'spress" table. It worked beautifully! The "'spress" chair and table were received with such rapture that we had to get

duplicates for the other small member of the family who was the particular crony of the proprietor of the new treasures.

When their mother and I returned from a row, we would often see the children waiting for us, running like sand-spiders along the beach. They always liked to swim in company with a grown-up of buoyant temperament and inventive mind, and the float offered limitless opportunities for enjoyment while bathing. All dutiful parents know the game of "stage-coach"; each child is given a name, such as the whip, the nigh leader, the off-wheeler, the old lady passenger, and, under penalty of paying a forfeit, must get up and turn round when the grown-up, who is improvising a thrilling story, mentions that particular object; and when the word "stage-coach" is mentioned, everybody has to get up and turn round. Well, we used to play stage-coach on the float while in swimming, and instead of tamely getting up and turning round, the child whose turn it was had to plunge overboard. When I mentioned "stage-coach," the water fairly foamed with vigorously kicking little legs; and then there was always a moment of interest while I counted, so as to be sure that the number of heads that came up corresponded with the number of children who had gone down.

No man or woman will ever forget the time when some child lies sick of a disease that threatens its life. Moreover, much less serious sickness is unpleasant enough at the time. Looking back, however, there are elements of comedy in certain of the less serious cases. I well remember one such instance which occurred when we were living in Washington, in a small house, with barely enough room for everybody when all the chinks were filled. Measles

descended on the household. In the effort to keep the children that were well and those that were sick apart, their mother and I had to camp out in improvised fashion. When the eldest small boy was getting well, and had
5 recovered his spirits, I slept on a sofa beside his bed—the sofa being so short that my feet projected over anyhow. One afternoon a toy organ was given to the small boy by a sympathetic friend. Next morning early I was waked to find the small boy very vivacious and requesting a
10 story. Having drowsily told the story, I said, "Now, father's told you a story, so you amuse yourself and let father go to sleep; " to which the small boy responded most virtuously, "Yes, father will go to sleep and I'll play the organ," which he did, at a distance of two feet from my
15 head. Later his sister, who had just come down with the measles, was put into the same room. The small boy was convalescing, and was engaged in playing on the floor with some tin ships, together with two or three pasteboard monitors and rams of my own manufacture. He
20 was giving a vivid rendering of Farragut° at Mobile Bay, from memories of how I told the story. My pasteboard rams and monitors were fascinating—if a naval architect may be allowed to praise his own work—and as property they were equally divided between the little girl and the
25 small boy. The little girl looked on with alert suspicion from the bed, for she was not yet convalescent enough to be allowed down on the floor. The small boy was busily reciting the phases of the fight, which now approached its climax, and the little girl evidently suspected that her
30 monitor was destined to play the part of victim.

Little boy. "And then they steamed bang into the monitor."

Little girl. "Brother, don't you sink my monitor!"

Little boy (without heeding, and hurrying toward the climax). "And the torpedo went at the monitor!"

Little girl. "My monitor is not to sink!"

Little boy, dramatically. "And bang the monitor sank!" 5

Little girl.· "It didn't do any such thing. My monitor always goes to bed at seven, and it's now quarter past. My monitor was in bed and *couldn't* sink!"

. When I was Assistant Secretary of the Navy, Leonard Wood and I used often to combine forces and take both 10 families of children out to walk, and occasionally some of their playmates. Leonard Wood's son, I found, attributed the paternity of all of those not of his own family to me. Once we were taking the children across Rock Creek on a fallen tree. I was standing on the middle of the log trying 15 to prevent any of the children from falling off, and while making a clutch at one peculiarly active and heedless child I fell off myself. As I emerged from the water I heard the little Wood boy calling frantically to the General: "Oh! oh! The father of all the children fell into 20 the creek!"—which made me feel like an uncommonly moist patriarch.

There could be no healthier and pleasanter place in which to bring up children than in that nook of old-time America around Sagamore Hill. Certainly I never knew 25 small people to have a better time or a better training for their work in after life than the three families of cousins at Sagamore Hill. It was real country, and—speaking from the somewhat detached point of view of the masculine parent—I should say there was just the proper mix- 30 ture of freedom and control in the management of the

children. They were never allowed to be disobedient or
to shirk lessons or work; and they were encouraged to
have all the fun possible. They often went barefoot,
especially during the many hours passed in various en-
5 thralling pursuits along and in the waters of the bay.
They swam, they tramped, they boated, they coasted and
skated in winter, they were intimate friends with the
cows, chickens, pigs, and other live stock. They had in
succession two ponies, General Grant and, when the
10 General's legs became such that he lay down too often and
too unexpectedly in the road, a calico pony named Algon-
quin, who is still living a life of honorable leisure in the
stable and in the pasture—where he has to be picketed,
because otherwise he chases the cows. Sedate pony Grant
15 used to draw the cart in which the children went driving
when they were very small, the driver being their old
nurse Mame, who had held their mother in her arms when
she was born, and who was knit to them by a tie as close
as any tie of blood. I doubt whether I ever saw Mame
20 really offended with them except once when, out of pure
but misunderstood affection, they named a pig after her!
They loved pony Grant. Once I saw the then little boy
of three hugging pony Grant's fore legs. As he leaned over,
his broad straw hat tilted on end, and pony Grant medi-
25 tatively munched the brim; whereupon the small boy
looked up with a wail of anguish, evidently thinking the
pony had decided to treat him like a radish.

The children had pets of their own, too, of course.
Among them guinea pigs were the stand-bys—their highly
30 unemotional nature fits them for companionship with ador-
ing but over-enthusiastic young masters and mistresses.
Then there were flying squirrels, and kangaroo rats, gentle

and trustful, and a badger whose temper was short but whose nature was fundamentally friendly. The badger's name was Josiah; the particular little boy whose property he was used to carry him about, clasped firmly around what would have been his waist if he had had any. Inas- 5 much as when on the ground the badger would play energetic games of tag with the little boy and nip his bare legs, I suggested that it would be uncommonly disagreeable if he took advantage of being held in the little boy's arms to bite his face; but this suggestion was repelled 10 with scorn as an unworthy assault on the character of Josiah. "He bites legs sometimes, but he never bites faces," said the little boy.

We also had a young black bear whom the children christened Jonathan Edwards,° partly out of compliment 15 to their mother, who was descended from that great Puritan divine, and partly because the bear possessed a temper in which gloom and strength were combined in what the children regarded as Calvinistic proportions. As for the dogs, of course there were many, and during their 20 lives they were intimate and valued family friends, and their deaths were household tragedies. One of them, a large yellow animal of several good breeds and valuable rather because of psychical than physical traits, was named "Susan" by his small owners, in commemoration 25 of another retainer, a white cow; the fact that the cow and the dog were not of the same sex being treated with indifference. Much the most individual of the dogs and the one with the strongest character was Sailor Boy, a Chespeake Bay dog. He had a masterful temper and a strong sense 30 of both dignity and duty. He would never let the other dogs fight, and he himself never fought unless circumstances

imperatively demanded it; but he was a murderous animal
when he did fight. He was not only exceedingly fond of the
water, as was to be expected, but passionately devoted to
gunpowder in every form, for he loved firearms and fairly
5 reveled in the Fourth of July celebrations—the latter being
rather hazardous occasions, as the children strongly objected to any "safe and sane" element being injected into
them, and had the normal number of close shaves with
rockets, Roman candles, and firecrackers.

10   One of the stand-bys for enjoyment, especially in rainy
weather,was the old barn. This had been built nearly a century previously, and was as delightful as only the pleasant-
est kind of old barn can be. It stood at the meeting-spot of
three fences. A favorite amusement used to be an obstacle
15 race when the barn was full of hay. The contestants were
timed and were started successively from outside the door.
They rushed inside, clambered over or burrowed through
the hay, as suited them best, dropped out of a place where
a loose board had come off, got over, through, or under the
20 three fences, and raced back to the starting point. When
they were little, their respective fathers were expected also
to take part in the obstacle race, and when with the advance of years the fathers finally refused to be contestants,
there was a general feeling of pained regret among the
25 children at such a decline in the sporting spirit.

Another famous place for handicap races was Cooper's
Bluff, a gigantic sand-bank rising from the edge of the
bay, a mile from the house. If the tide was high there
was an added thrill, for some of the contestants were sure
30 to run into the water.

As soon as the little boys learned to swim they were

allowed to go off by themselves in rowboats and camp
out for the night along the Sound. Sometimes I would go
along so as to take the smaller children. Once a schooner
was wrecked on a point half a dozen miles away. She
held together well for a season or two after having been 5
cleared of everything down to the timbers, and this gave
us a chance to make camping-out trips in which the girls
could also be included, for we put them to sleep in the
wreck, while the boys slept on the shore: squaw picnics,
the children called them.   10

We had a sleigh for winter; but if, when there was much
snow, the whole family desired to go somewhere, we would
put the body of the farm wagon on runners and all bundle
in together. We always liked snow at Christmas time,
and the sleigh-ride down to the church on Christmas eve. 15
One of the hymns always sung at this Christmas eve
festival begins, "It's Christmas eve on the river, it's Christmas eve on the bay." All good natives of the village
firmly believed that this hymn was written here, and with
direct reference to Oyster Bay; although if such were the 20
case the word "river" would have to be taken in a hyper-
bolic sense, as the nearest approach to a river is the village pond. I used to share this belief myself, until my
faith was shaken by a Denver lady who wrote that she
had sung that hymn when a child in Michigan, and that 25
at the present time her little Denver babies also loved
it, although in their case the river was not represented by
even a village pond.

As the children grew up, Sagamore Hill remained delightful for them. There were picnics and riding parties 30

there were dances in the north room—sometimes fancy
dress dances—and open air plays on the green tennis
court of one of the cousin's houses. The children are no
longer children now. Most of them are men and women,
5 working out their own fates in the big world; some in our
land, others across the great ocean or where the Southern Cross blazes in the tropic night. Some of them
have children of their own; some are working at one thing,
some at another; in cable ships, in business offices, in
10 factories, in newspaper offices, building steel bridges,
bossing gravel trains and steam shovels, or laying tracks
and superintending freight traffic. They have had their
share of accidents and escapes; as I write, word comes
from a far-off land that one of them, whom Seth Bullock
15 used to call "Kim"° because he was the friend of all mankind, while bossing a dangerous but necessary steel
structural job, has had two ribs and two back teeth
broken, and is back at work. They have known and they
will know joy and sorrow, triumph and temporary defeat.
20 But I believe they are all the better off because of their
happy and healthy childhood.

It is impossible to win the great prizes of life without
running risks, and the greatest of all prizes are those
connected with the home. No father and mother can
25 hope to escape sorrow and anxiety, and there are dreadful moments when death comes very near those we love,
even if for the time being it passes by. But life is a great
adventure, and the worst of all fears is the fear of living.
There are many forms of success, many forms of triumph.
30 But there is no other success, that in any shape or way
approaches that which is open to most of the many, many
men and women who have the right ideals. These are

the men and the women who see that it is the intimate and homely things that count most. They are the men and women who have the courage to strive for the happiness which comes only with labor and effort and self-sacrifice, and only to those whose joy in life springs in part from power of work and sense of duty.

HISTORY

THE BACKWOODSMEN OF THE ALLEGHANIES [1]

ALONG the western frontier of the colonies that were so soon to be the United States, among the foothills of the Alleghanies, on the slopes of the wooded mountains, and in the long trough-like valleys that lay between the ranges, dwelt a peculiar and characteristically American 5 people..

These frontier folk, the people of the up-country, or back-country, who lived near and among the forest-clad mountains, far away from the long-settled districts of flat coast plain and sluggish tidal river, were known to 10 themselves and to others as backwoodsmen. They all bore a strong likeness to one another in their habits of thought and ways of living, and differed markedly from the people of the older and more civilized communities to the eastward. The western border of our country was 15 then formed by the great barrier-chains of the Alleghanies, which ran north and south from Pennsylvania through Maryland, Virginia, and the Carolinas, the trend of the valleys being parallel to the seacoast, and the mountains rising highest to the southward. It was difficult to cross 20 the ranges from east to west, but it was both easy and natural to follow the valleys between. From Fort Pitt° to the high hill-homes of the Cherokees° this great tract of wooded and mountainous country possessed nearly the same features and characteristics, differing utterly 25 in physical aspect from the alluvial plains bordering the ocean.

[1] Reprinted by permission from *The Winning of the West*, copyrighted by G. P. Putnam's Sons.

So, likewise, the backwoods mountaineers who dwelt
near the great water-shed that separates the Atlantic
streams from the springs of the Watauga, the Kanawha,
and the Monongahela, were all cast in the same mould,
5 and resembled each other much more than any of them
did their immediate neighbors of the plains. The backwoodsmen of Pennsylvania had little in common with
the peaceful population of Quakers° and Germans who
lived between the Delaware and the Susquehanna; and
10 their near kinsmen of the Blue Ridge and the Great
Smoky Mountains were separated by an equally wide
gulf from the aristocratic planter communities that
flourished in the tide-water regions of Virginia and the
Carolinas. Near the coast the lines of division between
15 the colonies corresponded fairly well with the differences
between the populations; but after striking the foot-hills,
though the political boundaries continued to go east and
west, those both of ethnic and of physical significance
began to run north and south.
20   The backwoodsmen were Americans by birth and parentage, and of mixed race; but the dominant strain in
their blood was that of the Presbyterian Irish—the
Scotch-Irish,° as they were often called. Full credit has
been awarded the Roundhead° and the Cavalier° for
25 their leadership in our history; nor have we been altogether blind to the deeds of the Hollander and the Huguenot;° but it is doubtful if we have wholly realized the
importance of the part played by that stern and virile
people, the Irish, whose preachers taught the creed of
30 Knox° and Calvin°. These Irish representatives of the
Covenanters° were in the West almost what the Puritans
were in the Northeast, and more than the Cavaliers were

in the South. Mingled with the descendants of many
other races, they nevertheless formed the kernel of the
distinctively and intensely American stock who were the
pioneers of our people in their march westward, the
vanguard of the army of fighting settlers, who, with axe 5
and rifle, won their way from the Alleghanies to the Rio
Grande and the Pacific.

The Presbyterian Irish were themselves already a mixed
people. Though mainly descended from Scotch ancestors
who came originally from both lowlands and highlands, 10
from among both the Scotch Saxons and the Scotch Celts,—
many of them were of English, a few of French Huguenot,
and quite a number of true old Milesian Irish° extraction.
They were the Protestants of the Protestants; they detested
and despised the Catholics, whom their ancestors had 15
conquered, and regarded the Episcopalians, by whom they
themselves had been oppressed, with a more sullen, but
scarcely less intense, hatred. They were a truculent and
obstinate people, and gloried in the warlike renown of
their forefathers, the men who had followed Cromwell,° 20
and who had shared in the defence of Derry° and in the
victories of the Boyne° and Aughrim.°

They did not begin to come to America in any numbers
till after the opening of the eighteenth century; by 1730
they were fairly swarming across the ocean for the most 25
part in two streams, the larger going to the port of
Philadelphia, the smaller to the port of Charleston.
Pushing through the long-settled lowlands of the seacoast, they at once made their abode at the foot of the
mountains and became the outposts of civilization. From 30
Pennsylvania, whither the great majority had come, they
drifted south along the foothills, and down the long valleys,

till they met their brethren from Charleston who had pushed up into the Carolina back-country. In this land of hills, covered by unbroken forest, they took root and flourished, stretching in a broad belt from north to south, 5 a shield of sinewy men thrust in between the people of the seaboard and the red warriors of the wilderness. All through this region they were alike; they had as little kinship with the Cavalier as with the Quaker; the West was won by those who have been rightly called the Round-10 heads of the South, the same men who, before any others, declared for American independence.°

The two facts of most importance to remember in deal-ing with our pioneer history are, first, that the western portions of Virginia and the Carolinas were peopled by 15 an entirely different stock from that which had long existed in the tide-water regions of those colonies; and, secondly, that, except for those in the Carolinas who came from Charleston, the immigrants of this stock were mostly from the North, from their great breeding-ground and 20 nursery in western Pennsylvania.

That these Irish Presbyterians were a bold and hardy race is proved by their at once pushing past the settled regions, and plunging into the wilderness as the leaders of the white advance. They were the first and last set of 25 immigrants to do this; all others have merely followed in the wake of their predecessors. But, indeed, they were fitted to be Americans from the very start; they were kins-folk of the Covenanters; they deemed it a religious duty to interpret their own Bible, and held for a divine right the 30 election of their own clergy. For generations their whole ecclesiastic and scholastic systems had been fundamen-tally democratic. In the hard life of the frontier they lost

much of their religion, and they had but scant opportunity
to give their children the schooling in which they believed;
but what few meeting-houses and school-houses there were
on the border were theirs. The numerous families of
colonial English who came among them adopted their re- 5
ligion if they adopted any. The creed of the backwoodsman who had a creed at all was Presbyterianism; for the
Episcopacy of the tide-water lands obtained no foothold
in the mountains, and the Methodists and Baptists had
but just begun to appear in the West when the Revolution 10
broke out.

These Presbyterian Irish were, however, far from being
the only settlers on the border, although more than any
others they impressed the stamp of their peculiar character
on the pioneer civilization of the West and Southwest. 15
Great numbers of immigrants of English descent came
among them from the settled districts on the East; and
though these later arrivals soon became indistinguishable
from the people among whom they settled, yet they certainly sometimes added a tone of their own to backwoods 20
society, giving it here and there a slight dash of what we
are accustomed to consider the distinctively southern or
cavalier spirit. There was likewise a large German ad-
mixture not only from the Germans of Pennsylvania, but
also from those of the Carolinas. A good many Huguenots 25
likewise came, and a few Hollanders and even Swedes,
from the banks of the Delaware, or perhaps from farther
off still.

A single generation, passed under the hard conditions
of life in the wilderness, was enough to weld together into 30
one people the representatives of these numerous and
widely different races; and the children of the next gener-

ation became indistinguishable from one another. Long before the first Continental Congress assembled, the backwoodsmen, whatever their blood, had become Americans,
one in speech, thought, and character, clutching firmly the
5 land in which their fathers and grandfathers had lived
before them. They had lost all remembrance of Europe
and all sympathy with things European; they had become
as emphatically products native to the soil as were the
tough and supple hickories out of which they fashioned the
10 handles of their long, light axes. Their grim, harsh,
narrow lives were yet strangely fascinating and full of
adventurous toil and danger; none but natures as strong,
as freedom-loving, and as full of bold defiance as theirs
could have endured existence on the terms which these
15 men found pleasurable. Their iron surroundings made a
mould which turned out all alike in the same shape. They
resembled one another, and they differed from the rest
of the world—even the world of America, and infinitely
more, the world of Europe—in dress, in customs, and in
20 mode of life.

Where their lands abutted on the more settled districts
to the eastward, the population was of course thickest, and
their peculiarities least. Here and there at such points
they built small backwoods burgs or towns, rude, strag-
25 gling, unkempt villages, with a store or two, a tavern,—
sometimes good, often a "scandalous hog-sty," where travellers were devoured by fleas, and every one slept and ate in
one room,—a small log school-house, and a little church, pre-
sided over by a hard-featured Presbyterian preacher, gloomy,
30 earnest, and zealous, probably bigoted and narrow-minded,
but nevertheless a great power for good in the community.
However, the backwoodsmen as a class neither built

towns nor loved to dwell therein. They were to be seen
at their best in the vast, interminable forests that formed
their chosen home. They won and kept their lands by
force, and ever lived either at war or in dread of war.
Hence they settled always in groups of several families 5
each, all banded together for mutual protection. Their
red foes were strong and terrible, cunning in council,
dreadful in battle, merciless beyond belief in victory. The
men of the border did not overcome and dispossess cowards
and weaklings; they marched forth to spoil the stout- 10
hearted and to take for a prey the possessions of the men
of might. Every acre, every rood of ground which they
claimed had to be cleared by the axe and held with the
rifle. Not only was the chopping down of the forests the
first preliminary to cultivation, but it was also the surest 15
means of subduing the Indians, to whom the unending
stretches of choked woodland were an impenetrable cover
behind which to move unseen, a shield in making assaults,
and a strong tower of defence in repelling counter-attacks.
In the conquest of the West the backwoods axe, shapely, 20
well-poised, with long haft and light head, was a servant
hardly standing second even to the rifle; the two were
the national weapons of the American backwoodsman, and
in their use he has never been excelled.

When a group of families moved out into the wilderness 25
they built themselves a station or stockade fort: a square
palisade of upright logs, loop-holed, with strong block-
houses as bastions at the corners. One side at least was
generally formed by the backs of the cabins themselves,
all standing in a row; and there was a great door or gate, 30
that could be strongly barred in case of need. Often no
iron whatever was employed in any of the buildings. The

square inside contained the provision sheds and frequently
a strong central blockhouse as well. These forts, of
course, could not stand against cannon, and they were
always in danger when attacked with fire; but save for
5 this risk of burning they were very effectual defences
against men without artillery, and were rarely taken,
whether by whites or Indians, except by surprise. Few
other buildings have played so important a part in our
history as the rough stockade fort of the backwoods.
10   The families only lived in the fort when there was war
with the Indians, and even then not in the winter. At
other times they all separated out to their own farms,
universally called clearings, as they were always made by
first cutting off the timber. The stumps were left to dot
15 the fields of grain and Indian corn. The corn in especial
was the stand-by and invariable resource of the western
settler; it was the crop on which he relied to feed his
family, and when hunting or on a war-trail the parched
grains were carried in his leather wallet to serve often as
20 his only food. But he planted orchards and raised melons,
potatoes, and many other fruits and vegetables as well;
and he had usually a horse or two, cows, and perhaps hogs
and sheep, if the wolves and bears did not interfere. If he
was poor his cabin was made of unhewn logs, and held
25 but a single room; if well-to-do, the logs were neatly
hewed, and besides the large living- and eating-room with
its huge stone fireplace, there was also a small bedroom
and a kitchen, while a ladder led to the loft above, in
which the boys slept. The floors were made of puncheons,
30 great slabs of wood hewed carefully out, and the roof of
clapboards. Pegs of wood were thrust into the sides of
the house, to serve instead of a wardrobe; and buck

antlers, thrust into joists, held the ever-ready rifles. The table was a great clapboard set on four wooden legs; there were three-legged stools, and in the better sort of houses old-fashioned rocking-chairs. The couch or bed was warmly covered with blankets, bearskins, and deer-hides. 5

These clearings lay far apart from one another in the wilderness. Up to the door-sills of the log-huts stretched the solemn and mysterious forest. There were no openings to break its continuity; nothing but endless leagues on leagues of shadowy, wolf-haunted woodland. The great 10 trees towered aloft till their separate heads were lost in the mass of foliage above, and the rank underbrush choked the spaces between the trunks. On the higher peaks and ridge-crests of the mountains there were straggling birches and pines, hemlocks and balsam firs; elsewhere, oaks, 15 chestnuts, hickories, maples, beeches, walnuts, and great tulip-trees grew side by side with many other kinds. The sunlight could not penetrate the roofed archway of murmuring leaves; through the gray aisles of the forest men walked always in a kind of midday gloaming. Those who 20 had lived in the open plains felt when they came to the backwoods as if their heads were hooded. Save on the border of a lake, from a cliff-top, or on a bald knob—that is, a bare hill-shoulder,—they could not anywhere look out for any distance. 25

All the land was shrouded in one vast forest. It covered the mountains from crest to river-bed, filled the plains, and stretched in sombre and melancholy wastes towards the Mississippi. All that it contained, all that lay hid within it and beyond it, none could tell; men only knew 30 that their boldest hunters, however deeply they had penetrated, had not yet gone through it, that it was the home

of the game they followed and the wild beasts that preyed
on their flocks, and that deep in its tangled depths lurked
their red foes, hawk-eyed and wolf-hearted.

Backwoods society was simple, and the duties and rights
5 of each member of the family were plain and clear. The
man was the armed protector and provider, the bread-
winner; the woman was the housewife and child-bearer.
They married young and their families were large, for
they were strong and healthy, and their success in life
10 depended on their own stout arms and willing hearts.
There was everywhere great equality of conditions. Land
was plenty and all else scarce; so courage, thrift and industry were sure of their reward. All had small farms,
with the few stock necessary to cultivate them; the farms
15 being generally placed in the hollows, the division lines
between them, if they were close together, being the tops of
the ridges and the watercourses, especially the former.
The buildings of each farm were usually at its lowest
point, as if in the centre of an amphitheater. Each was
20 on an average of about four hundred acres, but sometimes
more. Tracts of low, swampy grounds, possibly some
miles from the cabin, were cleared for meadows, the fodder
being stacked, and hauled home in winter.

Each backwoodsman was not only a small farmer but
25 also a hunter; for his wife and children depended for their
meat upon the venison and bear's flesh procured by his
rifle. The people were restless and always on the move.
After being a little while in a place, some of the men would
settle down permanently, while others would again drift
30 off, farming and hunting alternately to support their
families. The backwoodsman's dress was in great part
borrowed from his Indian foes. He wore a fur cap or

felt hat, moccasins, and either loose, thin trousers, or else simply leggings of buckskin or elk-hide, and the Indian breech-clout. He was always clad in the fringed hunting-shirt, of homespun or buckskin, the most picturesque and distinctively national dress ever worn in 5 America. It was a loose smock or tunic, reaching nearly to the knees, and held in at the waist by a broad belt, from which hung the tomahawk and scalping-knife. His weapon was the long, small-bore, flint-lock rifle, clumsy, and ill-balanced, but exceedingly accurate. It was 10 very heavy, and when upright, reached to the chin of a tall man; for the barrel of thick, soft iron, was four feet in length, while the stock was short, and the butt scooped out. Sometimes it was plain, sometimes ornamented. It was generally bored out—or, as the expression then was, 15 "sawed out"—to carry a ball of seventy, more rarely of thirty or forty, to the pound; and was usually of backwoods manufacture. The marksman almost always fired from a rest, and rarely at a very long range; and the shooting was marvellously accurate. 20

In the backwoods there was very little money; barter was the common form of exchange, and peltries were often used as a circulating medium, a beaver, otter, fisher, dressed buckskin or large bearskin being reckoned as equal to two foxes or wildcats, four coons, or eight 25 minks. A young man inherited nothing from his father but his strong frame and eager heart; but before him lay a whole continent wherein to pitch his farm, and he felt ready to marry as soon as he became of age, even though he had nothing but his clothes, his horses, his axe, and 30 his rifle. If a girl was well off, and had been careful and industrious, she might herself bring a dowry, of a cow and a calf, a brood mare, a bed well stocked with blankets, and a chest containing her clothes—the latter not very elaborate, for a woman's dress consisted of a hat or poke bonnet, a "bed gown" perhaps a jacket, and a linsey 5 petticoat, while her feet were thrust into coarse shoe-packs or moccasins. Fine clothes were rare; a suit of such cost more than two hundred acres of good land.

The first lesson the backwoodsmen learnt was the necessity of self-help; the next, that such a community 10 could only thrive if all joined in helping one another. Log-rollings, house-raisings, house-warmings, corn-shuck-ings, quiltings, and the like were occasions when all the neighbors came together to do what the family itself could hardly accomplish alone. Every such meeting was 15 the occasion of a frolic and dance for the young people, whisky and rum being plentiful, and the host exerting his utmost power to spread the table with backwood delicacies—bear-meat and venison, vegetables from the "truck-patch," where squashes, melons, beans, and the 20 like were grown, wild fruits, bowls of milk, and apple pies, which were the acknowledged standard of luxury. At the better houses there was metheglin or small beer, cider, cheese, and biscuits. Tea was so little known that many of the backwoods people were not aware it was a beverage 25 and at first attempted to eat the leaves with salt or butter.

The young men prided themselves on their bodily strength, and were always eager to contend against one another in athletic games, such as wrestling, racing, jumping, and lifting flour-barrels; and they also sought 30 distinction in vieing with one another at their work. Sometimes they strove against one another singly, some-times they divided into parties, each bending all its energies to be first in shucking a given heap of corn or cutting (with sickles) an alloted patch of wheat. Among the men the bravos or bullies often were dandies also, in the backwoods fashions, wearing their hair long and delighting in the rude finery of hunting-shirts embroidered 5 with porcupine quills; they were loud, boastful, and profane, given to coarsely bantering one another. Brutally savage fights were frequent; the combatants, who were surrounded by rings of interested spectators, striking, kicking, biting, and gouging. The fall of one of them 10 did not stop the fight, for the man who was down was maltreated without mercy until he called "enough." The victor always bragged savagely of his prowess, often leaping on a stump, crowing and flapping his arms. This last was a thoroughly American touch; but otherwise 15 one of these contests was less a boxing match than a kind of backwoods *pankrâtion*,° no less revolting than its ancient prototype of Olympic fame. Yet, if the uncouth borderers were as brutal as the highly polished Greeks, they were more manly; defeat was not necessarily con- 20 sidered disgrace, a man often fighting when he was certain to be beaten, while the onlookers neither hooted nor pelted the conquered. We first hear of the noted Indian fighter, Simon Kenton,° as leaving a rival for dead after one of these ferocious duels, and fleeing from his home 25 in terror of the punishment that might follow the deed. Such fights were specially frequent when the backwoodsmen went into the little frontier towns to see horse-races or fairs.

A wedding was always a time of festival. If there was 30 a church anywhere near, the bride rode thither on horseback behind her father, and after the service her pillion°

was shifted to the bridegroom's steed. If, as generally
happened, there was no church, the groom and his friends,
all armed, rode to the house of the bride's father, plenty
of whisky being drunk, and the men racing recklessly
5 along the narrow bridle-paths, for there were few roads or
wheeled vehicles in the backwoods. At the bride's house
the ceremony was performed, and then a huge dinner was
eaten; after which the fiddling and dancing began, and
were continued all the afternoon, and most of the night
10 as well. A party of girls stole off the bride and put her
to bed in the loft above; and a party of young men then
performed the like service for the groom. The fun was
hearty and coarse, and the toasts always included one to
the young couple with the wish that they might have
15 many big children; for as long as they could remember
the backwoodsmen had lived at war while looking ahead
they saw no chance of its ever stopping, and so each son
was regarded as a future warrior, a help to the whole
community. The neighbors all joined again in chop-
20 ping and rolling the logs for the young couple's future
house, then in raising the house itself, and finally in feast-
ing and dancing at the house-warming.

Funerals were simple, the dead body being carried to
the grave in a coffin slung on poles and borne by four
25 men.

.There was not much schooling, and few boys or girls
learnt much more than reading, writing, and ciphering
up to the rule of three. Where the school-houses existed
they were only dark, mean log-huts, and, if in the south-
30 ern colonies, were generally placed in the so-called "old
fields," or abandoned farms grown up with pines. The
schoolmaster boarded about with the families; his learn-

ing was rarely great, nor was his discipline good, in spite
of the frequency and severity of the canings. The price
for such tuition was at the rate of twenty shillings a year,
in Pennsylvania currency.

Each family did everything that could be done for 5
itself. The father and sons worked with axe, hoe, and
sickle. Almost every house contained a loom, and almost every woman was a weaver. Linsey-woolsey, made
from flax grown near the cabin, and of wool from the
backs of the few sheep, was the warmest and most sub- 10
stantial cloth; and when the flax crop failed and the
flocks were destroyed by wolves, the children had but
scanty covering to hide their nakedness. The man tanned
the buckskin, the woman was tailor and shoemaker, and
made the deerskin sifters to be used instead of bolting- 15
cloths. There were a few pewter spoons in use; but the
table furniture consisted mainly of hand-made trenchers,
platters, noggins,° and bowls. The cradle was of peeled
hickory bark. Ploughshares had to be imported, but har-
rows and sleds were made without difficulty; and the coop- 20
er work was well done. Chaff beds were thrown on the
floor of the loft, if the house-owner was well off. Each
cabin had a hand-mill and a hominy-block; the last was
borrowed from the Indians, and was only a large block
of wood, with a hole burned in the top, as a mortar, where 25
the pestle was worked. If there were any sugar maples
accessible, they were tapped every year.

But some articles, especially salt and iron, could not
be produced in the backwoods. In order to get them
each family collected during the year all the furs possible, 30
these being valuable and yet easily carried on pack-horses,
the sole means of transport. Then, after seeding time,

in the fall, the people of a neighborhood ordinarily joined
in sending down a train of peltry-laden pack-horses to
some large seacoast or tidal-river trading town, where
their burdens were bartered for the needed iron and salt.
5 The unshod horses all had bells hung round their necks;
the clappers were stopped during the day, but when the
train was halted for the night, and the horses were hob-
bled and turned loose, the bells were once more un-
stopped. Several men accompanied each little caravan,
10 and sometimes they drove with them steers and hogs to
sell on the seacoast. A bushel of alum salt was worth a
good cow and calf, and as each of the poorly fed, undersized pack-animals could carry but two bushels, the
mountaineers prized it greatly, and, instead of salting or
15 pickling their venison, they jerked it by drying it in the
sun or smoking it over a fire.

The life of the backwoodsmen was one long struggle.
The forest had to be felled; droughts, deep snows, freshets,
cloudbursts, forest fires, and all the other dangers of a
20 wilderness life faced. Swarms of deer-flies, mosquitoes,
and midges rendered life a torment in the weeks of
hot weather. Rattlesnakes and copperheads were very
plentiful, and, the former especially constant sources
of danger and death. Wolves and bears were incessant
25 and inveterate foes of the live stock, and the cougar, or
panther, occasionally attacked man as well. More terrible still, the wolves sometimes went mad, and the men
who then encountered them were almost certain to be
bitten and to die of hydrophobia.

30   Every true backwoodsman was a hunter. Wild turkeys
were plentiful. The pigeons at times filled the woods
with clouds that hid the sun and broke down the branches

on their roosting-grounds as if a whirlwind had passed. The black and gray squirrels swarmed, devastating the corn-fields, and at times gathering in immense companies and migrating across mountain and river. The hunter's ordinary game was the deer, and after that the bear; the elk was already growing uncommon. No form of labor is harder than the chase, and none is so fascinating nor so excellent as a training-school for war. The successful still-hunter of necessity possessed skill in hiding and in creeping noiselessly upon the wary quarry, as well as in imitating the notes and calls of the different beasts and birds; skill in the use of the rifle and in throwing the tomahawk he already had; and he perforce acquired keenness of eye, thorough acquaintance with woodcraft, and the power of standing the severest strains of fatigue, hardship, and exposure. He lived out in the woods for many months with no food but meat, and no shelter whatever, unless he made a lean-to of brush or crawled into a hollow sycamore.

Such training stood the frontier folk in good stead when they were pitted against the Indians; without it they could not even have held their own, and the white advance would have been absolutely checked. Our frontiers were pushed westward by the warlike skill and adventurous personal prowess of the individual settlers; regular armies by themselves could have done little. For one square mile the regular armies added to our domain, the settlers added ten,—a hundred would probably be nearer the truth. A race of peaceful, unwarlike farmers would have been helpless before such foes as the red Indians, and no auxiliary military force could have protected them or enabled them to move westward. Colon-

ists fresh from the Old World, no matter how thrifty,
steady-going, and industrious, could not hold their own
on the frontier; they had to settle where they were protected from the Indians by a living barrier of bold and
5 self-reliant American borderers. The West would never
have been settled save for the fierce courage and the
eager desire to brave danger so characteristic of the
stalwart backwoodsmen.

These armed hunters, woodchoppers, and farmers
10 were their own soldiers. They built and manned their
own forts; they did their own fighting under their own
commanders. There were no regiments of regular troops
along the frontier. In the event of an Indian inroad
each borderer had to defend himself until there was time
15 for them all to gather together to repel or avenge it. Every
man was accustomed to the use of arms from his childhood; when a boy was twelve years old he was given a
rifle and made a fort-soldier, with a loophole where he
was to stand if the station was attacked. The war was
20 never-ending, for even the times of so-called peace were
broken by forays and murders; a man might grow from
babyhood to middle age on the border, and yet never
remember a year in which some one of his neighbors did
not fall a victim to the Indians.

25   There was everywhere a rude military organization,
which included all the able-bodied men of the community. Every settlement had its colonels and captains; but
these officers, both in their training and in the authority
they exercised, corresponded much more nearly to Indian
30 chiefs than to the regular army men whose titles they
bore. They had no means whatever of enforcing their
orders, and their tumultuous and disorderly levies of

sinewy riflemen were hardly as well disciplined as the Indians themselves. The superior officer could advise, entreat, lead, and influence his men, but he could not command them, or, if he did, the men obeyed him only just so far as it suited them. If an officer planned a scout or campaign, those who thought proper accompanied him, and the others stayed at home, and even those who went out came back if the fit seized them, or perchance followed the lead of an insubordinate junior officer whom they liked better then they did his superior. There was no compulsion to perform military duties beyond dread of being disgraced in the eyes of the neighbors, and there was no pecuniary reward for performing them; nevertheless the moral sentiment of a backwoods community was too robust to tolerate habitual remissness in military affairs, and the coward and laggard were treated with utter scorn, and were generally in the end either laughed out, or "hated out," of the neighborhood, or else got rid of in a still more summary manner. Among people naturally brave and reckless, this public opinion acted fairly effectively, and there was generally but little shrinking from military service.

A backwoods levy was formidable because of the high average courage and prowess of the individuals composing it; it was on its own ground much more effective than a like force of regular soldiers, but of course it could not be trusted on a long campaign. The backwoodsmen used their rifles better than the Indians, and also stood punishment better, but they never matched them in surprises nor in skill in taking advantage of cover, and very rarely equalled their discipline in the battle itself. After all, the pioneer was primarily a husbandman; the time spent in chopping trees and tilling the soil his foe spent in preparing for or practising forest warfare, and so the former, thanks to the exercise of the very qualities which in the end gave him the possession of the soil, could 5 not, as a rule, hope to rival his antagonist in the actual conflict itself. When large bodies of the red men and white borderers were pitted against each other, the former were if anything the more likely to have the advantage. But the whites soon copied from the Indians their system 10 of individual and private warfare, and they probably caused their foes far more damage and loss in this way than in the large expeditions. Many noted border scouts and Indian fighters—such men as Boon, Kenton, Wetzel, Brady, McCulloch, Mansker—grew to over- 15 match their Indian foes at their own game, and held themselves above the most renowned warriors. But these men carried the spirit of defiant self-reliance to such an extreme that their best work was always done when they were alone or in small parties of but four or 20 five. They made long forays after scalps and horses, going a wonderful distance, enduring extreme hardship, risking the most terrible of deaths, and harrying the hostile tribes into a madness of terror and revengeful hatred.

25   As it was in military matters, so it was with the administration of justice by the frontiersman; they had few courts, and knew but little law, and yet they contrived to preserve order and morality with rough effectiveness, by combining to frown down on the grosser misdeeds, 30 and to punish the more flagrant misdoers. Perhaps the spirit in which they acted can best be shown by the recital of an incident in the career of the three McAfee brothers,

who were among the pioneer hunters of Kentucky. Previous to trying to move their families out to the new country, they made a cache of clothing, implements, and provisions, which in their absence was broken into ·and plundered. They caught the thief, "a little diminu-5 tive, red-headed white man," a runaway convict servant from one of the tide-water counties of Virginia. In the first impulse of anger at finding that he was the criminal, one of the McAfees rushed at him to kill him with his tomahawk; but the weapon turned, the man was only 10 knocked down, and his assailant's gusty anger subsided as quickly as it had risen, giving way to a desire to do stern but fair justice. So the three captors formed themselves into a court, examined into the case, heard the man in his own defence, and after due consultation decided that 15 "according to their opinion of the laws he had forfeited his life, and ought to be hung," but none of them were willing to execute the sentence in cold blood, and they ended by taking their prisoner back to his master.

The incident was characteristic in more than one way. 20 The prompt desire of the backwoodsman to avenge his own wrong; his momentary furious anger, speedily quelled and replaced by a dogged determination to be fair but to exact full retribution; the acting entirely without regard to legal forms or legal officials, but yet in a spirit which 25 spoke well for the doer's determination to uphold the essentials that make honest men law-abiding; together with the good faith of the whole proceeding, and the amusing ignorance that it would have been in the least unlawful to execute their own rather harsh sentence—all 30 these were typical frontier traits. Some of the same traits appear in the treatment commonly adopted in

the backwoods to meet the case—of painfully frequent occurrence in the times of Indian wars—where a man taken prisoner by the savages, and supposed to be murdered, returned after two or three years' captivity, only
5 to find his wife married again. In the wilderness a husband was almost a necessity to a woman; her surroundings made the loss of the protector and provider an appalling calamity; and the widow, no matter how sincere her sorrow, soon remarried—for there were many suitors
10 where women were not over-plenty. If in such a case the one thought dead returned, the neighbors and the parties interested seem frequently to have held a sort of informal court, and to have decided that the woman should choose either of the two men she wished to be her
15 husband, the other being pledged to submit to the decision and leave the settlement. Evidently no one had the least idea that there was any legal irregularity in such proceedings.

The McAfees themselves and the escaped convict
20 servant whom they captured typify the two prominent classes of the backwoods people. The frontier, in spite of the outward uniformity of means and manners, is pre-eminently the place of sharp contrasts. The two extremes of society—the strongest, best, and most adven-
25 turous, and the weakest, most shiftless, and vicious—are which seem naturally to drift to the border. Most of the men who came to the backwoods to hew out homes and rear families were stern, manly, and honest; but there was also a large influx of people drawn from the worst immi-
30 grants that perhaps ever were brought to America—the mass of convict servants, redemptioners, and the like, who formed such an excessively undesirable substratum to the

otherwise excellent population of the tide-water regions in Virginia and the Carolinas. Many of the southern crackers or poor whites spring from this class, which also in the backwoods gave birth to generations of violent and hardened criminals, and to an even greater number 5 of shiftless, lazy, cowardly cumberers of the earth's surface. They had in many places a permanently bad effect upon the tone of the whole community.

Moreover, the influence of heredity was no more plainly perceptible than was the extent of individual variation. 10 If a member of a bad family wished to reform, he had every opportunity to do so; if a member of a good family had vicious propensities, there was nothing to check them. All qualities, good and bad, are intensified and accentuated in the life of the wilderness. The man who in 15 civilization is merely sullen and bad-tempered becomes a murderous, treacherous ruffian when transplanted to the wilds; while, on the other hand, his cheery, quiet neighbor develops into a hero, ready uncomplainingly to lay down his life for his friend. One who in an eastern city 20 is merely a backbiter and slanderer, in the western woods lies in wait for his foe with a rifle; sharp practice in the East becomes highway robbery in the West; but at the same time negative good-nature becomes active self-sacrifice, and a general belief in virtue is translated into 25 a prompt and determined war upon vice. The ne'er-do-well of a family who in one place has his debts paid a couple of times and is then forced to resign from his clubs and lead a cloudy but innocuous existence on a small pension, in the other abruptly finishes his career by being 30 hung for horse-stealing.

In the backwoods the lawless led lives of abandoned

wickedness; they hated good for good's sake, and did their utmost to destroy it. Where the bad element was large gangs of horse-thieves, highwaymen, and other criminals often united with the uncontrollable young men of vicious
5 tastes, who were given to gambling, fighting and the like. They then formed half-secret organizations, often of great extent and with wide ramifications; and if they could control a community they established a reign of terror, driving out both ministers and magistrates, and
10 killing without scruple those who interfered with them. The good men in such a case banded themselves together as regulators and put down the wicked with ruthless severity, by the exercise of lynch law, shooting and hanging the worst off-hand.

15　　Jails were scarce in the wilderness, and often were entirely wanting in a district, which, indeed, was quite likely to lack legal officers also. If punishment was inflicted at all it was apt to be severe, and took the form of death or whipping. An impromptu jury of neighbors
20 decided with a rough-and-ready sense of fair play and justice what punishment the crime demanded, and then saw to the execution of their own decree. Whipping was the usual reward of theft. Occasionally, torture was resorted to, but not often; and, to their honor be it said,
25 the backwoodsmen were horrified at the treatment accorded both to black slaves and to white convict servants in the lowlands.

　　They were superstitious, of course, believing in witchcraft and signs and omens; and it may be noted that
30 their superstition showed a singular mixture of old-world survivals and of practices borrowed from the savages or evolved by the very force of their strange surroundings.

At the bottom they were deeply religious in their tendencies; and although ministers and meeting-houses were rare, yet the backwoods cabins often contained Bibles, and the mothers used to instil into the minds of their children, reverence for Sunday, while many even of the 5 hunters refused to hunt on that day. Those of them who knew the right honestly tried to live up to it, in spite of the manifold temptations to backsliding offered by their lives of hard and fierce contention. But Calvinism, though more congenial to them than Episcopacy, and infinitely 10 more so than Catholicism, was too cold for the fiery hearts of the borderers; they were not stirred to the depths of their natures till other creeds, and, above all, Methodism, worked their way into the wilderness.

Thus the backwoodsmen lived on the clearings they 15 had hewed out of the everlasting forest; a grim, stern people, strong and simple, powerful for good and evil, swayed by gusts of stormy passion, the love of freedom rooted in their very hearts' core. Their lives were harsh and narrow, they gained their bread by their blood and 20 sweat, in the unending struggle with the wild ruggedness of nature. They suffered terrible injuries at the hands of the red men, and on their foes they waged a terrible warfare in return. They were relentless, revengeful, suspicious, knowing neither ruth nor pity; they were also upright, 25 resolute, and fearless, loyal to their friends, and devoted to their country. In spite of their many failings, they were of all men the best fitted to conquer the wilderness and hold it against all comers.

THE HISTORIAN OF THE FUTURE[1]

THE great historian of the future will have easy access to innumerable facts patiently gathered by tens of thousands of investigators, whereas the great historian of the past had very few facts, and often had to gather most 5 of these himself. The great historian of the future cannot be excused if he fails to draw on the vast storehouses of knowledge that have been accumulated, if he fails to profit by the wisdom and work of other men, which are now the common property of all intelligent men. He 10 must use the instruments which the historians of the past did not have ready to hand. Yet even with these instruments he cannot do as good work as the best of the elder historians unless he has vision and imagination, the power to grasp what is essential and to reject the 15 infinitely more numerous nonessentials, the power to embody ghosts, to put flesh and blood on dry bones, to make dead men living before our eyes. In short he must have the power to take the science of history and turn it into literature.

20 Those who wish history to be treated as a purely utilitarian science often decry the recital of the mighty deeds of the past, the deeds which always have aroused, and for a long period to come are likely to arouse, most interest. These men say that we should study not the 25 unusual but the usual. They say that we profit most by

[1] Reprinted from the version of the address, "History as Literature," which appeared in the Boston *Transcript*. The address is included in the volume *History as Literature*.

118

laborious research into the drab monotony of the ordinary, rather than by fixing our eyes on the purple patches that break it.   Beyond all question the great historian, of the future must keep ever in mind the relative importance of the usual and the unusual.   If he is a really great [5] historian, if he possesses the highest imaginative and literary quality, he will be able to interest us in the gray tints of the general landscape no less than in the flame hues of the jutting peaks.   It is even more essential to have such quality in writing of the commonplace than [10] in writing of the exceptional.   Otherwise no profit will come from study of the ordinary; for writings are useless unless they are read, and they cannot be read unless they are readable.   Furthermore, while doing full justice to the importance of the usual, of the commonplace, the [15] great historian will not lose sight of the importance of the heroic.

It is hard to tell just what it is that is most important to know.   The wisdom of one generation may seem the folly of the next.   This is just as true of the wisdom of [20] the dry-as-dusts as of the wisdom of those who write interestingly.   Moreover, while the value of the by-products of knowledge does not readily yield itself to quantitative expression, it is none the less real.   A utilitarian education should undoubtedly be the foun- [25] dation of all education.   But it is far from advisable, it is far from wise, to have it the end of all education. Technical training will more and more be accepted as the prime factor in our educational system, a factor as essential for the farmer, the blacksmith, the seamstress, [30] and the cook, as for the lawyer, the doctor, the engineer, and the stenographer.   For similar reasons the purely

practical and technical lessons of history, the lessons
that help us to grapple with our immediate social and
industrial problems, will also receive greater emphasis
than ever before. But if we are wise we will no more
5 permit this practical training to exclude knowledge of
that part of literature which is history than of that part
of literature which is poetry. Side by side with the need
for the perfection of the individual in the technique of
his special calling goes the need of broad human sympathy,
10 and the need of lofty and generous emotion in that in-
diividual. Only thus can the citizenship of the modern
state rise level to the complex modern social needs. . . .

The work of the archæologist, the work of the an-
thropologist, the work of the palæo-ethnologist—out of
15 all these a great literary historian may gather material
indispensable for his use. He, and we, ought fully to
acknowledge our debt to the collectors of these indispensable facts. The investigator in any line may do
work which puts us all under lasting obligations to him,
20 even though he be totally deficient in the art of literary
expression, that is, totally deficient in the ability to
convey vivid and lifelike pictures to others of the past
whose secrets he has laid bare. I would give no scanty
or grudging acknowledgment to the deeds of such a man.
25 He does a lasting service; whereas the man who tries to
make literary expression cover his ignorance or mis-
reading of facts renders less than no service. But the
service done is immeasurably increased in value when
the man arises who from his study of a myriad dead
30 fragments is able to paint some living picture of the
past.

This is why the record as great writers preserve it has a value immeasurably beyond what is merely lifeless. Such a record pulses with immortal life. It may recount the deed or the thought of a hero at some supreme moment. It may be merely the portrayal of homely every-5 day life. This matters not, so long as in either event the genius of the historian enables him to paint in colors that do not fade. The cry of the Ten Thousand° when they first saw the sea still stirs the hearts of men. The ruthless death scene between Jehu° and Jezebel; wicked 10 Ahab,° smitten by the chance arrow, and propped in his chariot until he died at sundown; Josiah,° losing his life because he would not heed the Pharaoh's solemn warning, and mourned by all the singing men and all the singing women—the fates of these kings and of this king's 15 daughter, are part of the common stock of knowledge of mankind. They were petty rulers of petty principalities; yet, compared with them, mighty conquerors, who added empire to empire, Shalmaneser° and Sargon, Amenhotep and Rameses, are but shadows; for the deeds 20 and the deaths of the kings of Judah and Israel are written in words that, once read, cannot be forgotten. The Peloponnesian War° bulks of unreal size to-day because it once seemed thus to bulk to a master mind. Only a great historian can fittingly deal with a very great sub-25 ject; yet because the qualities of chief interest in human history can be shown on a small field no less than on a large one, some of the greatest historians have treated subjects that only their own genius rendered great.

So true is this that if great events lack a great historian, 30 and a great poet writes about them, it is the poet who fixes them in the mind of mankind, so that in after-time

importance the real has become the shadow and the
shadow the reality. Shakespeare has definitely fixed the
character of the Richard III,° of whom ordinary men
think and speak. Keats° forgot even the right name of
5 the man who first saw the Pacific Ocean; yet it is his
lines which leap to our minds when we think of the
"wild surmise" felt by the indomitable explorer-conqueror
from Spain when the vast new sea burst on his vision.

When, however, the great historian has spoken, his
10 work will never be undone. No poet can ever supersede
what Napier° wrote of the storming of Badajoz, of the
British infantry at Albuera, and of the light artillery
at Fuentes d'Oñoro. After Parkman° had written of
Montcalm° and Wolfe° there was left for other writers
15 only what Fitzgerald° left for other translators of Omar
Khayyam. Much new light has been thrown on the
history of the Byzantine Empire by the many men who
have studied it of recent years; we read each new writer
with pleasure and profit; and after reading each we take
20 down a volume of Gibbon,° with renewed thankfulness
that a great writer was moved to do a great task.

The greatest of future archæologists will be the great
historian who instead of being a mere antiquarian delver
in dust heaps has the genius to reconstruct for us the
25 immense panorama of the past. He must possess knowledge. He must possess that without which knowledge
is of so little use, wisdom. What he brings from the
charnel-house he must use with such potent wizardry that
we shall see the life that was and not the death that is.
30 For remember that the past was life just as much as the
present is life. Whether it be Egypt, or Mesopotamia,
or Scandinavia with which he deals, the great historian, if

the facts permit him, will put before us the men and women
as they actually lived so that we shall recognize them
for what they were, living beings.   Men like Maspero°,
Breasted,° and Weigall° have already begun this work for
the countries of the Nile and the Euphrates.   For Scan- 5
dinavia the groundwork was laid long ago in the *Heim-
skringla°* and in such sagas° as those of Burnt Njal and Gisli
Soursop.   Minute descriptions of mummies and of the
furniture of tombs help us as little to understand the Egypt
of the mighty days, as to sit inside the tomb of Mount 10
Vernon° would help us to see Washington the soldier
leading to battle his scarred and tattered veterans, or
Washington the statesman, by his serene strength of
character, rendering it possible for his countrymen to
establish themselves as one great nation.   15

The great historian must be able to paint for us the
life of the plain people, the ordinary men and women,
of the time of which he writes.   He can do this only if
he possesses the highest kind of imagination.   Collections
of figures no more give us a picture of the past than the 20
reading of a tariff report on hides or woolens gives us an
idea of the actual lives of the men and women who live
on ranches or work in factories.   The great historian will
in as full measure as possible present to us the every-day
life of the men and women of the age which he describes. 25
Nothing that tells of this life will come amiss to him.   The
instruments of their labor and the weapons of their warfare, the wills that they wrote, the bargains that they made,
and the songs that they sang when they feasted and made
love; he must use them all.   He must tell us of the toil 30
of the ordinary man in ordinary times, and of the play
by which that ordinary toil was broken.   He must never

forget that no event stands out entirely isolated. He must trace from its obscure and humble beginnings each of the movements that in its hour of triumph has shaken the world.

5 Yet he must not forget that the times that are extraordinary need especial portrayal. In the revolt against the old tendency of historians to deal exclusively with the spectacular and the exceptional, to treat only of war and oratory and government, many modern writers 10 have gone to the opposite extreme. They fail to realize that in the lives of nations as in the lives of men there are hours so fraught with weighty achievement, with triumph or defeat, with joy or sorrow, that each such hour may determine all the years that are to come there-15 after, or may outweigh all the years that have gone before. In the writings of our historians, as in the lives of our ordinary citizens, we can neither afford to forget that it is the ordinary every-day life which counts most; nor yet that seasons come when ordinary qualities count 20 for but little in the face of great contending forces of good and of evil, the outcome of whose strife determines whether the nation shall walk in the glory of the morning or in the gloom of spiritual death.

The historian must deal with the days of common 25 things, and deal with them so that they shall interest us in reading of them as our own common things interest us as we live among them. He must trace the changes that come almost unseen, the slow and gradual growth that transforms for good or for evil the children and grand-30 children so that they stand high above or far below the level on which their forefathers stood. He must also trace the great cataclysms that interrupt and divert this gradual development. He can no more afford to be blind to one class of phenomena than to the other. He must ever remember that while the worst offense of which he can be guilty is to write vividly and inaccurately, yet that unless he writes vividly he cannot write truthfully; 5 for no amount of dull, painstaking detail will sum up as the whole truth unless the genius is there to paint the truth.

There can be no better illustration of what I mean than is afforded by the history of Russia during the last 10 thousand years. The historian must trace the growth of the earliest Slav communities of the forest and the steppe, the infiltration of Scandinavian invaders who gave them their first power of mass action, and the slow, chaotic development of the little communes into barbarous 15 cities and savage princedoms. In later Russian history he must show us priest and noble, merchant and serf, changing slowly from the days when Ivan the Terrible° warred against Bátory, the Magyar king of Poland, until the present moment, when with half-suspicious eyes the 20 people of the Czar watch their remote Bulgarian kinsmen standing before the last European stronghold of the Turk. During all these centuries there were multitudes of wars, foreign and domestic, any or all of which were of little moment compared to the slow working of the 25 various forces that wrought in the times of peace. But there was one period of storm and overthrow so terrible that it affected profoundly for all time the whole growth of the Russian people, in inmost character no less than in external dominion. Early in the thirteenth century the 30 genius of Jenghiz Khan° stirred the Mongol horsemen of the mid-Asian pastures to a movement as terrible to

civilization as the lava flow of a volcano.to the lands around the volcano's foot. When that century opened, ·the Mongols were of no more weight in the world than the Touaregs° of the Sahara are to-day. Long before the
5 century had closed they had ridden from the Yellow Sea to the Adriatic and the Persian Gulf. They had crushed Christian and Moslem° and Buddhist° alike beneath the iron cruelty of their sway. They had conquered China as their successors conquered India. They
10 sacked Baghdad, the seat of the Khalif. In mid-Europe their presence for a moment caused the same horror to fall on the warring adherents of the pope and the kaiser. To Europe they were a scourge so frightful, so irresistible, that the people cowered before them as if they
15 had been demons. No European army of that day, of any nation, was able to look them in the face on a stricken field. Bestial in their lives, irresistible in battle, merciless in victory, they trampled the lands over which they rode into bloody mire beneath the hoofs of their horses. The
20 squat, slit-eyed, brawny horse-bowmen drew a red furrow across Hungary, devasted Poland, and in Silesia overthrew the banded chivalry of Germany. But it was in Russia that they did their worst. They not merely conquered Russia, but held the Russians as cowering and
25 abject serfs for two centuries. Every feeble effort at resistance was visited with such bloodthirsty vengeance that finally no Russian ventured ever to oppose them at all. But the princes of the cities soon found that the beast-like fury of the conquerors when their own desires
30 were thwarted, was only equalled by their beast-like indifference to all that was done among the conquered people themselves, and that they were ever ready to hire

themselves out to aid each Russian against his brother. Under this régime the Russian who rose was the Russian who with cringing servility to his Tartar overlords combined ferocious and conscienceless greed in the treatment of his fellow-Russians. Moscow came to the front 5 by using the Tartar to help conquer the other Russian cities, paying as a price abject obedience to all Tartar demands. In the long run the fierce and pliant cunning of the conquered people proved too much for the short-sighted and arrogant brutality of the conquerors. The 10 Tartar power, the Mongolian power, waned. Russia became united, threw off the yoke, and herself began a career of aggression at the expense of her former conquerors. But the reconquest of racial independence, vitally necessary though it was to Russia, had been paid 15 for by the establishment of a despotism Asiatic rather than European in its spirit and working.

The true historian will bring the past before our eyes as if it were the present. He will make us see as living men the hard-faced archers of Agincourt,° and the war- 20 worn spearmen who followed Alexander° down beyond the rim of the known world. We shall hear grate on the coast of Britain the keels of the Low-Dutch sea-thieves° whose children's children were to inherit unknown continents.° We shall thrill to the triumphs of Hannibal.° 25 Gorgeous in our sight will rise the splendor of dead cities, and the might of the elder empires of which the very ruins crumbled to dust ages ago. Along ancient trade routes, across the world's waste spaces, the caravans shall move; and the admirals of uncharted seas shall furrow the oceans 30 with their lonely prows. Beyond the dim centuries we shall see the banners float above armed hosts. We shall

see conquerors riding forward to victories that have
changed the course of time. We shall listen to the
prophecies of forgotten seers. Ours shall be the dreams
of dreamers who dreamed greatly, who saw in their vision
5 peaks so lofty that never yet have they been reached by
the sons and daughters of men. Dead poets shall sing
to us the deeds of men of might and the love and the
beauty of women. We shall see the dancing girls of
Memphis.° The scent of the flowers in the Hanging
10 Gardens of Babylon° will be heavy to our senses.
We shall sit at feast with the kings of Nineveh° when
they drink from ivory and gold. With Queen Maeve°
in her sun parlor we shall watch the nearing chariots of
the champions. For us the war-horns of King Olaf°
15 shall wail across the flood, and the harps sound high at
festivals in forgotten halls. The frowning strongholds
of the barons of old shall rise before us, and the white
palace-castles from whose windows Syrian princes once
looked across the blue Ægean. We shall know the valor
20 of the two-sworded Samurai.° Ours shall be the hoary
wisdom and the strange, crooked folly of the immemorial civilizations which tottered to a living death in
India and in China. We shall see the terrible horsemen
of Timur the Lame° ride over the roof of the world; we
25 shall hear the drums beat as the armies of Gustavus° and
Frederick° and Napoleon° drive forward to victory. Ours
shall be the woe of burgher and peasant, and ours the
stern joy when freemen triumph and justice comes to
her own. The agony of the galley-slaves shall be ours,
30 and the rejoicing when the wicked are brought low and
the men of evil days have their reward. We shall see
the glory of triumphant violence, and the revel of those

who do wrong in high places; and the broken-hearted despair that lies beneath the glory and the revel. We shall also see the supreme righteousness of the wars for freedom and justice, and know that the men who fell in these wars made all mankind their debtors.   5

Some day the historians will tell us of these things. Some day, too, they will tell our children of the age and the land in which we now live. They will portray the conquest of the continent. They will show the slow beginnings of settlement, the growth of the fishing and trad- 10 ing towns on the seacoast, the hesitating early ventures into the Indian-haunted forest. Then they will show the backwoodsmen, with their long rifles and their light axes, making their way with labor and peril through the wooded wilderness° to the Mississippi; and then the endless march 15 of the white-topped wagon-trains across plain and mountain to the coast of the greatest of the five great oceans. They will show how the land which the pioneers won slowly and with incredible hardship was filled in two generations by the overflow from the countries of western 20 and central Europe. The portentous growth of the cities will be shown, and the change from a nation of farmers to a nation of business men and artisans, and all the far-reaching consequences of the rise of the new industrialism. The formation of a new ethnic type in this melting-pot 25 of the nations will be told. The hard materialism of our age will appear, and also the strange capacity for lofty idealism which must be reckoned with by all who would understand the American character. A people whose heroes are Washington and Lincoln, a peaceful people who 30 fought to a finish one of the bloodiest of wars, waged solely for the sake of a great principle and a noble idea, surely possess an emergency standard far above mere money-getting.

Those who tell the Americans of the future what the Americans of to-day and of yesterday have done, will perforce tell much that is unpleasant. This is but saying that they will describe the arch-typical civilization of this age. Nevertheless when the tale is finally told, I believe that it will show that the forces working for good in our national life outweigh the forces working for evil, and that, with many blunders and shortcomings, with much halting and turning aside from the path, we shall yet in the end prove our faith by our works, and show in our lives our belief that righteousness exalteth a nation.

ADVENTURE

BEAR HUNTING EXPERIENCES [1]

EARLY next morning we were over at the elk carcass, and, as we expected, found that the bear had eaten his fill at it during the night. His tracks showed him to be an immense fellow, and were so fresh that we doubted if he had left long before we arrived; and we made up our 5 minds to follow him up and try to find his lair. The bears that lived on these mountains had evidently been little disturbed; indeed, the Indians and most of the white hunters are rather chary of meddling with "Old Ephraim," as the mountainmen style the grizzly, unless they get him 10 at a disadvantage; for the sport is fraught with some danger and but small profit. The bears thus seemed to have very little fear of harm, and we thought it likely that the bed of the one who had fed on the elk would not be far away. , 15

My companion was a skilful tracker, and we took up the trail at once. For some distance it led over the soft, yielding carpet of moss and pine needles, and the footprints were quite easily made out, although we could follow them but slowly; for we had, of course, to keep a sharp 20 lookout ahead and around us as we walked noiselessly on in the sombre half-light always prevailing under the great pine trees, through whose thickly interlacing branches stray but few beams of light, no matter how bright the sun may be outside. We made no sound ourselves, and every 25 little sudden noise sent a thrill through me as I peered about with each sense on the alert. Two or three of the

[1] Reprinted by permission from *Hunting Trips of a Ranchman*, copyright by G. P. Putnam's Sons.

ravens that we had scared from the carcass flew overhead, croaking hoarsely; and the pine tops moaned and sighed in the slight breeze—for pine trees seem to be ever in motion, no matter how light the wind.

5 After going a few hundred yards the tracks turned off. on a well-beaten path made by the elk; the woods were in many places cut up by these game-trails, which had often become as distinct as ordinary foot-paths. The beast's footprints were perfectly plain in the dust, and he had 10 lumbered along up the path until near the middle of the hill-side, where the ground broke away and there were hollows and bowlders. Here there had been a windfall, and the dead trees lay among the living, piled across one another in all directions; while between and around them 15 sprouted up a thick growth of young spruces and other evergreens. The trail turned off into the tangled thicket, within which it was almost certain we would find our quarry. We could still follow the tracks, by the slight scrapes of the claws on the bark or by the bent and broken 20 twigs, and we advanced with noiseless caution, slowly climbing over the dead tree trunks and upturned stumps, and not letting a branch rustle or catch on our clothes. When in the middle of the thicket we crossed what was almost a breastwork of fallen logs, and Merrifield, who 25 was leading, passed by the upright stem of a great pine. As soon as he was by it he sank suddenly on one knee, turning half round, his face fairly aflame with excitement; and as I strode past him, with my rifle at the ready, there, not ten steps off, was the great bear, slowly rising from 30 his bed among the young spruces. He had heard us, but apparently hardly knew exactly where or what we were, for he reared up on his haunches sideways to us. Then he

saw us and dropped down again on all-fours, the shaggy hair on his neck and shoulders seeming to bristle as he turned toward us. As he sank down on his forefeet I had raised the rifle; his head was bent slightly down, and when I saw the top of the white bead fairly between his small, glit- 5 tering, evil eyes, I pulled trigger. Half rising up, the huge beast fell over on his side in the death-throes, the ball having gone into his brain, striking as fairly between the eyes as if the distance had been measured by a carpenter's rule.

The whole thing was over in twenty seconds from the 10 time I caught sight of the game; indeed, it was over so quickly that the grizzly did not have time to show fight at all or come a step toward us. It was the first I had ever seen, and I felt not a little proud, as I stood over the great brindled bulk which lay stretched out at length in the cool 15 shade of the evergreens. He was a monstrous fellow, much larger than any I have seen since, whether alive or brought in dead by the hunters. As near as we could estimate (for of course we had nothing with which to weigh more than very small portions), he must have weighed about 20 twelve hundred pounds, and, though this is not as large as some of his kind are said to grow in California, it is yet a very unusual size for a bear. He was a good deal heavier than any of our horses, and it was with the greatest difficulty that we were able to skin him. He 25 must have been very old, his teeth and claws being all worn down and blunted; but nevertheless he had been living in plenty, for he was as fat as a prize-hog, the layers on his back being a finger's length in thickness. He was still in the summer coat, his hair being short, 30 and in color a curious brindled brown, somewhat like that of certain bull-dogs, while all the bears we shot afterward

had the long thick winter fur, cinnamon or yellowish brown. By the way, the name of this bear has reference to its character and not to its color, and should, I suppose, be properly spelt grisly°—in the sense of horrible, exactly as we
5 speak of a "grisly spectre"—and not grizzly; but perhaps the latter way of spelling it is too well established to be now changed.

In killing dangerous game, steadiness is more needed than good shooting. No game is dangerous unless a man
10 is close up, for nowadays hardly any wild beast will charge from a distance of a hundred yards, but will rather try to run off; and if a man is close it is easy enough for him to shoot straight if he does not lose his head. A bear's brain is about the size of a pint bottle; and any one can hit a
15 pint bottle off-hand at thirty or forty feet. I have had two shots at bears at close quarters, and each time I fired into the brain, the bullet in one case striking fairly between the eyes, as told above, and in the other going in between the eye and ear. A novice at this kind of sport
20 will find it best and safest to keep in mind the old Norse viking's advice in reference to a long sword: "If you go in close enough your sword will be long enough." If a poor shot goes in close enough he will find that he shoots straight enough.
25 I was very proud over my first bear; but Merrifield's chief feeling seemed to be disappointment that the animal had not had time to show fight. He was rather a reckless fellow, and very confident in his own skill with the rifle; and he really did not seem to have any more fear of the grizzlies
30 than if they had been so many jack-rabbits. I did not at all share his feelings, having a hearty respect for my foes' prowess, and in following and attacking them always took

all possible care to get the chances on my side. Merrifield was sincerely sorry that we never had to stand a regular charge; while on this trip we killed five grizzlies with seven bullets, and except in the case of the she and cub, spoken of further on, each was shot about as quickly as 5 it got sight of us.

A day or two after the death of the big bear, we went out one afternoon on horseback, intending merely to ride down to see a great canyon lying some six miles west of our camp; indeed, we went more to look at the scenery 10 than for any other reason, though, of course, neither of us ever stirred out of camp without his rifle. We rode down the valley in which we had camped, through alternate pine groves and open glades, until we reached the canyon, and then skirted its brink for a mile or so. It was 15 a great chasm, many miles in length, as if the table-land had been rent asunder by some terrible and unknown force; its sides were sheer walls of rock, rising three or four hundred feet straight up in the air, and worn by the weather till they looked like the towers and battlements 20 of some vast fortress. Between them at the bottom was a space, in some places nearly a quarter of a mile wide, in others very narrow, through whose middle foamed a deep rapid torrent of which the sources lay far back among the snow-topped mountains around Cloud Peak. In this val- 25 ley, dark-green, sombre pines stood in groups, stiff and erect; and here and there among them were groves of poplar and cotton-wood, with slender branches and trembling leaves, their bright green already changing to yellow in the sharp fall weather. We went down to where the 30 mouth of the canyon opened out, and rode our horses to the end of a great jutting promontory of rock, thrust

out into the plain; and in the cold, clear air we looked far
over the broad valley of the Big Horn as it lay at our very
feet, walled in on the other side by the distant chain of
the Rocky Mountains.

5 Turning our horses, we rode back along the edge of
another canyon-like valley, with a brook flowing down its
centre, and its rocky sides covered with an uninterrupted
pine forest—the place of all others in whose inaccessible
wildness and ruggedness a . bear would find a safe
10 retreat.   After some time we came to where other valleys,
with steep, grass-grown sides, covered with sage-brush,
branched out from it, and we followed one of these out.
There was plenty of elk sign about, and we saw several
black-tail deer. These last were very common on the
15 mountains, but we had not hunted them at all, as we were
in no need of meat. But this afternoon we came across a
buck with remarkably fine antlers, and accordingly I shot
it, and we stopped to cut off and skin out the horns,
throwing the reins over the heads of the horses and
20 leaving them to graze by themselves. The body lay near
the crest of one side of a deep valley, or ravine, which
headed up on the plateau a mile to our left. Except for
scattered trees and bushes the valley was bare; but there
was heavy timber along the crests of the hills on its
25 opposite side. It took some time to fix the head properly,
and we were just ending when Merrifield sprang to his feet
and exclaimed "Look at the bears!" pointing down into
the valley below us. Sure enough there were two bears
(which afterwards proved to be an old she and a nearly
30 full-grown cub) traveling up the bottom of the valley,
much too far off for us to shoot. Grasping our rifles and
throwing off our hats we started off as hard as we could

run, diagonally down the hill-side, so as to cut them off. It was some little time before they saw us, when they made off at a lumbering gallop up the valley. It would seem impossible to run into two grizzlies in the open, but they were going up hill, and we down, and moreover the old one kept stopping. The cub would forge ahead and could probably have escaped us, but the mother now and then stopped to sit up on her haunches and look round at us, when the cub would run back to her. The upshot was that we got ahead of them, when they turned and went straight up one hill-side as we ran straight down the other behind them. By this time I was pretty nearly done out, for running along the steep ground through the sage-brush was most exhausting work; and Merrifield kept gaining on me and was well in front. Just as he disappeared over a bank, almost at the bottom of the valley, I tripped over a bush and fell full-length. When I got up I knew I could never make up the ground I had lost, and besides could hardly run any longer; Merrifield was out of sight below, and the bears were laboring up the steep hill-side directly opposite and about three hundred yards off, so I sat down and began to shoot over Merrifield's head, aiming at the big bear. She was going very steadily and in a straight line, and each bullet sent up a puff of dust where it struck the dry soil, so that I could keep correcting my aim; and the fourth ball crashed into the old bear's flank. She lurched heavily forward, but recovered herself and reached the timber, while Merrifield, who had put on a spurt, was not far behind.

I toiled up the hill at a sort of trot, fairly gasping and sobbing for breath; but before I got to the top I heard a couple of shots and a shout. The old bear had turned as soon as

she was in the timber, and came toward Merrifield, but he
gave her the death-wound by firing into her chest, and then
shot at the young one, knocking it over.   When I came
up he was just walking toward the latter to finish it with
5 the revolver, but it suddenly jumped up as lively as
ever and made off at a great pace—for it was nearly full-
grown.   It was impossible to fire where the tree trunks
were so thick, but there was a small opening across which
it would have to pass, and collecting all my energies I
10 made a last run, got into position, and covered the opening with my rifle.   The instant the bear appeared I fired,
and it turned a dozen somersaults down-hill, rolling over
and over; the ball had struck it near the tail and had
ranged forward through the hollow of the body.   Each of
15 us had thus given the fatal wound to the bear into which
the other had fired the first bullet.   The run, though short,
had been very sharp, and over such awful country that
we were completely fagged out, and could hardly speak
for lack of breath.   The sun had already set, and it was
20 too late to skin the animals; so we merely dressed them,
caught the ponies—with some trouble, for they were
frightened at the smell of the bear's blood on our hands—
and rode home through the darkening woods.   Next day
we brought the teamster and two of the steadiest pack-
25 horses to the carcasses, and took the skins into camp.

GETTING CHRISTMAS DINNER ON A RANCH [1]

ONE December, while I was out on my ranch, so much work had to be done that it was within a week of Christmas before we were able to take any thought for the Christmas dinner. The winter set in late that year, and there had been comparatively little cold weather, but 5 one day the ice on the river had been sufficiently strong to enable us to haul up a wagonload of flour, with enough salt pork to last through the winter, and a very few tins of canned goods, to be used at special feasts. We had some bushels of potatoes, the heroic victors of a struggle 10 for existence in which the rest of our garden vegetables had succumbed to drought, frost, and grasshoppers; and we also had some wild plums and dried elk venison. But we had no fresh meat, and so one day my foreman and I agreed to make a hunt on the morrow.   15

Accordingly one of the cowboys rode out in the frosty afternoon to fetch in the saddleband from the plâteau three miles off, where they were grazing. It was after sunset when he returned. I was lounging out by the corral, my wolf-skin cap drawn down over my ears, and 20 my hands thrust deep into the pockets of my fur coat, gazing across the wintry landscape. Cold red bars in the winter sky marked where the sun had gone down behind a row of jagged, snow-covered buttes.

Turning to go into the little bleak log house, as the 25 dusk deepened, I saw the horses trotting homeward in a long file, their unshod hoofs making no sound in the

[1] Reprinted by permission from *Everybody's Magazine*, vol. ix, page 851.

light snow which covered the plain, turning it into a
glimmering white waste wherein stood dark islands of
leafless trees, with trunks and branches weirdly dis-
torted. The cowboy, with bent head, rode behind the
5 line of horses, sometimes urging them on by the shrill
cries known to cattlemen; and as they neared the corral
they broke into a gallop, ran inside, and then halted in
a mass. The frost lay on their shaggy backs, and little
icicles hung from their nostrils.

10   Choosing out two of the strongest and quietest, we
speedily roped them and led them into the warm log
stable, where they were given a plentiful supply of the
short, nutritious buffalo-grass hay, while the rest of the
herd were turned loose to shift for themselves. Then
15 we went inside the house to warm our hands in front of
the great pile of blazing logs, and to wait impatiently
until the brace of prairie chickens I had shot that afternoon should be fixed for supper. Then our rifles and
cartridge belts were looked to, one of the saddles which
20 had met with an accident was overhauled, and we were
ready for bed.

It was necessary to get to the hunting grounds by
sunrise, and it still lacked a couple of hours of dawn when
the foreman wakened me as I lay asleep beneath the
25 buffalo robes. Dressing hurriedly and breakfasting on
a cup of coffee and some mouthfuls of bread and jerked
elk meat, we slipped out to the barn, threw the saddles
on the horses, and were off.

The air was bitterly chill; the cold had been severe
30 for two days, so that the river ice would again bear horses.
Beneath the light covering of powdery snow we could
feel the rough ground like wrinkled iron under the horses'

hoofs. There was no moon, but the stars shone beautifully down through the cold, clear air, and our willing
horses galloped swiftly across the long bottom on which
the ranch-house stood, threading their way deftly among
the clumps of sprawling sagebush.   5

A mile off we crossed the river, the ice cracking with
noises like pistol shots as our horses picked their way
gingerly over it. On the opposite side was a dense
jungle of bullberry bushes, and on breaking through
this we found ourselves galloping up a long, winding 10
valley, which led back many miles into the hills. The
crannies and little side ravines were filled with brushwood and groves of stunted ash. By this time there
was a faint flush of gray in the east, and as we rode
silently along we could make out dimly the tracks made 15
by the wild animals as they had passed and repassed in
the snow. Several times we dismounted to examine
them. A couple of coyotes, possibly frightened by our
approach, had trotted and loped up the valley ahead of
us, leaving a trail like that of two dogs; the sharper, more 20
delicate footprints of a fox crossed our path; and outside one long patch of brushwood a series of round im-
prints in the snow betrayed where a bobcat—as plains-
men term the small lynx—had been lurking around to
try to pick up a rabbit or a prairie fowl.   25

As the dawn reddened, and it became light enough to
see objects some little way off, we began to sit erect in
our saddles and to scan the hillsides sharply for sight
of feeding deer. Hitherto we had seen no deer tracks
save inside the bullberry bushes by the river, and we 30
knew that the deer that lived in that impenetrable
jungle were cunning whitetails which in such a place

could be hunted only by aid of a hound. But just before sunrise we came on three lines of heart-shaped foot-
marks in the snow, which showed where as many deer
had just crossed a little plain ahead of us. They were
5 walking leisurely, and from the lay of the land we believed
that we should find them over the ridge, where there was
a brush coulee.

Riding to one side of the trail, we topped the little
ridge just as the sun flamed up, a burning ball of
10 crimson, beyond the snowy waste at our backs. Almost
immediately afterward my companion leaped from his
horse and raised his rifle, and as he pulled the trigger I saw
through the twigs of a brush patch on our left the erect,
startled head of a young black-tailed doe as she turned
15 to look at us, her great mule-like ears thrown forward.
The ball broke her neck, and she turned a complete somer-
sault downhill, while a sudden smashing of underbrush
told of the flight of her terrified companions.

We both laughed and called out "dinner" as we sprang
20 down toward her, and in a few minutes she was dressed
and hung up by the hind legs on a small ash tree. The
entrails and viscera we threw off to one side, after carefully poisoning them from a little bottle of strychnine
which I had in my pocket. Almost every cattleman
25 carries poison and neglects no chance of leaving out wolf
bait, for the wolves are sources of serious loss to the un-
fenced and unhoused flocks and herds. In this instance
we felt particularly revengeful because it was but a few
days since we had lost a fine yearling heifer. The tracks
30 on the hillside where the carcass lay when we found it,
told the story plainly. The wolves, two in number, had
crept up close before being discovered, and had then raced

down on the astounded heifer almost before she could get fairly started. One brute had hamstringed her with a snap of his vise-like jaws, and once down, she was torn open in a twinkling.

No sooner was the sun up than a warm west wind 5 began to blow in our faces. The weather had suddenly changed, and within an hour the snow was beginning to thaw and to leave patches of bare ground on the hillsides. We left out coats with our horses and struck off on foot for a group of high buttes cut up by 10 the cedar canyons and gorges, in which we knew the old bucks loved to lie. It was noon before we saw anything more. We lunched at a clear spring—not needing much time, for all we had to do was to drink a draught of icy water and munch a strip of dried venison. Shortly after- 15 ward, as we were moving along a hillside with silent caution, we came to a sheer canyon of which the opposite face was broken by little ledges grown up with wind-beaten cedars. As we peeped over the edge, my companion touched my arm and pointed silently to one of the ledges, 20 and instantly I caught the glint of a buck's horns as he lay half behind an old tree trunk. A slight shift of position gave me a fair shot slanting down between his shoulders, and though he struggled to his feet, he did not go fifty yards after receiving the bullet. 25

This was all we could carry. Leading the horses around, we packed the buck behind my companion's saddle, and then rode back for the doe, which I put behind mine. But we were not destined to reach home without a slight adventure. When we got to the river we rode boldly on 30 the ice, heedless of the thaw; and about midway there was a sudden, tremendous crash, and men, horses, and

deer were scrambling together in the water amid slabs
of floating ice. However, it was shallow, and no worse
results followed than some hard work and a chilly bath.
But what cared we?   We were returning triumphant with
5 our Christmas dinner.

CITIZENSHIP

TRUE AMERICANISM [1]

PATRIOTISM was once defined as "the last refuge of a scoundrel;" and somebody has recently remarked that when Dr. Johnson° gave this definition he was ignorant of the infinite possibilities contained in the word "reform." Of course both gibes were quite justifiable, in so far as 5 they were aimed at people who use noble names to cloak base purposes. Equally of course the man shows little wisdom and a low sense of duty who fails to see that love of country is one of the elemental virtues, even though scoundrels play upon it for their own selfish ends; and, 10 inasmuch as abuses continually grow up in civic life as in all other kinds of life, the statesman is indeed a weakling who hesitates to reform these abuses because the word "reform" is often on the lips of men who are silly or dishonest.   15

What is true of patriotism and reform is true also of Americanism. There are plenty of scoundrels always ready to try to belittle reform movements or to bolster up existing iniquities in the name of Americanism; but this does not alter the fact that the man who can do most 20 in this country is and must be the man whose Americanism is most sincere and intense. Outrageous though it is to use a noble idea as the cloak for evil, it is still worse to assail the noble idea itself because it can thus be used. The men who do iniquity in the name of patriotism, of 25 reform, of Americanism, are merely one small division of the class that has always existed and will always exist,—

[1] Reprinted by permission from *American Ideals and Other Essays*, copyright by G. P. Putnam's Sons.

the class of hypocrites and demagogues, the class that is
always prompt to steal the watchwords of righteousness
and use them in the interests of evil-doing.

The stoutest and truest Americans are the very men
5 who have the least sympathy with the people who invoke
the spirit of Americanism to aid what is vicious in our
government, or to throw obstacles in the way of those who
strive to reform it. It is contemptible to oppose a movement for good because that movement has already suc-
10 ceeded somewhere else, or to champion an existing abuse
because our people have always been wedded to it. To
appeal to national prejudice against a given reform movement is in every way unworthy and silly. It is as childish
to denounce free trade because England has adopted it
15 as to advocate it for the same reason. It is eminently
proper, in dealing with the tariff, to consider the effect of
tariff legislation in time past upon other nations as will
as the effect upon our own; but in drawing conclusions it
is in the last degree foolish to try to excite prejudice against
20 one system because it is in vogue in some given country, or
to try to excite prejudice in its favor because the econo-
mists of that country have found that it was suited to their
own peculiar needs. In attempting to solve our difficult
problem of municipal government it is mere folly to refuse
25 to profit by whatever is good in the examples of Man-
chester° and Berlin because these cities are foreign, exactly as it is mere folly blindly to copy their examples
without reference to our own totally different conditions.
As for the absurdity of declaimimg against civil-service
30 reform, for instance, as "Chinese," because written ex-
aminations have been used in China, it would be quite as
wise to declaim against gunpowder because it was first

utilized by the same people. In short, the man who, whether from mere dull fatuity or from an active interest in misgovernment, tries to appeal to American prejudice against things foreign, so as to induce Americans to oppose any measure for good, should be looked on by his 5 fellow-countrymen with the heartiest contempt. So much for the men who appeal to the spirit of Americanism to sustain us in wrong-doing. But we must never let our contempt for these men blind us to the nobility of the idea which they strive to degrade. 10

We Americans have many grave problems to solve, many threatening evils to fight, and many deeds to do, if,. as we hope and believe, we have the wisdom, the strength, the courage, and the virtue to do them. But we must face facts as they are. We must neither surrender 15 ourselves to a foolish optimism, nor succumb to a timid and ignoble pessimism. Our nation is that one among all the nations of the earth which holds in its hands the fate of the coming years. We enjoy exceptional advantages, and are menaced by exceptional dangers; 20 and all signs indicate that we shall either fail greatly or succeed greatly. I firmly believe that we shall succeed; but we must not foolishly blink the dangers by which we are threatened, for that is the way to fail. On the contrary, we must soberly set to work to find out all 25 we can about the existence and extent of every evil, must acknowledge it to be such, and must then attack it with unyielding resolution. There are many such evils, and each must be fought after a separate fashion; yet there is one quality which we must bring to the solution of every 30 problem,—that is, an intense and fervid Americanism. We shall never be successful over the dangers that con-

front us; we shall never achieve true greatness, nor reach
the lofty ideal which the founders and preservers of our
mighty Federal Republic have set before us, unless we
are Americans in heart and soul, in spirit and purpose,
5 keenly alive to the responsibility implied in the very name
of American, and proud beyond measure of the glorious
privilege of bearing it.

There are two or three sides to the question of Americanism, and two or three senses in which the word
10 "Americanism" can be used to express the antithesis of
what is unwholesome and undesirable.   In the first place we
wish to be broadly American and national, as opposed to
being local or sectional.   We do not wish, in politics, in
literature, or in art, to develop that unwholesome parochial
15 spirit, that over-exaltation of the little community at the
expense of the great nation, which produces what has been
described as the patriotism of the village, the patriotism
of the belfry.   Politically, the indulgence of this spirit was
the chief cause of the calamities which befell the ancient
20 republics of Greece,° the mediæval republics of Italy,°
and the petty States of Germany° as it was in the last
century.   It is this spirit of provincial patriotism, this
inability to take a view of broad adhesion to the whole
nation that has been the chief among the causes that have
25 produced such anarchy in the South American States,
and which have resulted in presenting to us, not one great
Spanish-American federal nation stretching from the
Rio Grande to Cape Horn, but a squabbling multitude
of revolution-ridden States, not one of which stands even
30 in the second rank as a power.   However, politically this
question of American nationality has been settled once
for all.   We are no longer in danger of repeating in our

history the shameful and contemptible disasters that have befallen the Spanish possessions on this continent since they threw off the yoke of Spain. Indeed there is, all through our life, very much less of this parochial spirit than there was formerly. Still there is an occasional outcrop- 5 ping here and there; and it is just as well that we should keep steadily in mind the futility of talking of a Northern literature or a Southern literature, an Eastern or a Western school of art or science. The "Sewanee Review" and the "Overland Monthly," like the "Century" and the 10 "Atlantic," do good work, not merely for one section of the country, but for American literature as a whole. Their success really means as much for Americans who happen to live in New York or Boston as for Americans who happen to live in the Gulf States or on the Pacific slope. Joel 15 Chandler Harris° is emphatically a national writer; so is Mark Twain.° They do not write merely for Georgia or Missouri, any more than for Illinois or Connecticut; they write as Americans and for all people who can read English. It is of very great consequence that we should have 20 a full and ripe literary development in the United States, but it is not of the least consequence whether New York, or Boston, or Chicago, or San Francisco becomes the literary centre of the United States.

There is a second side to this question of a broad Amer- 25 icanism, however. The patriotism of the village or the belfry is bad, but the lack of all patriotism is even worse. There are philosophers who assure us that, in the future, patriotism will be regarded not as a virtue at all, but merely as a mental stage in the journey toward a state 30 of feeling when our patriotism will include the whole human race and all the world. This may be so; but the

age of which these philosophers speak is still several æons
distant.   In fact, philosophers of this type are so very
advanced that they are of no practical service to the present generation.   It may be that in ages so remote that we
5 cannot now understand any of the feelings of those who
will dwell in them, patriotism will no longer be regarded as
a virtue, exactly as it may be that in those remote ages
people will look down upon and disregard monogamic
marriage; but as things now are and have been for two
10 or three thousand years past, and are likely to be for two
or three thousand years to come, the words "home" and
"country" mean a great deal.   Nor do they show any
tendency to lose their significance.   At present, treason,
like adultery, ranks as one of the worst of all possible
15 crimes.

One may fall very far short of treason and yet be an
undesirable citizen in the community.   The man who
becomes Europeanized, who loses his power of doing
good work on this side of the water, and who loses his
20 love for his native land, is not a traitor; but he is a silly
and undesirable citizen.   He is as emphatically a noxious
element in our body politic as is the man who comes here
from abroad and remains a foreigner.   Nothing will more
quickly or more surely disqualify a man from doing good
25 work in the world than the acquirement of that flaccid
habit of mind which its possessors style cosmopolitanism.

It is not only necessary to Americanize the immigrants
of foreign birth who settle among us, but it is even more
necessary for those among us who are by birth and descent
30 already Americans not to throw away our birthright, and,
with incredible and contemptible folly, wander back to
bow down before the alien gods whom our forefathers

forsook. It is hard to believe that there is any necessity to warn Americans that, when they seek to model themselves on the lines of other civilizations, they make themselves the butts of all right-thinking men; and yet the necessity certainly exists to give this warning to many of 5 our citizens who pride themselves on their standing in the world of art and letters, or, perchance, on what they would style their social leadership in the community. It is always better to be an original than an imitation, even when the imitation is of something better than the original; 10 but what shall we say of the fool who is content to be an imitation of something worse? Even if the weaklings who seek to be other than Americans were right in deeming other nations to be better than their own, the fact yet remains that to be a first-class American is fifty-fold 15 better than to be a second-class imitation of a Frenchman or Englishman. As a matter of fact, however, those of our countrymen who do believe in American inferiority are always individuals who, however cultivated, have some organic weakness in their moral or mental make-up; 20 and the great mass of our people, who are robustly patriotic, and who have sound, healthy minds, are justified in regarding these feeble renegades with a half-impatient and half-amused scorn.

We believe in waging relentless war on rank-growing 25 evils of all kinds, and it makes no difference to us if they happen to be of purely native growth. We grasp at any good, no matter whence it comes. We do not accept the evil attendant upon another system of government as an adequate excuse for that attendant upon our own; the 30 fact that the courtier is a scamp does not render the demagogue any the less a scoundrel. But it remains true that,

in spite of all our faults and shortcomings, no other land
offers such glorious possibilities to the man able to take
advantage of them, as does ours; it remains true that
no one of our people can do any work really worth doing
5 unless he does it primarily as an American. It is because
certain classes of our people still retain their spirit of
colonial dependence on, and exaggerated deference to,
European opinion, that they fail to accomplish what they
ought to. It is precisely along the lines where we have
10 worked most independently that we have accomplished the
greatest results; and it is in those professions where there
has been no servility to, but merely a wise profiting by,
foreign experience, that we have produced our greatest
men. Our soldiers and statesmen and orators; our explor-
15 ers, our wilderness-winners and commonwealth-builders;
the men who have made our laws and seen that they were
executed; and the other men whose energy and ingenuity
have created our marvellous material prosperity,—all
these have been men who have drawn wisdom from the
20 experience of every age and nation, but who have nevertheless thought, and worked, and conquered, and lived,
and died, purely as Americans; and on the whole they
have done better work than has been done in any other
country during the short period of our national life.
25   On the other hand, it is in those professions where our
people have striven hardest to mould themselves in conventional European forms that they have suceeded least;
and this holds true to the present day, the failure being of
course most conspicuous where the man takes up his abode
30 in Europe; where he becomes a second-rate European,
because he is over-civilized, over-sensitive, over-refined,
and has lost the hardihood and manly courage by which

alone he can conquer in the keen struggle of our national life. Be it remembered, too, that this same being does not really become a European; he only ceases being an American, and becomes nothing. He throws away a great prize for the sake of a lesser one, and does not even get the lesser one. The painter who goes to Paris, not merely to get two or three years' thorough training in his art, but with the deliberate purpose of taking up his abode there, and with the intention of following in the ruts worn deep by ten thousand earlier travellers, instead of striking off to rise or fall on a new line, thereby forfeits all chance of doing the best work. He must content himself with aiming at that kind of mediocrity which consists in doing fairly well what has already been done better; and he usually never even sees the grandeur and picturesqueness lying open before the eyes of every man who can read the book of America's past and the book of America's present. Thus it is with the undersized man of letters, who flees his country because he, with his delicate, effeminate sensitiveness, finds the conditions of life on this side of the water crude and raw; in other words, because he finds that he cannot play a man's part among men, and so goes where he will be sheltered from the winds that harden stouter souls. This *emigré* may write graceful and pretty verses, essays, novels; but he will never do work to compare with that of his brother, who is strong enough to stand on his own feet, and do his work as an American. Thus it is with the scientist who spends his youth in a German university, and can thenceforth work only in the fields already fifty times furrowed by the German ploughs. Thus it is with that most foolish of parents who sends his children to be educated abroad, not

knowing—what every clear-sighted man from Washington
and Jay down has known—that the American who is to
make his way in America should be brought up among his
fellow Americans.   It is among the people who like to
5 consider themselves, and, indeed, to a large extent are, the
leaders of the so-called social world, especially in some of
the northeastern cities, that this colonial habit of thought,
this thoroughly provincial spirit of admiration for things
foreign, and inability to stand on one's own feet, becomes
10 most evident and most despicable.   We thoroughly believe in every kind of honest and lawful pleasure, so long
as the getting it is not made man's chief business; and we
believe heartily in the good that can be done by men of
leisure who work hard in their leisure, whether at politics
15 or philanthropy, literature or art.   But a leisure class
whose leisure simply means idleness is a curse to the community, and in so far as its members distinguish themselves chiefly by aping the worst—not the best—traits of
similar people across the water, they become both comic
20 and noxious elements of the body politic.
   The third sense in which the word "Americanism" may
be employed is with reference to the Americanizing of the
newcomers to our shores.   We must Americanize them in
every way, in speech, in political ideas and principles, and
25 in their way of looking at the relations between Church and
State.   We welcome the German or the Irishman who becomes an American.   We have no use for the German or
Irishman who remains such.   We do not wish German-
Americans and Irish-Americans who figure as such in our
30 social and political life; we want only Americans, and, provided they are such, we do not care whether they are of native or of Irish or of German ancestry.   We have no room in

any healthy American community for a German-American vote or an Irish-American vote, and it is contemptible demagogy to put planks into any party platform with the purpose of catching such a vote. We have no room for any people who do not act and vote simply as Americans, and as nothing else. Moreover, we have as little use for people who carry religious prejudices into our politics as for those who carry prejudices of caste or nationality. We stand unalterably in favor of the public-school system in its entirety. We believe that the English, and no other language, is that in which all the school exercises should be conducted. We are against any division of the school fund, and against any appropriation of public money for sectarian purposes. We are against any recognition whatever by the State in any shape or form of State-aided parochial schools. But we are equally opposed to any discrimination against or for a man because of his creed. We demand that all citizens, Protestant and Catholic, Jew and Gentile, shall have fair treatment in every way; that all alike shall have their rights guaranteed them. The very reasons that make us unqualified in our opposition to State-aided sectarian schools make us equally bent that, in the management of our public schools, the adherents of each creed shall be given exact and equal justice, wholly without regard to their religious affiliations; that trustees, superintendents, teachers, scholars, all alike, shall be treated without any reference whatsoever to the creed they profess. We maintain that it is an outrage, in voting for a man for any position, whether State or national. to take into account his religious faith, provided only he is a good American. When a secret society does what in some places the American Protective Association seems

to have done, and tries to proscribe Catholics both politically and socially, the members of such society show that they themselves are as utterly un-American, as alien to our school of political thought, as the worst immigrants
5 who land on our shores. This conduct is equally base and contemptible; they are the worst foes of our public-school system, because they strengthen the hands of its ultra-montane enemies; they should receive the hearty condemnation of all Americans who are truly patriotic.

10 The mighty tide of immigration to our shores has brought in its train much of good and much of evil; and whether the good or the evil shall predominate depends mainly on whether these newcomers do or do not throw themselves heartily into our national life, cease to be
15 European, and become Americans like the rest of us. More than a third of the people of the Northern States are of foreign birth or parentage. An immense number of them have become completely Americanized, and these stand on exactly the same plane as the descend-
20 ants of any Puritan, Cavalier, or Knickerbocker among us, and do their full and honorable share of the nation's work. But where immigrants, or the sons of immigrants, do not heartily and in good faith throw in their lot with us, but cling to the speech, the customs,
25 the ways of life, and the habits of thought of the Old World which they have left, they thereby harm both themselves and us. If they remain alien elements, unassimilated, and with interests separate from ours, they are mere obstructions to the current of our national life, and, more-
30 over, can get no good from it themselves. In fact, though we ourselves also suffer from their perversity, it is they who really suffer most. It is an immense benefit to the

European immigrant to change him into an American citizen. To bear the name of American is to bear the most honorable of titles; and whoever does not so believe has no business to bear the name at all, and, if he comes from Europe, the sooner he goes back there the better. Besides, the man who does not become Americanized nevertheless fails to remain a European and becomes nothing at all. The immigrant cannot possibly remain what he was, or continue to be a member of the Old World society. If he tries to retain his old language, in a few generations it becomes a barbarous jargon; if he tries to retain his old customs and ways of life, in a few generations he becomes an uncouth boor. He has cut himself off from the Old World, and cannot retain his connection with it; and if he wishes ever to amount to anything he must throw himself heart and soul, and without reservation, into the new life to which he has come.

So, from his own standpoint, it is beyond all question the wise thing for the immigrant to become thoroughly Americanized. Moreover, from our standpoint, we have a right to demand it. We freely extend the hand of welcome and of good-fellowship to every man, no matter what his creed or birthplace, who comes here honestly intent on becoming a good United States citizen like the rest of us; but we have a right, and it is our duty, to demand that he shall indeed become so, and shall not confuse the issues with which we are struggling by introducing among us Old-World quarrels and prejudices. There are certain ideas which he must give up. For instance, he must learn that American life is incompatible with the existence of any form of anarchy, or, indeed,

of any secret society having murder for its aim, whether
at home or abroad; and he must learn that we exact
full religious toleration and the complete separation of
Church and State.   Moreover, he must not bring in his
5 Old World race and national antipathies, but must
merge them into love for our common country, and
must take pride in the things which we can all take
pride in.   He must revere only our flag; not only must
it come first, but no other flag should even come second.
10 He must learn to celebrate Washington's birthday rather
than that of the Queen or Kaiser, and the Fourth of
July instead of St. Patrick's Day.   Our political and
social questions must be settled on their own merits, and
not complicated by quarrels between England and Ireland,
15 or France and Germany, with which we have nothing to
do: it is an outrage to fight an American political campaign with reference to questions of European politics.
Above all, the immigrant must learn to talk and think
and *be* United States.
20   The immigrant of to-day can learn much from the
experience of the immigrants of the past, who came to
America prior to the Revolutionary War.   Many of our
most illustrious Revolutionary names were borne by men
of Huguenot blood—Jay,° Sevier,° Marion,° Laurens.°
25 But the Huguenots were, on the whole, the best immigrants we have ever received; sooner than any other, and
more completely, they became American in speech, conviction, and thought.   The Hollanders took longer than
the Huguenots to become completely assimilated; never-
30 theless they in the end became so, immensely to their
own advantage.   One of the leading Revolutionary gen-
erals, Schuyler,° and one of the Presidents of the United

States, Van Buren,° were of Dutch blood; but they rose
to their positions, the highest in the land, because they
had become Americans and had ceased being Hollanders.
If they had remained members of an alien body, cut off
by their speech and customs and belief from the rest of 5
the American community, Schuyler would have lived his
life as a boorish, provincial squire, and Van Buren would
have ended his days a small tavern-keeper. So it is with
the Germans of Pennsylvania. Those of them who became Americanized have furnished to our history a mul- 10
titude of honorable names, from the days of the Mühlen-
bergs° onward; but those who did not become Americanized
form to the present day an unimportant body, of no
significance in American existence. So it is with the
Irish, who gave to Revolutionary annals such names as 15
Carrol° and Sullivan,° and to the Civil War men like
Sheridan° and Shields,°—all men who were Americans
and nothing else: while the Irish who remain such, and
busy themselves solely with alien politics, can have only
an unhealthy influence upon American life, and can 20
never rise as do their compatriots who become straight-
out Americans. Thus it has ever been with all people
who have come hither, of whatever stock or blood.

But I wish to be distinctly understood on one point.
Americanism is a question of spirit, convictions, and pur- 25
pose, not of creed or birthplace. The politician who bids
for the Irish or German vote, or the Irishman or German
who votes as an Irishman or German, is despicable, for
all citizens of this commonwealth should vote solely as
Americans; but he is not a whit less despicable than the 30
voter who votes against a good American, merely because that American happens to have been born in Ire-

land or Germany. Know-nothingism, in any form, is as utterly un-American as foreignism. It is a base outrage to oppose a man because of his religion or birthplace, and all good citizens will hold any such effort in
5 abhorrence. A Scandinavian, a German, or an Irishman who has really become an American has the right to stand on exactly the same footing as any native-born citizen in the land, and is just as much entitled to the friendship and support, social and political, of his
10 neighbors. Among the men with whom I have been thrown in close personal contact socially, and who have been among my staunchest friends and allies politically, are not a few Americans who happen to have been born on the other side of the water, in Germany, Ireland,
15 Scandinavia; and I know no better men in the ranks of our native-born citizens.

In closing, I cannot better express the ideal attitude that should be taken by our fellow-citizens of foreign birth than by quoting the words of a representative
20 American, born in Germany, the Honorable Richard Guenther, of Wisconsin. In a speech spoken at the time of the Samoan trouble,° he said:

" We know as well as any other class of American citizens where our duties belong. We will work for our country
25 in time of peace and fight for it in time of war, if a time of war should ever come. When I say our country, I mean, of course, our adopted country. I mean the United States of America. After passing through the crucible of naturalization, we are no longer Germans; we are
30 Americans. Our attachment to America cannot be measured by the length of our residence here. We are Americans from the moment we touch the American

shore until we are laid in American graves. We will fight for America whenever necessary. America, first, last, and all the time. America against Germany, America against the world; America, right or wrong; always America. We are Americans." 5

All honor to the man who spoke such words as those; and I believe they express the feelings of the great majority of those among our fellow-American citizens who were born abroad. We Americans can only do our allotted task well if we face it steadily and bravely, seeing but 10 not fearing the dangers. Above all we must stand shoulder to shoulder, not asking as to the ancestry or creed of our comrades, but only demanding that they be in very truth Americans, and that we all work together, heart, hand, and head, for the honor and the greatness 15 of our common country.

THE STRENUOUS LIFE [1]

GENTLEMEN:—In speaking to you, men of the greatest city of the West, men of the State which gave to the country Lincoln and Grant, men who preëminently and distinctly embody all that is most American in the American character, I wish to preach not the doctrine of ignoble ease but the doctrine of the strenuous life; the life of toil and effort; of labor and strife; to preach that highest form of success which comes not to the man who desires mere easy peace but to the man who does not shrink from danger, from hardship, or from bitter toil, and who out of these wins the splendid ultimate triumph.

A life of ignoble ease, a life of that peace which springs merely from lack either of desire or of power to strive after great things, is as little worthy of a nation as of an individual. I ask only that what every self-respecting American demands from himself, and from his sons, shall be demanded of the American nation as a whole. Who among you would teach your boys that ease, that peace is to be the first consideration in your eyes—to be the ultimate goal after which they strive? You men of Chicago have made this city great, you men of Illinois have done your share, and more than your share, in making America great, because you neither preach nor practice such a doctrine. You work yourselves, and you bring up your sons to work. If you are rich, and are worth your salt, you will teach your sons that though they may have leisure, it is not to be spent in idleness; for wisely used leisure

[1] Reprinted by permission from *The Strenuous Life*, copyrighted by The Century Company.

merely means that those who possess it, being free from
the necessity of working for their livelihood, are all the
more bound to carry on some kind of non-remunerative
work in science, in letters, in art, in exploration, in historical research—work of the type we most need in this 5
country, the successful carrying out of which reflects most
honor upon the nation.

We do not admire the man of timid peace. We admire
the man who embodies victorious effort; the man who
never wrongs his neighbor; who is prompt to help a 10
friend; but who has those virile qualities necessary to win
in the stern strife of actual life. It is hard to fail; but it
is worse never to have tried to succeed. In this life we
get nothing save by effort. Freedom from effort in the
present, merely means that there has been stored up 15
effort in the past. A man can be freed from the necessity
of work only by the fact that he or his fathers before him
have worked to good purpose. If the freedom thus pur-
chased is used aright, and the man still does actual work,
though of a different kind, whether as a writer or a general, 20
whether in the field of politics or in the field of exploration and adventure, he shows he deserves his good fortune.
But if he treats this period of freedom from the need of
actual labor as a period not of preparation but of mere
enjoyment, he shows that he is simply a cumberer on the 25
earth's surface; and he surely unfits himself to hold his
own with his fellows if the need to do so should again
arise. A mere life of ease is not in the end a satisfactory
life, and above all it is a life which ultimately unfits those
who follow it for serious work in the world.   30

As it is with the individual so it is with the nation. It
is a base untruth to say that happy is the nation that has

no history. Thrice happy is the nation that has a glorious history. Far better it is to dare mighty things, to win glorious triumphs, even though checkered by failure, than to take rank with those poor spirits who neither enjoy
5 much nor suffer much because they live in the gray twilight that knows neither victory nor defeat. If in 1861 the men who loved the Union had believed that peace was the end of all things and war and strife a worst of all things, and had acted up to their belief, we would have
10 saved hundreds of thousands of lives, we would have saved hundreds of millions of dollars. Moreover, besides saving all the blood and treasure we then lavished, we would have prevented the heart-break of many women, the dissolution of many homes; and we would have spared the
15 country those months of gloom and shame when it seemed as if our armies marched only to defeat. We could have avoided all this suffering simply by shrinking from strife. And if we had thus avoided it we would have shown that we were weaklings and that we were unfit to stand among
20 the great nations of the earth. Thank God for the iron in the blood of our fathers, the men who upheld the wisdom of Lincoln and bore sword or rifle in the armies of Grant! Let us, the children of the men who proved themselves equal to the mighty days—let us, the children
25 of the men who carried the great Civil War to a triumphant conclusion, praise the God of our fathers that the ignoble counsels of peace were rejected, that the suffering and loss, the blackness of sorrow and despair, were unflinchingly faced and the years of strife endured; for in
30 the end the slave was freed, the Union restored, and the mighty American Republic placed once more as a helmeted queen among nations.

We of this generation do not have to face a task such as that our fathers faced, but we have our tasks, and woe to us if we fail to perform them! We cannot, if we would, play the part of China, and be content to rot by inches in ignoble ease within our borders, taking no interest in what goes on beyond them; sunk in a scrambling commercialism; heedless of the higher life, the life of aspiration, of toil and risk; busying ourselves only with the wants of our bodies for the day; until suddenly we should find, beyond a shadow of question, what China has already found, that in this world the nation that has trained itself to a career of unwarlike and isolated ease is bound in the end to go down before other nations which have not lost the manly and adventurous qualities. If we are to be a really great people, we must strive in good faith to play a great part in the world. We cannot avoid meeting great issues. All that we can determine for ourselves is whether we shall meet them well or ill. Last year we could not help being brought face to face with the problem of war with Spain. All we could decide was whether we should shrink like cowards from the contest or enter into it as beseemed a brave and high-spirited people; and, once in, whether failure or success should crown our banners. So it is now. We cannot avoid the responsibilities that confront us in Hawaii, Cuba, Porto Rico, and the Philippines. All we can decide is whether we shall meet them in a way that will redound to the national credit, or whether we shall make of our dealings with these new problems a dark and shameful page in our history. To refuse to deal with them at all merely amounts to dealing with them badly. We have a given problem to solve. If we undertake the solution there is, of course, always dan-

ger that we may not solve it aright, but to refuse to undertake the solution simply renders it certain that we cannot
possibly solve it aright.

The timid man, the lazy man, the man who distrusts
5 his country, the overcivilized man, who has lost the great
fighting, masterful virtues, the ignorant man and the man
of dull mind, whose soul is incapable of feeling the mighty
lift that thrills "stern men with empires in their brains"—
all these, of course, shrink from seeing the nation under-
10 take its new duties; shrink from seeing us build a navy and
army adequate to our needs; shrink from seeing us do
our share of the world's work by bringing order out of
chaos in the great, fair tropic islands from which the valor
of our soldiers and sailors has driven the Spanish flag.
15 These are the men who fear the strenuous life, who fear
the only national life which is really worth leading. They
believe in that cloistered life which saps the hardy virtues
in a nation, as it saps them in the individual; or else they
are wedded to that base spirit of gain and greed which
20 recognizes in commercialism the be-all and end-all of
national life, instead of realizing that, though an indispensable element, it is after all but one of the many elements that go to make up true national greatness. No
country can long endure if its foundations are not laid
25 deep in the material prosperity which comes from thrift,
from business energy and enterprise, from hard unsparing
effort in the fields of industrial activity; but neither was
any nation ever yet truly great if it relied upon material
prosperity alone. All honor must be paid to the archi-
30 tects of our material prosperity; to the great captains of
industry who have built our factories and our railroads;
to the strong men who toil for wealth with brain or hand;

for great is the debt of the nation to these and their kind. But our debt is yet greater to the men whose highest type is to be found in a statesman like Lincoln, a soldier like Grant. They showed by their lives that they recognized the law of work, the law of strife; they toiled to win a 5 competence for themselves and those dependent upon them; but they recognized that there were yet other and even loftier duties—duties to the nation and duties to the race.

We cannot sit huddled within our own borders and 10 avow ourselves merely an assemblage of well-to-do hucksters who care nothing for what happens beyond. Such a policy would defeat even its own end; for as the nations grow to have ever wider and wider interests and are brought into closer and closer contact, if we are to hold our own 15 in the struggle for naval and commercial supremacy, we must build up our power without our own borders. We must build the Isthmian canal, and we must grasp the points of vantage which will enable us to have our say in deciding the destiny of the oceans of the East and the 20 West. . . .

I preach to you, then, my countrymen, that our country calls not for the life of ease, but for the life of strenuous endeavor. The Twentieth Century looms before us big with the fate of many nations. If we stand idly by, if 25 we seek merely swollen, slothful ease, and ignoble peace, if we shrink from the hard contests where men must win at hazard of their lives and at the risk of all they hold dear, then the bolder and stronger peoples will pass us by and will win for themselves the domination of the world. 30 Let us therefore boldly face the life of strife, resolute to do our duty well and manfully; resolute to uphold righteousness by deed and by word; resolute to be both honest and brave, to serve high ideals, yet to use practical methods. Above all, let us shrink from no strife, moral or physical, within or without the nation, provided we 5 are certain that the strife is justified; for it is only through strife, through hard and dangerous endeavor, that we shall ultimately win the goal of true national greatness.

OUR RESPONSIBILITIES AS A NATION

No people on earth have more cause to be thankful
than ours, and this is said reverently, in no spirit of
boastfulness in our own strength, but with gratitude
to the Giver of Good, who has blessed us with the
conditions which have enabled us to achieve so large a 5
measure of well-being and of happiness. To us as a people it has been granted to lay the foundations of our national life in a new continent. We are the heirs of the
ages, and yet we have had to pay few of the penalties
which in old countries are exacted by the dead hand of 10
a bygone civilization. We have not been obliged to fight
for our existence against any alien race; and yet our
life has called for the vigor and effort without which the
manlier and hardier virtues wither away. Under such
conditions it would be our own fault if we failed; and the 15
success which we have had in the past, the success which
we confidently believe the future will bring, should cause
in us no feeling of vain glory, but rather a deep and
abiding realization of all which life has offered us; a full
acknowledgment of the responsibility which is ours; and 20
a fixed determination to show that under a free government a mighty people can thrive best, alike as regards the
things of the body and the things of the soul.

Much has been given to us, and much will rightly be
expected from us. We have duties to others and duties 25
to ourselves; and we can shirk neither. We have become a great nation, forced by the fact of its greatness
into relations with the other nations of the earth; and
we must behave as beseems a people with such responsi-

173

bilities.   Toward all other nations, large and small, our attitude must be one of cordial and sincere friendship. We must show not only in our words but in our deeds that we are earnestly desirous of securing their good will
5 by acting toward them in a spirit of just and generous recognition of all their rights.   But justice and generosity in a nation, as in an individual, count most when shown not by the weak but by the strong.   While ever careful to refrain from wronging others, we must be no less in-
10 sistent that we are not wronged ourselves.   We wish peace; but we wish the peace of justice, the peace of righteousness.   We wish it because we think it is right and not because we are afraid.   No weak nation that acts manfully and justly should ever have cause to fear
15 us, and no strong power should ever be able to single us out as a subject for insolent aggression.

Our relations with the other Powers of the world are important; but still more important are our relations among ourselves.   Such growth in wealth, in population,
20 and in power as this nation has seen during the century and a quarter of its national life is inevitably accompanied by a like growth in the problems which are ever before every nation that rises to greatness.   Power invariably means both responsibility and danger.   Our forefathers
25 faced certain perils which we have outgrown.   We now face other perils, the very existence of which it was im-possible that they should foresee.   Modern life is both complex and intense, and the tremendous changes wrought by the extraordinary industrial development of the last
30 half century are felt in every fiber of our social and political being.   Never before have men tried so vast and formidable an experiment as that of administering

the affairs of a continent under the form of a democratic republic. The conditions, which have told for our marvelous material well-being, which have developed to a very high degree our energy, self-reliance, and individual initiative, have also brought the care and anxiety inseparable from the accumulation of great wealth in industrial centers. Upon the success of our experiment much depends; not only as regards our own welfare, but as regards the welfare of mankind. If we fail, the cause of free self-government throughout the world will rock to its foundations; and therefore our responsibility is heavy, to ourselves, to the world as it is to-day, and to the generations yet unborn. There is no good reason why we should fear the future but there is every good reason why we should face it seriously, neither hiding from ourselves the gravity of the problems before us nor fearing to approach these problems with the unbending, unflinching purpose to solve them aright.

Yet, after all, though the problems are new, though the tasks set before us differ from the tasks set before our fathers who founded and preserved this Republic, the spirit in which these tasks must be undertaken and these problems faced, if our duty is to be well done, remains essentially unchanged. We know that self-government is difficult. We know that no people needs such high traits of character as that people which seeks to govern its affairs aright through the freely expressed will of the freemen who compose it. But we have faith that we shall not prove false to the memories of the men of the mighty past. They did their work, they left us the splendid heritage we now enjoy. We in our turn have an assured confidence that we shall be able to

leave this heritage unwasted and enlarged to our children and our children's children. To do so we must show, not merely in great crises, but in the everyday affairs of life, the qualities of practical intelligence, of courage, of
5 hardihood and endurance, and above all the power of devotion to a lofty ideal, which made great the men who founded this Republic in the days of Washington, which made great the men who preserved this Republic in the days of Abraham Lincoln.

THE MAN WITH THE MUCK-RAKE

Over a century ago Washington laid the corner-stone of the Capitol° in what was then little more than a tract of wooded wilderness here beside the Potomac. We now find it necessary to provide by great additional buildings for the business of the Government. This growth in the 5 need for the housing of the Government is but a proof· and example of the way in which the Nation has grown and the sphere of action of the National Government has grown. We now administer the affairs of a Nation in which the extraordinary growth of population has been 10 outstripped by the growth of wealth and the growth in complex interests. The natural problems that face us to-day are not such as they were in Washington's time, but the underlying facts of human nature are the same now as they were then. Under altered external form we war 15 with the same tendencies toward evil that were evident in Washington's time, and are helped by the same tendencies for good. It is about some of these that I wish to say a word to-day.

In Bunyan's° "Pilgrim's Progress" you may recall the 20 description of the Man with the Muck-rake,° the man who could look no way but downward, with the muck-rake in his hand; who was offered a celestial crown for his muck-rake, but who would neither look up nor regard the crown he was offered, but continued to rake to him- 25 self the filth of the floor.

In "Pilgrim's Progress" the Man with the Muck-rake is set forth as the example of him whose vision is fixed on carnal instead of on spiritual things. Yet he also typifies

177

the man who in this life consistently refuses to see aught
that is lofty, and fixes his eyes with solemn intentness
only on that which is vile and debasing. Now, it is very
necessary that we should not flinch from seeing what is
5 vile and debasing. There is filth on the floor, and it must
be scraped up with the muck-rake; and there are times
and places where this service is the most needed of all
the services that can be performed. But the man who
never does anything else, who never thinks or speaks or
10 writes save of his feats with the muck-rake, speedily
becomes, not a help to society, not an incitement to good,
but one of the most potent forces for evil.

There are, in the body politic, economic, and social,
many and grave evils, and there is urgent necessity for
15 the sternest war upon them. There should be relentless
exposure of and attack upon every evil man, whether
politician or business man, every evil practice, whether
in politics, in business, or in social life. I hail as a bene-
factor every writer or speaker, every man who, on the
20 platform, or in book, magazine, or newspaper, with merciless severity makes such attack, provided always that he
in his turn remembers that the attack is of use only if it
is absolutely truthful. The liar is no whit better than the
thief, and if his mendacity takes the form of slander, he
25 may be worse than most thieves. It puts a premium upon
knavery untruthfully to attack an honest man, or even
with hysterical exaggeration to assail a bad man with
untruth. An epidemic of indiscriminate assault upon
character does no good, but very great harm. The soul of
30 every scoundrel is gladdened whenever an honest man is
assailed, or even when a scoundrel is untruthfully assailed.

Now, it is easy to twist out of shape what I have just

said, easy to affect to misunderstand it, and, if it is slurred over in repetition, not difficult really to misunderstand it. Some persons are sincerely incapable of understanding that to denounce mud-slinging does not mean the indorsement of whitewashing; and both the interested 5 individuals who need whitewashing, and those others who practice mud-slinging, like to encourage such confusion of ideas. One of the chief counts against those who make indiscriminate assault upon men in business or men in public life is that they invite a reaction which 10 is sure to tell powerfully in favor of the unscrupulous scoundrel who really ought to be attacked, who ought to be exposed, who ought, if possible, to be put in the penitentiary. If Aristides° is praised overmuch as just, people get tired of hearing it; and overcensure of the unjust finally 15 and from similar reasons results in their favor.

Any excess is almost sure to invite a reaction; and, unfortunately, the reaction, instead of taking the form of punishment of those guilty of the excess, is very apt to take the form either of punishment of the unoffending 20 or of giving immunity, and even strength, to offenders. The effort to make financial or political profit out of the destruction of character can only result in public calamity. Gross and reckless assaults on character, whether on the stump or in newspaper, magazine, or book, create a morbid 25 and vicious public sentiment, and at the same time act as a profound deterrent to able men of normal sensitiveness and tend to prevent them from entering the public service at any price. As an instance in point, I may mention that one serious difficulty encountered in getting 30 the right type of men to dig the Panama Canal° is the certainty that they will be exposed, both without, and, I

am sorry to say, sometimes within, Congress, to utterly
reckless assaults on their character and capacity.

At the risk of repetition let me say again that my plea
is, not for immunity to but for the most unsparing ex-
5 posure of the politician who betrays his trust, of the big
business man who makes or spends his fortune in illegiti-
mate or corrupt ways. There should be a resolute effort
to hunt every such man out of the position he has disgraced. Expose the crime, and hunt down the criminal;
10 but remember that even in the case of crime, if it is attacked in sensational, lurid, and untruthful fashion, the
attack may do more damage to the public mind than the
crime itself. It is because I feel that there should be no
rest in the endless war against the forces of evil that I
15 ask that the war be conducted with sanity as well as with
resolution. The men with the muck-rakes are often indispensable to the well-being of society; but only if they
know when to stop raking the muck, and to look upward
to the celestial crown above them, to the crown of worthy
20 endeavor. There are beautiful things above and round
about them; and if they gradually grow to feel that the
whole world is nothing but muck, their power of usefulness is gone. If the whole picture is painted black, there
remains no hue whereby to single out the rascals for dis-
25 tinction from their fellows. Such painting finally induces
a kind of moral color-blindness; and people affected by it
come to the conclusion that no man is really black, and
no man really white, but that all are gray. In other words,
they believe neither in the truth of the attack, nor in the
30 honesty of the man who is attacked; they grow as suspicious of the accusation as of the offence; it becomes well-
nigh hopeless to stir them either to wrath against wrong-

doing or to enthusiasm for what is right; and such a mental attitude in the public gives hope to every knave, and is the despair of honest men.

To assail the great and admitted evils of our political and industrial life with such crude and sweeping gener- 5 alizations as to include decent men in the general condemnation means the searing of the public conscience. There results a general attitude either of cynical belief in and indifference to public corruption or else of a distrustful inability to discriminate between the good and 10 the bad. Either attitude is fraught with untold damage to the country as a whole. The fool who has not sense to discriminate between what is good and what is bad is well-nigh as dangerous as the man who does discriminate and yet chooses the bad. There is nothing more 15 distressing to every good patriot, to every good American, than the hard, scoffing spirit which treats the allegation of dishonesty in a public man as a cause for laughter. Such laughter is worse than the crackling of thorns° under a pot, for it denotes not merely the vacant mind, but the 20 heart in which high emotions have been choked before they could grow to fruition.

There is any amount of good in the world, and there never was a time when loftier and more disinterested work for the betterment of mankind was being done than now. 25 The forces that tend for evil are great and terrible but the forces of truth and love and courage and honesty and generosity and sympathy are also stronger than ever before. It is a foolish and timid, no less than a wicked thing, to blink the fact that the forces of evil are strong, 30 but it is even worse to fail to take into account the strength of the forces that tell for good. Hysterical sensationalism is the very poorest weapon wherewith to fight for lasting righteousness. The men who, with stern sobriety and truth, assail the many evils of our time, whether in the public press, or in magazines, or in books, are the leaders 5 and allies of all engaged in the work for social and political betterment. But if they give good reason for distrust of what they say, if they chill the ardor of those who demand truth as a primary virtue, they thereby betray the good cause, and play into the hands of the very men 10 against whom they are nominally at war.

In his "Ecclesiastical Polity"° that fine old Elizabethan divine, Bishop Hooker, wrote:

"He that goeth about to persuade a multitude that they are not so well governed as they ought to be shall 15 never want attentive and favorable hearers, because they know the manifold defects whereunto every kind of regimen is subject; but the secret lets and difficulties, which in public proceedings are innumerable and inevitable, they have not ordinarily the judgment to consider."

20   This truth should be kept constantly in mind by every ' free people desiring to preserve the sanity and poise indispensable to the permanent success of self-government. Yet, on the other hand, it is vital not to permit this spirit of sanity and self-command to degenerate into mere mental 25 stagnation. Bad though a state of hysterical excitement is, and evil though the results are which· come from the violent oscillations such excitement invariably produces, yet a sodden acquiescence in evil is even worse. At this moment we are passing through a period of great unrest— 30 social, political, and industrial unrest. It is of the utmost importance for our future that this should prove to be not the unrest of mere rebelliousness against life, of mere dis-

satisfaction with the inevitable inequality of conditions, but the unrest of a resolute and eager ambition to secure the betterment of the individual and the Nation. So far as this movement of agitation throughout the country takes the form of a fierce discontent with evil, of a deter- 5 mination to punish the authors of evil, whether in industry or politics, the feeling is to be heartily welcomed as a sign of healthy life.

If, on the other hand, it turns into a mere crusade of appetite against appetite, a contest between the brutal 10 greed of the "have-nots" and the brutal greed of the "haves," then it has no significance for good, but only for evil. If it seeks to establish a, line of cleavage, not along the line which divides good men from bad, but along that other line, running at right angles thereto, which 15 divides those who are well off from those who are less well off, then it will be fraught with immeasurable harm to the body politic.

We can no more and no less afford to condone evil in the man of capital than evil in the man of no capital. The 20 wealthy man who exults because there is a failure of justice in the effort to bring some trust magnate to an account for his misdeeds is as bad as, and no worse than, the so-called labor leader who clamorously strives to excite a foul class feeling on behalf of some other labor leader who 25 is implicated in murder. One attitude is as bad as the other and no worse; in each case the accused is entitled to exact justice; and in neither case is there need of action by others which can be construed into an expression of sympathy for crime. There is nothing more anti-social 30 in a democratic republic like ours than such vicious class-consciousness. The multi-millionaires who band together

to prevent the enactment of proper laws for the supervision
of the use of wealth, or to assail those who resolutely enforce such laws, or to exercise a hidden influence upon the
political destinies of parties or individuals in their own
5 personal interest, are a menace to the whole community;
and a menace at least as great is offered by those laboring
men who band together to defy the law, and by their
openly used influence to coerce law-upholding public
officials. The apologists for either class of offenders are
10 themselves enemies of good citizenship; and incidentally
they are also, to a peculiar degree, the enemies of every
honest-dealing corporation and every law-abiding labor
union.

It is a prime necessity that if the present unrest is to
15 result in permanent good the emotion shall be translated into action, and that the action shall be marked by
honesty, sanity, and self-restraint. There is mighty
little good in a mere spasm of reform. The reform that
counts is that which comes through steady, continuous
20 growth; violent emotionalism leads to exhaustion.

It is important to this people to grapple with the
problems connected with the amassing of enormous fortunes, and the use of those fortunes, both corporate
and individual, in business. We should discriminate in
25 the sharpest way between fortunes well won and fortunes
ill won; between those gained as an incident to performing great services to the community as a whole, and those
gained in evil fashion by keeping just within the limits
of mere law-honesty. Of course no matter of charity in
30 spending such fortunes in any way compensates for mis-
conduct in making them. As a matter of personal conviction, and without pretending to discuss the details

or formulate the system; I feel that we shall ultimately have to consider the adoption of some such scheme as that of a progressive tax on all fortunes, beyond a certain amount, either given in life or devised or bequeathed upon death to any individual—a tax so framed as to put5 it out of the power of the owner of one of these enormous fortunes to hand on more than a certain amount to any one individual; the tax, of course, to be imposed by the National and not the State Government. Such taxation should, of course, be aimed merely at the inherit-10 ance or transmission in their entirety of those fortunes swollen beyond all healthy limits.

Again, the National Government must in some form exercise supervision over corporations engaged in inter-State business—and all large corporations are engaged in15 inter-State business,—whether by license or otherwise, so as to permit us to deal with the far-reaching evils of over-capitalization. This year we are making a beginning in the direction of serious effort to settle some of these economic problems by the railway rate legislation. Such20 legislation, if so framed, as I am sure it will be, as to secure definite and tangible results, will amount to something of itself; and it will amount to a great deal more in so far as it is taken as a first step in the direction of a policy of superintendence and control over corporate25 wealth engaged in inter-State commerce, this superintendence and control not to be exercised in a spirit of malevolence toward the men who have created the secure definite and tangible results, will amount to some wealth, but with the firm purpose both to do justice to30 them and to see that they in their turn do justice to the public at large.

The first requisite in the public servants who are to deal in this shape with corporations, whether as legislators or as executives, is honesty. This honesty can be no respecter of persons. There can be no such thing as unilateral honesty. The danger is not really from corrupt corporations: it springs from the corruption itself, whether exercised for or against corporations.

The eighth commandment reads, "Thou shalt not steal." It does not read, "Thou shalt not steal from the rich man." It does not read, "Thou shalt not ' steal from the poor man." It reads simply and plainly, "Thou shalt not steal." No good whatever will come from that warped and mock morality which denounces the misdeeds of men of wealth and forgets the misdeeds practiced at their expense; which denounces bribery, but blinds itself to blackmail; which foams with rage if a corporation secures favors by improper methods, and merely leers with hideous mirth if the corporation is itself wronged. The only public servant who can be trusted honestly to protect the rights of the public against the misdeeds of a corporation is that public man who will just as surely protect the corporation itself from wrongful aggression. If a public man is willing to yield to popular clamor and do wrong to the men of wealth or to rich corporations, it may be set down as certain that if the opportunity comes he will secretly and furtively do wrong to the public in the interest of a corporation.

But, in addition to honesty, we need sanity. No honesty will make a public man useful if that man is timid or foolish, if he is a hot-headed zealot or an impracticable visionary. As we strive for reform we find that it is not at all merely the case of a long uphill pull. On the contrary, there is almost as much of breeching work as of collar work; to depend only on traces means that there will soon be a runaway and an upset. The men of wealth who to-day are trying to prevent the regulation and control of their business in the interest of the public by 5 the proper Government authorities will not succeed, in my judgment, in checking the progress of the movement. But if they did succeed they would find that they had sown the wind and would surely reap the whirlwind, for they would ultimately provoke the violent excesses which 10 accompany a reform coming by convulsion instead of . by steady and natural growth.

On the other hand, the wild preachers of unrest and discontent, the wild agitators against the entire existing order, the men who act crookedly, whether because 15 of sinister design or from mere puzzle-headedness, the men who preach destruction without proposing any substitute for what they intend to destroy, or who propose a substitute which would be far worse than the existing evils—all these men are the most dangerous opponents of 20 real reform. If they get their way, they will lead the people into a deeper pit than any into which they could fall under the present system. If they fail to get their way, they will still do incalculable harm by provoking the kind of reaction which, in its revolt against the senseless 25 evil of their teaching, would enthrone more securely than ever the very evils which their misguided followers believe they are attacking.

More important than aught else is the development of the broadcast sympathy of man for man. The welfare of 30 the wage-worker, the welfare of the tiller of the soil—upon this depends the welfare of the entire country; their good is not to be sought in pulling down others; but their good must be the prime object of all our statesmanship.

Materially we must strive to secure a broader economic opportunity for all men, so that each shall have a better chance to show the stuff of which he is made. Spiritually and ethically we must strive to bring about clean living and right thinking. We appreciate that the things of the body are important; but we appreciate also that the things of the soul are immeasurably more important. The foundation stone of national life is, and ever must be, the high individual character of the average citizen.

THE DEVELOPMENT OF THE AMERICAN NATION

At the outset I wish to say a word of special greeting to the representatives of the foreign governments here present. They have come to assist us in celebrating ° what was in very truth the birthday of this nation, for it was here that the colonists first settled,° whose incoming, 5 whose growth from their own loins and by the addition of newcomers from abroad, was to make the people which one hundred and sixty-nine years later assumed the solemn responsibilities and weighty duties of complete independence.   10

In welcoming all of you I must say a special word, first to the representative of the people of Great Britain and Ireland. The fact that so many of our people, of whom as it happens I myself am one, have but a very small portion of English blood in our veins, in no way alters the 15 other fact that this nation was founded by Englishmen, by the Cavalier and the Puritan.° Their tongue, law, literature, the fund of their common thought, made an inheritance which all of us share, and marked deep the lines along which we have developed. It was the men of 20 English stock who did most in casting the mold into which our national character was run.

Let me furthermore greet all of you, the representatives of the people of continental Europe. From almost every nation of Europe we have drawn some part of our blood, 25 some part of our traits. This mixture of blood has gone on from the beginning, and with it has gone on a kind of development unexampled among peoples of the stock from

189

which we spring; and hence to-day we differ sharply from,
and yet in some ways are fundamentally akin to, all of
the nations of Europe.

Again, let me bid you welcome, representatives of our
5 sister Republics of this continent. In the larger aspect,
your interests and ours are identical. Your problems and
ours are in large part the same; and as we strive to settle
them, I pledge you herewith on the part of this nation the
heartiest friendship and good will.

10 Finally, let me say a special word of greeting to those
representatives of the Asiatic nations who make up that
newest East which is yet the most ancient East, the East
of time immemorial. In particular, let me express a word
of hearty welcome to the representative of the mighty
15 island empire of Japan; that empire, which, in learning
from the West, has shown that it had so much, so very
much, to teach the West in return.

To all of you here gathered I express my thanks for
your coming, and I extend to you my earnest wishes for
20 the welfare of your several nations. The world has moved
so far that it is no longer necessary to believe that one
nation can rise only by thrusting another down. All far-
sighted statesmen, all true patriots, now earnestly wish
that the leading nations of mankind, as in their several
25 ways they struggle constantly toward a higher civilization, a higher humanity, may advance hand in hand,
united only in a generous rivalry to see which can best do
its allotted work in the world. I believe that there is a rising tide in human thought which tends for righteous in-
30 ternational peace; a tide which it behooves us to guide
through rational channels to sane conclusions; and all of
us here present can well afford to take to heart St. Paul's

counsel: "If it be possible, as much as lieth in you, live peaceably with all men."

We have met to-day to celebrate the opening of the Exposition which itself commemorates the first permanent settlement of men of our stock in Virginia, the first be-5 ginning of what has since become this mighty Republic. Three hundred years ago a handful of English adventurers, who had crossed the ocean in what we should now call cockle-boats, as clumsy as they were frail, landed in the great wooded wilderness, the Indian-haunted waste, 10 which then stretched down to the water's edge along the entire Atlantic coast. They were not the first men of European race to settle in what is now the United States, for there were already Spanish settlements in Florida and on the headwaters of the Rio Grande; and the French, 15 who at almost the same time were struggling up the St. Lawrence, were likewise destined to form permanent settlements on the Great Lakes and in the valley of the Mississippi before the people of English stock went westward of the Alleghenies. Moreover, both the Dutch and 20 the Swedes were shortly to found colonies between the two sets of English colonies, those that grew up around the Potomac and those that grew up on what is now the New England Coast. Nevertheless, this landing at Jamestown possesses for us of the United States an alto-25 gether peculiar significance, and this without regard to our several origins. The men who landed at Jamestown and those who, thirteen years later, landed at Plymouth, all of English stock, and their fellow-settlers who during the next few decades streamed in after them, were those 30 who took the lead in shaping the life history of this people in the colonial and revolutionary days. It was they who bent into definite shape our nation while it was still young enough most easily, most readily, to take on the characteristics which were to become part of its permanent life habit.

5 Yet let us remember that while this early English colonial stock has left deeper than all others upon our national life the mark of its strong twin individualities, the mark of the Cavalier and of the Puritan—nevertheless, this stock, not only from its environment but also from the 10 presence with it of other stocks, almost from the beginning began to be differentiated strongly from any European people. As I have already said, about the time the first English settlers landed here, the Frenchman and the Spaniard, the Swede and the Dutchman, also came hither 15 as permanent dwellers, who left their seed behind them to help shape and partially to inherit our national life. The German, the Irishman, and the Scotchman came later, but still in colonial times. Before the outbreak of the Revolution the American people, not only because of 20 their surroundings, physical and spiritual, but because of the mixture of blood that had already begun to take place, represented a new and distinct ethnic type. This type has never been fixed in blood. All through the colonial days new waves of immigration from time to time 25 swept hither across the ocean, now from one country, now from another. The same thing has gone on ever since our birth as a nation; and for the last sixty years the tide of immigration has been at the full. The newcomers are soon absorbed into our eager national life, and are 30 radically and profoundly changed thereby, the rapidity of their assimilation being marvelous. But each group of newcomers, as it adds its blood to the life, also changes

it somewhat, and this change and growth and development have gone on steadily, generation by generation, throughout three centuries.

The pioneers of our people who first landed on these shores on that eventful day three centuries ago, had be- 5 fore them a task which during the early years was of heartbreaking danger and difficulty. The conquest of a new continent is iron work. People who dwell in old civilizations and find that therein so much of humanity's lot is hard, are apt to complain against the conditions as 10 being solely due to man and to speak as if life could be made easy and simple if there were but a virgin continent in which to work. It is true that the pioneer life was simpler, but it was certainly not easier. As a matter of fact, the first work of the pioneers in taking possession 15 of a lonely wilderness is so rough, so hard, so dangerous that all but the strongest spirits fail. The early iron days of such a conquest search out alike the weak in body and the weak in soul. In the warfare against the rugged sternness of primeval Nature, only those can conquer 20 who are themselves unconquerable. It is not until the first bitter years have passed that the life becomes easy enough to invite a mass of newcomers, and so great are the risk, hardship, and toil of the early years that there always exists a threat of lapsing back from civilization. 25

The history of the pioneers of Jamestown, of the founders of Virginia, illustrates the truth of all this. Famine and pestilence and war menaced the little band of daring men who had planted themselves alone on the edge of a frowning continent. Moreover, as men ever 30 find, whether in the tiniest frontier community or in the vastest and most highly organized and complex civilized

society, their worst foes were in their own bosoms. Dis-
sension, distrust, the inability of some to work and the
unwillingness of others, jealousy arrogance and envy,
folly and laziness—in short all the shortcomings with
5 which we have to grapple now, were faced by those
pioneers, and at moments threatened their whole enterprise with absolute ruin. It was some time before the
ground on which they had landed supported them, in
spite of its potential fertility, and they looked across the
10 sea for supplies. At one moment so hopeless did they become that the whole colony embarked, and was only saved
from abandoning the country by the opportune arrival of
help from abroad.

At last they took root in the land, and were already
15 prospering when the Pilgrims landed at Plymouth. In a
few years a great inflow of settlers began. Four of the
present States of New England were founded. Virginia
waxed apace. The Carolinas grew up to the south of it,
and Maryland to the north of it. The Dutch colonies
20 between, which had already absorbed the Swedish, were
in their turn absorbed by the English. Pennsylvania was
founded and, later still, Georgia. There were many wars
with the Indians and with the dauntless captains whose
banners bore the lilies of France. At last the British flag
25 flew without a rival in all eastern North America. Then
came the successful struggle for national independence.

For half a century after we became a separate nation
there was comparatively little immigration to this country.
Then the tide once again set hither, and has flowed in
30 ever-increasing size until in each of the last three years
a greater number of people came to these shores than
had landed on them during the entire colonial period.

Generation by generation these people have been absorbed into the national life. Generally their sons, almost always their grandsons, are indistinguishable from one another and from their fellow-Americans descended from the colonial stock. For all alike the problems of our existence are fundamentally the same, and for all alike these problems change from generation to generation.

In the colonial period, and for at least a century after its close, the conquest of the continent, the expansion of our people westward, to the Alleghenies, then to the Mississippi, then to the Pacific, was always one of the most important tasks, and sometimes the most important, in our national life. Behind the first settlers the conditions grew easier, and in the older-settled regions of all the colonies life speedily assumed much of comfort and something of luxury; and though generally it was on a much more democratic basis than life in the Old World, it was by no means democratic when judged by our modern standards; and here and there, as in the tidewater regions of Virginia, a genuine aristocracy grew and flourished. But the men who first broke ground in the virgin wilderness, whether on the Atlantic coast, or in the interior, fought hard for mere life. In the early stages the frontiersman had to do battle with the savage, and when the savage was vanquished there remained the harder strain of war with the hostile forces of soil and climate, with flood, fever, and famine. There was sickness, and bitter weather; there were no roads; there was a complete lack of all but the very roughest and most absolute necessaries. Under such circumstances the men and women who made ready the continent for civilization were able themselves to spend but little time in doing

aught but the rough work which was to make smooth
the ways of their successors.   In consequence observers
whose insight was spoiled by lack of sympathy always
found both the settlers and their lives unattractive and
5 repellent.   In Martin Chuzzlewit° the description of
America, culminating in the description of the frontier
town of Eden, was true and lifelike from the standpoint
of one content to look merely at the outer shell; and yet
it was a community like Eden that gave birth to Abraham
10 Lincoln; it was men such as were therein described from
whose loins Andrew Jackson° sprang.

Hitherto each generation among us has had its allotted
task, now heavier, now lighter.   In the Revolutionary
War the business was to achieve independence.   Immedi-
15 ately afterwards there was an even more momentous
task; that to achieve the national unity and the capacity
for orderly development, without which our liberty, our
independence, would have been a curse and not a blessing.
In each of these two contests, while there were many
20 great leaders from many different States, it is but fair to
say that the foremost place was taken by the soldiers and
the statesmen of Virginia; and to Virginia was reserved
the honor of producing the hero of both movements, the
hero of the war, and of the peace that made good the re-
25 sults of the war—George Washington; while the two
great political tendencies of the time can be symbolized
by the names of two other great Virginians—Jefferson°
and Marshall°—from one of whom we inherit the abiding
trust in the people which is the foundation stone of de-
30 mocracy, and from the other the power to develop on behalf of the people a coherent and powerful government, a
genuine and representative nationality.

Two generations passed before the second great crisis of our history had to be faced. Then came the Civil War, terrible and bitter in itself and in its aftermath, but a struggle from which the Nation finally emerged united in fact as well as in name, united forever. Oh, my hearers, my fellow countrymen, great indeed has been our good fortune; for as time clears away the mists that once shrouded brother from brother and made each look "as through a glass darkly" at the other, we can all feel the same pride in the valor, the devotion and the fealty toward the right as it was given to each to see the right, shown alike by the men who wore the blue and by the men who wore the gray. Rich and prosperous though we are as a people, the proudest heritage that each of us has, no matter where he may dwell, North or South, East or West, is the immaterial heritage of feeling, the right to claim as his own all the valor and all the steadfast devotion to duty shown by the men of both the great armies, of the soldiers whose leader was Grant° and the soldiers whose leader was Lee.° The men and the women of the Civil War did their duty bravely and well in the days that were dark and terrible and splendid. We, their descendants, who pay proud homage to their memories, and glory in the feats of might of one side no less than of the other, need to keep steadily in mind that the homage which counts is the homage of heart and of hand, and not of the hps, the homage of deeds and not of words only. We, too, in our turn, must prove our truth by our endeavor. We must show ourselves worthy sons of the men of the mighty days by the way in which we meet the problems of our own time. We carry our heads high because our fathers did well in the years that tried men's souls; and we must in our turn so bear ourselves that the children who come after us may feel that we too have done our duty.

We can not afford to forget the maxim° upon which Washington insisted, that the surest way to avert war is 5 to be prepared to meet it. Nevertheless the duties that most concern us of this generation are not military, but social and industrial. Each community must always dread the evils which spring up as attendant upon the very qualities which give it success. We of this mighty 10 western Republic have to grapple with the dangers that spring from popular self-government tried on a scale incomparably vaster than ever before in the history of mankind, and from an abounding material prosperity greater also than anything which the world has hitherto 15 seen.

As regards the first set of dangers, it behooves us to remember that men can never escape being governed. Either they must govern themselves or they must submit to being governed by others. If from lawlessness or fickle- 20 ness, from folly or self-indulgence, they refuse to govern themselves, then most assuredly in the end they will have to be governed from the outside. They can prevent the need of government from without only by showing that they possess the power of government from within. A 25 sovereign can not make excuses for his failures; a sovereign must accept the responsibility for the exercise of the power that inheres in him; and where, as is true in our Republic, the people are sovereign, then the people must show a sober understanding and a sane and steadfast pur- 30 pose if they are to preserve that orderly liberty upon which as a foundation every republic must rest.

In industrial matters our enormous prosperity has

brought with it certain grave evils. It is our duty to try
to cut out these evils without at the same time destroying our well-being itself. This is an era of combination
alike in the world of capital and in the world of labor.
Each kind of combination can do good, and yet each, 5
however powerful, must be opposed when it does ill. At
the moment the greatest problem before us is how to exercise such control over the business use of vast wealth,
individual, but especially corporate, as will insure its not
being used against the interest of the public, while yet 10
permitting such ample legitimate profits as will encourage
individual initiative. It is our business to put a stop to
abuses and to prevent their recurrence, without showing
a spirit of mere vindictiveness for what has been done in
the past. In John Morley's brilliant sketch° of Burke he 15
lays especial stress upon the fact that Burke more than
almost any other thinker or politician of his time realized
the profound lesson that in politics we are concerned not
with barren rights but with duties; not with abstract
truth, but with practical morality. He especially eulo- 20
gizes the way in which in his efforts for economic reform,
Burke combined unshakable resolution in pressing the
reform with a profound temperateness of spirit which
made him, while bent on the extirpation of the evil system,
refuse to cherish an unreasoning and vindictive ill will 25
toward the men who had benefited by it. Said Burke,
"If I can not reform with equity, I will not reform at
all. . . . (There is) a state to preserve as well as a state
to reform."

This is the exact spirit in which this country should move 30
to the reform of abuses of corporate wealth. The wrong-
doer, the man who swindles and cheats, whether on a big

scale or a little one, shall receive at our hands mercy as scant as if he committed crimes of violence or brutality. We are unalterably determined to prevent wrongdoing in the future; we have no intention of trying to wreak such an indiscriminate vengeance for wrongs done in the past as would confound the innocent with the guilty. Our purpose is to build up rather than to tear down. We show ourselves the truest friends of property when we make it evident that we will not tolerate the abuses of property. We are steadily bent on preserving the institution of private property; we combat every tendency toward reducing the people to economic servitude; and we care not whether the tendency is due to a sinister agitation directed against all property, or whether it is due to the actions of those members of the predatory classes whose anti-social power is immeasurably increased because of the very fact that they possess wealth.

Above all, we insist that while facing changed conditions and new problems, we must face them in the spirit which our forefathers showed when they founded and preserved this Republic. The corner-stone of the Republic lies in our treating each man on his worth as a man, paying no heed to his creed, his birthplace, or his occupation, asking not whether he is rich or poor, whether he labors with head or hand; asking only whether he acts decently and honorably in the various relations of his life, whether he behaves well to his family, to his neighbors, to the State. We base our regard for each man on the essentials and not the accidents. We judge him not by his profession, but by his deeds; by his conduct, not by what he has acquired of this world's goods. Other republics have fallen, because the citizens gradually grew to consider the interests of a class before the interests of the whole; for when such was the case it mattered little whether it was the poor who plundered the rich or the rich who exploited the poor; in either event the end of the Republic was at hand. We are resolute in our purpose not to fall into such a pit. This great Republic of ours shall never become the government of a plutocracy, and it shall never become the government of a mob. God willing, it shall remain what our fathers who founded it meant it to be— a government in which each man stands on his worth as a man, where each is given the largest personal liberty consistent with securing the well-being of the whole, and where, so far as in us lies, we strive continually to secure for each man such equality of opportunity that in the strife of life he may have a fair chance to show the stuff that is in him. We are proud of our schools and of the trained intelligence they give our children the opportunity to acquire. But what we care for most is the character of the average man; for we believe that if the average of character in the individual citizen is sufficiently high, if he possesses those qualities which make him worthy of respect in his family life and in his work outside, as well as the qualities which fit him for success in the hard struggle of actual existence—that if such is the character of our individual citzenship, there is literally no height of triumph unattainable in this vast experiment of government by, of, and for a free people.

CONSERVATION OF NATURAL RESOURCES

Governors of the Several States and Gentlemen:

I welcome you to this conference at the White House. You have come hither at my request so that we may join together to consider the question of the conservation and use of the great fundamental sources of wealth of this
5 nation. So vital is this question that for the first time in our history the chief executive officers of the states separately and of the states together forming the nation have met to consider it.

With the Governors come men from each state chosen
10 for their special acquaintance with the terms of the problem that is before us. Among them are experts in natural resources and representatives of national organizations concerned in the development and use of these resources; the Senators and Representatives in Congress; the Su-
15 preme Court, the Cabinet and the Inland Waterways Commission have likewise been invited to the conference, which is therefore national in a peculiar sense.

This conference on the conservation of natural resources is in effect a meeting of the representatives of all
20 the people of the United States called to consider the weightiest problem now before the nation, and the occasion for the meeting lies in the fact that the natural resources of our country are in danger of exhaustion if we permit the old wasteful methods of exploiting them longer
25 to continue.

With the rise of peoples from savagery to civilization, and with the consequent growth in the extent and variety of the needs of the average man, there comes a steadily

increasing growth of the amount demanded by this average
man from the actual resources of the country. Yet, rather
curiously, at the same time the average man is likely to
lose his realization of this dependence upon nature.

Savages, and very primitive peoples generally, concern 5
themselves only with superficial natural resources; with
those which they obtain from the actual surface of the
ground. As peoples become a little less primitive their
industries, although in a rude manner, are extended to
resources below the surface; then, with what we call civil- 10
ization and the extension of knowledge, more resources
come into use, industries are multiplied and foresight
begins to become a necessary and prominent factor in
life. Crops are cultivated, animals are domesticated and
metals are mastered. 15

Every step of the progress of mankind is marked by
the discovery and use of natural resources previously
unused. Without such progressive knowledge and utilization of natural resources population could not grow, nor
industries multiply, nor the hidden wealth of the earth 20
be developed for the benefit of mankind.

From the first beginnings of civilization, on the banks
of the Nile and the Euphrates, the industrial progress of
the world has gone on slowly, with occasional setbacks,
but on the whole steadily, through tens of centuries to 25
the present day. But of late the rapidity of the progress
has increased at such a rate that more space has been
actually covered during the century and a quarter occupied
by our national life than during the preceding six thousand
years that take us back to the earliest monuments of 30
Egypt, to the earliest cities of the Babylonian plain.

When the founders of this nation met at Independence

Hall in Philadelphia the conditions of commerce had not
fundamentally changed from what they were when the
Phœnician keels first furrowed the lonely waters of the
Mediterranean. The differences were those of degree,
5 not of kind, and they were not in all cases even those of
degree. Mining was carried on fundamentally as it had
been carried on by the Pharaohs in the countries adjacent
to the Red Sea.

The wares of the merchants of Boston, of Charleston,
10 like the wares of the merchants of Nineveh and Sidon, if
they went by water were carried by boats propelled by
sails or oars; if they went by land were carried in wagons
drawn by beasts of draft or in packs on the backs of beasts
of burden. The ships that crossed the high seas were bet-
15 ter than the ships that had once crossed the Ægean, but
they were of the same type, after all—they were wooden
ships propelled by sails; and on land the roads were not
as good as the roads of the Roman Empire, while the service of the posts was probably inferior.

20   In Washington's time anthracite coal was known only
as a useless black stone; and the great fields of bituminous
coal were undiscovered. As steam was unknown, the use
of coal for power production was undreamed of. Water
was practically the only source of power, save the labor of
25 men and animals; and this power was used only in the
most primitive fashion. But a few small iron deposits
had been found in this country, and the use of iron by our
countrymen was very small. Wood was practically the
only fuel, and what lumber was sawed was consumed
30 locally, while the forests were regarded chiefly as obstructions to settlement and cultivation.

Such was the degree of progress to which civilized mankind had attained when this nation began its career. It is almost impossible for us in this day to realize how little our Revolutionary ancestors knew of the great store of natural resources whose discovery and use have been such vital factors in the growth and greatness of this nation, 5 and how little they required to take from this store in order to satisfy their needs.

Since then our knowledge and use of the resources of the present territory of the United States have increased a hundredfold. Indeed, the growth of this nation by 10 leaps and bounds makes one of the most striking and important chapters in the history of the world. Its growth has been due to the rapid development, and, alas! that it should be said, to the rapid destruction, of our natural resources. Nature has supplied to us in the United States, 15 and still supplies to us, more kinds of resources in a more lavish degree than has ever been the case at any other time or with any other people. Our position in the world has been attained by the extent and thoroughness of the control we have achieved over Nature; but we are more, and 20 not less, dependent upon what she furnishes than at any previous time of history since the days of primitive man.

Yet our fathers, though they knew so little of the resources of the country, exercised a wise forethought in reference thereto. Washington clearly saw that the per- 25 petuity of the states could only be secured by union and that the only feasible basis of union was an economic one; in other words, that it must be based on the development and use of their natural resources. Accordingly, he helped to outline a scheme of commercial development, and by 30 his influence an interstate waterways commission was appointed by Virginia and Maryland.

It met near where we are now meeting, in Alexandria, adjourned to Mount Vernon, and took up the consideration of interstate commerce by the only means then available, that of water. Further conferences were arranged, 5 first at Annapolis and then at Philadelphia. It was in Philadelphia that the representatives of all the states met for what was in its original conception merely a waterways conference; but when they had closed their deliberations the outcome was the Constitution which made the states 10 into a nation.

The Constitution of the United States thus grew in large part out of the necessity for united action in the wise use of one of our natural resources. The wise use of all of our natural resources, which are our national resources 15 as well, is the great material question of to-day. I have asked you to come together now because the enormous consumption of these resources, and the threat of imminent exhaustion of some of them, due to reckless and wasteful use, once more call for common effort, common action. 20 Since the days when the Constitution was adopted, steam and electricity have revolutionized the industrial world. Nowhere has the revolution been so great as in our own country. The discovery and utilization of mineral fuels and alloys have given us the lead over all other 25 nations in the production of steel. The discovery and utilization of coal and iron have given us our railways, and have led to such industrial development as has never before been seen. The vast wealth of lumber in our forests, the riches of our soils and mines, the discovery 30 of gold and mineral oils, combined with the efficiency of our transportation, have made the conditions of our life unparalleled in comfort and convenience.

The steadily increasing drain on these natural resources has promoted to an extraordinary degree the
complexity of our industrial and social life. Moreover,
this unexampled development has had a determining
effect upon the character and opinions of our people. The 5
demand for efficiency in the great task has given us vigor,
effectiveness, decision and power, and a capacity for
achievement which in its own lines has never ·yet been
matched. So great and so rapid has been our material
growth that there has been a tendency to lag behind in 10
spiritual and moral growth; but that is not the subject
upon which I speak to you to-day.

Disregarding for the moment the question of moral purpose, it is safe to say that the prosperity of our people
depends directly on the energy and intelligence with 15
which our natural resources are used. It is equally clear
that these resources are the final basis of national power
and perpetuity. Finally, it is ominously evident that
these resources are in the course of rapid exhaustion.

This nation began with the belief that its landed posses- 20
sions were illimitable and capable of supporting all the
people who might care to make our country their home;
but already the limit of unsettled land is in sight, and
indeed but little land fitted for agriculture now remains
unoccupied save what can be reclaimed by irrigation and 25
drainage. We began with an unapproached heritage of
forests; more than half of the timber is gone. We began
with coal fields more extensive than those of any other
nation and with iron ores regarded as inexhaustible, and
many experts now declare that the end of both iron and 30
coal is in sight.

The mere increase in our consumption of coal during

1907 over 1906 exceeded the total consumption in 1876, the centennial year. The enormous stores of mineral oil and gas are largely gone. Our natural waterways are not gone, but they have been so injured by neglect and by the division of responsibility and utter lack of system in dealing with them that there is less navigation on them now than there was fifty years ago. Finally, we began with soils of unexampled fertility and we have so impoverished them by injudicious use and by failing to check erosion that their crop-producing power is diminishing instead of increasing. In a word, we have thoughtlessly, and to a large degree unnecessarily, diminished the resources upon which not only our prosperity but the prosperity of our children must always depend.

We have become great because of the lavish use of our resources, and we have just reason to be proud of our growth. But the time has come to inquire seriously what will happen when our forests are gone, when the coal, the iron, the oil and the gas are exhausted, when the soils shall have been still further impoverished and washed into the streams, polluting the rivers, denuding the fields and obstructing navigation. These questions do not relate only to the next century or to the next generation. It is time for us now as a nation to exercise the same reasonable foresight in dealing with our great natural resources that would be shown by any prudent man in conserving and wisely using the property which contains the assurance of well-being for himself and his children.

The natural resources I have enumerated can be divided into two sharply distinguished classes accordingly as they are or are not capable of renewal. Mines if used must necessarily be exhausted. The minerals do not and can not renew themselves. Therefore, in dealing with the coal, the oil, the gas, the iron, the metals generally, all that we can do is to try to see that they are wisely used. The exhaustion is certain to come in time.

The second class of resources consists of those which can not only be used in such manner as to leave them undiminished for our children, but can actually be improved by wise use. The soil, the forests, the waterways, come in this category. In dealing with mineral resources, man is able to improve on nature only by putting the resources to a beneficial use, which in the end exhausts them; but in dealing with the soil and its products man can improve on nature by compelling the resources to renew and even reconstruct themselves in such manner as to serve increasingly beneficial uses—while the living waters can be so controlled as to multiply their benefits.

Neither the primitive man nor the pioneer was aware of any duty to posterity in dealing with the renewable resources. When the American settler felled the forests he felt that there was plenty of forest left for the sons who came after him. When he exhausted the soil of his farm he felt that his son could go West and take up another. So it was with his immediate successors. When the soil washed from the farmer's fields choked the neighboring river he thought only of using the railway rather than boats for moving his produce and supplies.

Now all this is changed. On the average the son of the farmer of to-day must make his living on his father's farm. There is no difficulty in doing this if the father will exercise wisdom. No wise use of a farm exhausts its fertility. So with the forests. We are on the verge of a timber famine in this country, and it is unpardonable for the nation or the states to permit any further cutting of our timber save in accordance with a system which will provide that the next generation shall see the timber increased instead of diminished. Moreover, we can add enormous tracts of the most valuable possible agricultural land to the national domain by irrigation in the arid and semi-arid regions, and by drainage of great tracts of swamp land in the humid regions. We can enormously increase our transportation facilities by the canalization of our rivers so as to complete a great system of waterways on the Pacific, Atlantic and Gulf coasts and in the Mississippi Valley, from the Great Plains to the Alleghenies and from the northern lakes to the mouth of the mighty Father of Waters. But all these various uses of our natural resources are so closely connected that they should be co-ordinated, and should be treated as part of one coherent plan and not in haphazard and piecemeal fashion.

It is largely because of this that I appointed the Waterways Commission last year, and that I have sought to perpetuate its work. I wish to take this opportunity to express in heartiest fashion my acknowledgment to all the members of the commission. At great personal sacrifice of time and effort they have rendered a service to the public for which we cannot be too grateful. Especial credit is due to the initiative, the energy, the devotion to duty and the far-sightedness of Gifford Pinchot,° to whom we owe so much of the progress we have already made in handling this matter of the co-ordination and conservation of natural resources. If it had not been for him this convention neither would nor could have been called.

We are coming to recognize as never before the right of the nation to guard its own future in the essential matter of natural resources. In the past we have admitted the right of the individual to injure the future of the Republic for his own present profit. The time has come 5 for a change. As a people we have the right and the duty, second to none other but the right and duty of obeying the moral law, of requiring and doing justice, to protect ourselves and our children against the wasteful development of our natural resources, whether that waste is caused 10 by the actual destruction of such resources or by making them impossible of development hereafter.

Any right-thinking father earnestly desires and strives to leave his son both an untarnished name and a reasonable equipment for the struggle of life. So this nation 15 as a whole should earnestly desire and strive to leave to the next generation the national honor unstained and the national resources unexhausted. There are signs that both the nation and the states are waking to a realization of this great truth. On March 10, 1908, the Supreme Court 20 of Maine rendered an exceedingly important judicial decision. This opinion was rendered in response to questions as to the right of the Legislature to restrict the cutting of trees on private land for the prevention of drouths and floods, the preservation of the natural water supply 25 and the prevention of the erosion of such lands and the consequent filling up of rivers, ponds and lakes. The forests and water power of Maine constitute the larger part of her wealth and form the basis of her industrial life, and the question submitted by the Maine Senate 30 to the Supreme Court and the answer of the Supreme Court alike bear testimony to the wisdom of the people

of Maine and clearly define a policy of conservation of
natural resources the adoption of which is of vital importance not merely to Maine but to the whole country.

Such a policy will preserve soil, forests, water power
5 as a heritage for the children and the children's children
of the men and women of this generation; for any enactment that provides for the wise utilization of the forests,
whether in public or private ownership, and for the conservation of the water resources of the country must nec-
10 essarily be legislation that will promote both private and
public welfare; for flood prevention, water power development, preservation of the soil and improvement of
navigable rivers are all promoted by such a policy of
forest conservation.

15   The opinion of the Maine Supreme bench sets forth
unequivocally the principle that the property rights of
the individual are subordinate to the rights of the community, and especially that the waste of wild timber land
derived originally from the state, involving as it would
20 the impoverishment of the state and its people and thereby
defeating one great purpose of government, may properly
be prevented by state restrictions.

The court says that there are two reasons why the right
of the public to control and limit the use of private prop-
25 erty is peculiarly applicable to property in land: "First,
such property is not the result of productive labor, but
is derived solely from the state itself, the original owner;
second, the amount of land being incapable of increase,
if the owners of large tracts can waste them at will with-
30 out state restrictions, the state and its people may be
helplessly impoverished and one great purpose of government defeated. . . . We do not think the proposed

legislation would operate to 'take' private property within the inhibition of the Constitution. While it might restrict the owner of wild and uncultivated lands in his use of them, might delay his taking some of the product, might delay his anticipated profits and even thereby 5 might cause him some loss of profit, it would nevertheless leave him his lands, their product and increase, untouched, and without diminution of title, estate or quantity. He would still have large measures of control and large opportunity to realize values. He might suffer 10 delay—but not deprivation. . . . The proposed legislation . . . would be within the legislature power and would not operate as a taking of private property for which compensation must be made."

The Court of Errors and Appeals of New Jersey has 15 adopted a similar view, which has recently been sustained by the Supreme Court of the United States. In delivering the opinion of the court on April 6, 1908, Mr. Justice Hohnes said: "The state as quasi-sovereign and representative of the interests of the public has a standing 20 in court to protect the atmosphere, the water and the forests within its territory, irrespective of the assent or dissent of the private owners of the land most immediately concerned. . . . It appears to us that few public interests are more obvious, indisputable and independent 25 of particular theory than the interest of the public of a state to maintain the rivers that are wholly within it substantially undiminished, except by such drafts upon them as the guardian of the public welfare may permit for the purpose of turning them to a more perfect use. 30 This public interest is omnipresent wherever there is a state, and grows more pressing as population grows. . . .

We are of opinion, further, that the constitutional power of the state to insist that its natural advantages shall remain unimpaired by its citizens is not dependent upon any nice estimate of the extent of present use or specula-
5 tion as to future needs. The legal conception of the necessary is likely to be confined to somewhat rudimentary wants, and there are benefits from a great river that might escape a lawyer's view. But the state is not required to submit even to an æsthetic analysis. Any analysis may
10 be inadequate. It finds itself in possession of what all admit to be a great public good, and what it has it may keep and give no one a reason for its will."

These decisions reach the root of the idea of conservation of our resources in the interests of our people.

15   Finally, let us remember that the conservation of our natural resources, though the gravest problem of to-day, is yet but part of another and greater problem to which this nation is not yet awake, but to which it will awake in time, and with which it must hereafter grapple if it is
20 to live—the problem of national efficiency, the patriotic duty of insuring the safety and continuance of the nation. When the people of the United States consciously undertake to raise themselves as citizens, and the nation and the states in their several spheres, to the highest pitch
25 of excellence in private, state and national life, and to do this because it is the first of all the duties of true patriotism, then and not till then the future of this nation in quality and in time will be assured.

DUTIES OF THE CITIZEN

STRANGE and impressive associations rise in the mind of a man from the New World who speaks before this august body in this ancient institution of learning. Before his eyes pass the shadows of mighty kings and warlike nobles, of great masters of law and theology; through 5 the shining dust of the dead centuries he sees crowded figures that tell of the power and learning and splendor of times gone by; and he sees also the innumerable host of humble students to whom clerkship meant emancipation, to whom it was well-nigh the only outlet from the dark 10 thraldom of the Middle Ages.

This was the most famous university° of medieval Europe at a time when no one dreamed that there was a new world to discover. Its services to the cause of human knowledge already stretched far back into the remote past at 15 the time when my forefathers, three centuries ago, were among the sparse band of traders, ploughmen, woodchoppers and fisherfolk who, in hard struggle with the iron unfriendliness of the Indian-haunted land, were laying the foundations of what has now become the giant 20 republic of the West. To conquer a continent, to tame the shaggy roughness of wild nature, means grim warfare; and the generations engaged in it cannot keep, still less add to, the stores of garnered wisdom which once were theirs, and which are still in the hands of their brethren 25 who dwell in the old land. To conquer the wilderness means to wrest victory from the same hostile forces with which mankind struggled in the immemorial infancy of our race. The primeval conditions must be met by pri-

215

meval qualities which are incompatible with the retention
of much that has been painfully acquired by humanity
as through the ages it has striven upward toward civilization. In conditions so primitive there can be but a prim-
5 itive culture. At first only the rudest schools can be
established, for no others would meet the needs of the
hard-driven, sinewy folk who thrust forward the frontier
in the teeth of savage man and savage nature; and many
years elapse before any of these schools can develop into
10 seats of higher learning and broader culture.

The pioneer days pass; the stump-dotted clearings
expand into vast stretches of fertile farm land; the stock-
aded clusters of log cabins change into towns; the hunters
of game, the fellers of trees, the rude frontier traders and
15 tillers of the soil, the men who wander all their lives long
through the wilderness as the heralds and harbingers of an
oncoming civilization, themselves vanish before the civilization for which they have prepared the way. The children of their successors and supplanters, and then their
20 children and children's children, change and develop with
extraordinary rapidity. The conditions accentuate vices
and virtues, energy and ruthlessness, all the good qualities
and all the defects of an intense individualism, self-reliant,
self-centered, far more conscious of its rights than of its
25 duties, and blind to its own shortcomings. To the hard
materialism of the frontier days succeeds the hard materialism of an industrialism even more intense and ab-
sorbing than that of the older nations; although these
themselves have likewise already entered on the age of a
30 complex and predominantly industrial civilization.

As the country grows, its people, who have won success
in so many lines, turn back to try to recover the possessions

of the mind and the spirit which perforce their fathers threw aside in order better to wage the first rough battles for the continent their children inherit. The leaders of thought and of action grope their way forward to a new life, realizing, sometimes dimly, sometimes clearsightedly, 5 that the life of material gain, whether for a nation or an individual, is of value only as a foundation, only as there is added to it the uplift that comes from devotion to loftier ideals. The new life thus sought can in part be developed afresh from what is round about in the New 10 World; but it can be developed in full only by freely drawing upon the treasure houses of the Old World, upon the treasures stored in the ancient abodes of wisdom and learning, such as this where I speak to-day. It is a mistake for any nation merely to copy another; but it is an 15 even greater mistake, it is a proof of weakness in any nation, not to be anxious to learn from another and willing and able to adapt that learning to the new national conditions and make it fruitful and productive therein. It is for us of the New World to sit at the feet of the Gam- 20 aliel° of the Old; then, if we have the right stuff in us, we can show that Paul in his turn can become a teacher as well as a scholar.

To-day I shall speak to you on the subject of individual citizenship, the one subject of vital importance to you, 25 my hearers, and to me and my countrymen, because you and we are citizens of great democratic republics. A democratic republic such as each of ours—an effort to realize in its full sense government by, of and for the people—represents the most gigantic of all possible social 30 experiments, the one fraught with greatest possibilities alike for good and for evil. The success of republics like

yours and like ours means the glory, and our failure the
despair, of mankind; and for you and for us the question
of the quality of the individual citizen is supreme.   Under
other forms of government, under the rule of one man or of
5 a very few men, the quality of the rulers is all-important.
If, under such governments, the quality of the rulers is
high enough, then the nation may for generations lead a
brilliant career and add substantially to the sum of world
achievement, no matter how low the quality of the aver-
10 age citizen; because the average citizen is an almost negligible quantity in working out the final results of that type
of national greatness.

But with you and with us the case is different.   With
you here, and with us in my own home, in the long run,
15 success or failure will be conditioned upon the way in
which the average man, the average woman, does his or
her duty, first in the ordinary, every-day affairs of life,
and next in those great occasional crises which call for
the heroic virtues.   The average citizen must be a good
20 citizen if our republics are to succeed.   The stream will
not permanently rise higher than the main source; and
the main source of national power and national greatness
is found in the average citizenship of the nation.   Therefore it behooves us to do our best to see that the standard
25 of the average citizen is kept high; and the average cannot be kept high unless the standard of the leaders is
very much higher.

It is well if a large proportion of the leaders in any republic, in any democracy, are, as a matter of course, drawn
30 from the classes represented in this audience to-day; but
only provideed that those classes possess the gifts of
sympathy with plain people and of devotion to great

ideals. You and those like you have received special advantages; you have all· of you had the opportunity for mental training; many of you have had leisure; most of you have had a chance for the enjoyment of life far greater than comes to the majority of your fellows. To you and your kind much has been given, and from you much should be expected. Yet there are certain failings against which it is especially incumbent that both men of trained and cultivated intellect and men of inherited wealth and position, should especially guard themselves, because to these failings they are especially liable; and if yielded to their—your—chances of useful service are at an end.·

Let the man of learning, the man of lettered leisure, beware of that queer and cheap temptation to pose to himself and to others as the cynic, as the man who has outgrown emotions·and beliefs, the man to whom good and evil are as one. The poorest way to face life is to face it with a sneer. There are many men who feel a kind of twisted pride in cynicism; there are many who confine themselves to criticism of the way others do what they themselves dare not even attempt. There is no more unhealthy being, no man less worthy of respect, than he who either really holds, or feigns to hold, an attitude of sneering disbelief toward all that is great and lofty, whether in achievement or in that noble effort which, even if it fail, comes second to achievement. A cynical habit of thought and speech, a readiness to criticise work which the critic himself never tries to perform, an intellectual aloofness which will not accept contact with life's realities—all these are marks, not, as the possessor would fain think, of superiority, but of weakness. They mark the men unfit to bear their part manfully in the stern strife of living, who seek, in the affectation of comtempt for the achievements of others, to hide from others and from themselves their own weakness. The rôle is 5 easy; there is none easier, save only the rôle of the man who sneers alike at both criticism and performance.

It is not the critic who counts; not the man who points out how the strong man stumbles or where the doer of deeds could have done them better. The credit belongs 10 to the man who is actually in the arena, whose face is marred by dust and sweat and blood; who strives valiantly; who errs, and comes short again and again, because there is no effort without error and shortcoming; but who does actually strive to do the deeds; who knows 15 the great enthusiasms, the great devotions; who spends himself in a worthy cause; who at the best knows in the end the triumph of high achievement, and who at the worst, if he fails, at least fails while daring greatly, so that his place shall never be with those cold and timid 20 souls who know neither victory nor defeat. Shame on the man of cultivated taste who permits refinement to develop into a fastidiousness that unfits him for doing the rough work of a workaday world! Among the free peoples who govern themselves there is but a small field 25 of usefulness open for the men of cloistered life, who shrink from contact with their fellows. Still less room is there for those who deride or slight what is done by those who actually bear the brunt of the day; nor yet for those others who always profess that they would like to take action, 30 if only the conditions of life were not what they actually are. The man who does nothing cuts the same sordid figure in the pages of history, whether he be cynic, or

fop or voluptuary. There is little use for the being whose
tepid soul knows nothing of the great and generous emotion, of the high pride, the stern belief, the lofty enthusiasm, of the men who quell the storm and ride the thunder.
Well for these men if they succeed; well also, though not 5
so well, if they fail, given only that they have nobly ventured, and have put forth all their heart and strength·
It is warworn Hotspur,° spent with hard fighting, he of
the many errors and the valiant end, over whose memory
we love to linger, not over the memory of the young lord 10
who "but for the vile guns would have been a soldier."

France has taught many lessons to other nations; surely
one of the most important is the lesson her whole history
teaches, that a high artistic and literary development is
compatible with notable leadership in arms and state- 15
craft. The brilliant gallantry of the French soldier has
for many centuries been proverbial, and during these
same centuries at every court in Europe the "freemasons
of fashion" have treated the French tongue as their common speech; while every artist and man of letters, and 20
every man of science able to appreciate that marvelous instrument of precision, French prose, has turned
toward France for aid and inspiration. How long the
leadership in arms and letters has lasted is curiously
illustrated by the fact that the earliest masterpiece in a 25
modern tongue is the splendid French epic ° which tells of
Roland's doom and the vengeance of Charlemagne when
the lords of the Frankish host were stricken at Ronces-
valles.

Let those who have keep, let those who have not strive 30
to attain a high standard of cultivation and scholarship.
Yet let us remember that these stand second to certain

other things.   There is need of a sound body; and even
more need of a sound mind.   But above mind and above
body stands character—the sum of those qualities which
we mean when we speak of a man's force and courage, of
5 his good faith and sense of honor.   I believe in exercise
for the body, always provided that we keep in mind that
physical development is a means and not an end.   I believe, of course, in giving to all the people a good education.
But the education must contain much besides book learn-
10 ing in order to be really good.   We must ever remember
that no keenness and subtleness of intellect, no polish,
no cleverness, in any way makes up for the lack of the
great solid qualities.   Self-restraint, self-mastery, common
sense, the power of accepting individual responsibility and
15 yet of acting in conjunction with others, courage and
resolution—these are the qualities which mark a masterful people.   Without them no people can control itself,
or save itself from being controlled from the outside.   I
speak to a brilliant assemblage; I speak in a great univer-
20 sity which represents the flower of the highest intellectual development; I pay all homage to intellect, and to
elaborate and specialized training of the intellect; and
yet I know I shall have the assent of all you present when
I add that more important still are the commonplace,
25 everyday qualities and virtues.

Such ordinary, everyday qualities include the will and
the power to work, to fight at need and to have plenty
of healthy children.   The need that the average man
shall work is so obvious as hardly to warrant insistence.
30 There are a few persons in every country so born that they
can lead lives of leisure.   These fill a useful function if
they make it evident that leisure does not mean idleness;

for some of the most valuable work needed by civilization is essentially non-remunerative in its character, and of course the people who do this work should in large part be drawn from those to whom remuneration is an object of indifference. But the average man must earn his own 5 livelihood. He should be trained to do so, and he should be trained to feel that he occupies a contemptible position if he does not do so—that he is not an object of envy if he is idle, at whichever end of the social scale he stands, but an object of contempt, an object of derision. 10

In the next place, the good man should be both a strong and brave man; that is, he should be able to fight, he should be able to serve his country as a soldier should the need arise. There are well meaning philosophers who declaim against the unrighteousness of war. They are 15 right only if they lay all their emphasis upon the unrighteousness. War is a dreadful thing, and unjust war is a crime against humanity. But it is such a crime because it is unjust, not because it is war. The choice must ever be in favor of righteousness, and this whether the alter- 20 native be peace or whether the alternative be war. The question must not be merely, Is there to be peace or war? The question must be, Is the right to prevail? Are the great laws of righteousness once more to be fulfilled? And the answer from a strong and virile people must be "Yes," 25 whatever the cost. Every honorable effort should always be made to avoid war, just as every honorable effort should always be made by the individual in private life to keep out of a brawl, to keep out of trouble; but no self-respecting individual, no self-respecting nation, can 30 or ought to submit to wrong.

Finally, even more important than ability to work, even

more important than ability to fight at need, is it to remember that the chief of blessings for any nation is that
it shall leave its seed to inherit the land. It was the crown
of blessings in Biblical times and it is the crown of bless-
5 ings now. The greatest of all curses is the curse of sterility, and the severest of all condemnations should be that
visited upon wilful sterility. The first essential in any
civilization is that the man and the woman shall be father
and mother of healthy children, so that the race shall in-
10 crease and not decrease. If this is not so, if through no
fault of the society there is failure to increase, it is a great
misfortune. If the failure is due to deliberate and wilful
fault, then it is not merely a misfortune, it is one of those
crimes of ease and self-indulgence, of shrinking from pain
15 and effort and risk, which in the long run Nature pun-
ishes more heavily than any other. If we of the great
republics, if we, the free people who claim to have emanci-
pated ourselves from the thraldom of wrong and error,
bring down on our heads the curse that comes upon the
20 wilfully barren, then it will be an idle waste of breath to
prattle of our achievements, to boast of all that we have
done. No refinement of life, no delicacy of taste, no material progress, no sordid heaping up of riches, no sensuous
development of art and literature, can in any way com-
25 pensate for the loss of the great fundamental virtues,
and of these great fundamental virtues the greatest is
the race's power to perpetuate the race.

Character must show itself in the man's performance
both of the duty he owes himself and of the duty he owes
30 the state. The man's foremost duty is owed to himself
and his family; and he can do this duty only by earning
money, by providing what is essential to material well-

being; it is only after this has been done that he can hope
to build a higher superstructure on the solid material
foundation; it is only after this has been done that he can
help in movements for the general well-being. He must
pull his own weight first, and only after this can his sur- 5
plus strength be of use to the general public. . It is not
good to excite that bitter laughter which expresses contempt, and contempt is what we feel for the being whose
enthusiasm to benefit mankind is such that he is a burden
to those nearest him; who wishes to do great things for 10
humanity in the abstract, but who cannot keep his wife
in comfort or educate his children.

Nevertheless, while laying all stress on this point, while
not merely acknowledging but insisting upon the fact that
there must be a basis of material well-being for the in- 15
dividual, as for the nation, let us with equal emphasis
insist that this material well-being represents nothing but
the foundation, and that the foundation, though indispensable, is worthless unless upon it is raised the superstructure of a higher life. 20

That is why I decline to recognize the mere multi-
millionaire, the man of mere wealth, as an asset of value
to any country, and especially as not an asset to my own
country. If he has earned or uses his wealth in a way
that makes him of real benefit, of real use—and such is 25
often the case—why, then he does become an asset of
worth. But it is the way in which it has been earned or
used and not the mere fact of wealth that entitles him to
the credit. There is need in business, as in most other
forms of human activity, of the great guiding intelli- 30
gences. Their places cannot be supplied by any number
of lesser intelligences. It is a good thing that they should

have ample recognition, ample reward. But we must not transfer our admiration to the reward instead of to the deed rewarded; and if what should be the reward exists without the service having been rendered, then ad-
5 miration will come only from those who are mean of soul. The truth is that after a certain measure of tangible material success or reward has been achieved the question of increasing ,it becomes of constantly less importance compared to other things that can be done in life. It is a
10 bad thing for a nation to raise and to admire a false standard of success and there can be no falser standard than that set by the deification of material well-being in and for itself. The man who for any cause for which he is himself accountable has failed to support himself and those
15 for whom he is responsible ought to feel that he has fallen lamentably short in his prime duty. But the man who, having far surpassed the limit of providing for the wants, both of body and mind, of himself and of those depending upon him, then piles up a great fortune, for the acquisi-
20 tion or retention of which he returns no corresponding benefit to the nation as a whole, should himself be made to feel that, so far from being a desirable he is an unworthy citizen of the community, that he is to be neither admired nor envied, that his right thinking fellow countrymen put
25 him low in the scale of citizenship and leave him to be consoled by the admiration of those whose level of purpose is even lower than his own.

My position as regards the moneyed interests can be put in a few words. In every civilized society property
30 rights must be carefully safeguarded. Ordinarily, and in the great majority of cases, human rights and property rights are fundamentally, and in the long run, identi-

cal; but when it clearly appears that there is a real conflict between them, human rights must have the upper
hand, for property belongs to man and not man to
property.

In fact, it is essential to good citizenship clearly to un- 5
derstand that there are certain qualities which we in a
democracy are prone to admire in and of themselves,
which ought by rights to be judged admirable or the reverse solely from the standpoint of the use made of them.
Foremost among these I should include two very distinct 10
gifts—the gift of money making and the gift of oratory.
Money making, the money touch, I have spoken of above.
It is a quality which in a moderate degree is essential.
It may be useful when developed to a very great degree,
but only if accompanied and controlled by other qual- 15
ities; and without such control the possessor tends to develop into one of the least attractive types produced by
a modern industrial democracy. So it is with the orator.
It is highly desirable that a leader of opinion in a democracy should be able to state his views clearly and con- 20
vincingly. But all that the oratory can do of value to the
community is to enable the man thus to explain himself;
if it enables the orator to persuade his hearers to put false
values on things it merely makes him a power for mischief.
Some excellent public servants have not the gift at all, 25
and must rely upon their deeds to speak for them; and
unless the oratory does represent genuine conviction,
based on good common sense and able to be translated
into efficient performance, then the better the oratory
the greater the damage to the public it deceives. Indeed, 30
it is a sign of marked political weakness in any commonwealth if the people tend to be carried away by mere

oratory, if they tend to value words in and for themselves, as divorced from the deeds for which they are supposed to stand. The phrase maker, the phrase monger, the ready talker, however great his power, whose speech does not 5 make for courage, sobriety and right understanding, is simply a noxious element in the body politic, and it speaks ill for the public if he has influence over them. To admire the gift of oratory without regard to the moral quality behind the gift is to do wrong to the republic.

10 Of course, all that I can say of the orator applies with even greater force to the orator's latter-day and more influential brother, the journalist. The power of the journalist is great, but he is entitled neither to respect nor admiration because of that power unless it is used 15 aright. He can do, and he often does, great good. He can do, and he often does, infinite mischief. All journalists, all writers, for the very reason that they appreciate the vast possibilities of their profession, should bear testimony against those who deeply discredit it. Offences against 20 taste and morals, which are bad enough in a private citizen, are infinitely worse if made into instruments for debauching the community through a newspaper. Mendacity, slander, sensationalism, inanity, vapid triviality, all are potent factors for the debauchery of the public mind 25 and conscience. The excuse advanced for vicious writing, that the public demands it and that the demand must be supplied, can no more be admitted than if it were advanced by the purveyors of food who sell poisonous adulterations.

30 In short, the good citizen in a republic must realize that he ought to possess two sets of qualities, and that neither avails without the other. He must have those qualities

which make for efficiency; and he must also have those qualities which direct the efficiency into channels for the public good. He is useless if he is inefficient. There is nothing to be done with that type of citizen of whom all that can be said is that he is harmless. Virtue which is dependent upon a sluggish circulation is not impressive. There is little place in active life for the timid good' man. The man who is saved by weakness from robust' wickedness is likewise rendered immune from the robuster virtues. The good citizen in a republic must first of all be able to hold his own. He is no good citizen unless he has the ability which will make him work hard and which at need will make him fight hard. He is not a good citizen unless he is an efficient citizen.

But if a man's efficiency is not guided and regulated by a moral sense, then the more efficient he is the worse he is, the more dangerous to the body politic. Courage, intellect, all the masterful qualities, serve but to make a man more evil if they are used merely for that man's own advancement, with brutal indifference to the rights of others. It speaks ill for the community if the community worships these qualities and treats their possessors as heroes, regardless of whether the qualities are used rightly or wrongly. It makes no difference as to the precise way in which this sinister efficiency is shown. It makes no difference whether such a man's force and ability betray themselves in the career of money maker or politician, soldier or orator, journalist or popular leader. If the man works for evil, then the more successful he is the more he should be despised and condemned by all upright and farseeing men. To judge a man merely by success is an abhorrent wrong; and if the people at large habitually so

judge men, if they grow to condone wickedness because the wicked man triumphs, they show their inability to understand that in the last analysis free institutions rest upon the character of citizenship, and that by such admi-
5 ration of evil they prove themselves unfit for liberty.

The homely virtues of the household, the ordinary workaday virtues which make the woman a good house-wife and house mother, which make the man a hard worker, a good husband and father, a good soldier at need, stand
10 at the bottom of character. But of course many others must be added thereto if a state is to be not only free, but great. Good citizenship is not good citizenship if exhibited only in the home. There remain the duties of the individual in relation to the state, and these duties are none too
15 easy under the conditions which exist where the effort is made to carry on free government in a complex industrial civilization. Perhaps the most important thing the ordinary citizen, and, above all, the leader of ordinary citizens, has to remember in political life is that he must
20 not be a sheer doctrinaire. The closest philosopher, the refined and cultured individual who from his library tells how men ought to be governed under ideal conditions, is of no use in actual governmental work; and the one-sided fanatic, and still more the mob leader, and the insincere
25 man who to achieve power promises what by no possibility can be performed, are not merely useless but noxious.

The citizen must have high ideals, and yet he must be able to achieve them in practical fashion. No permanent good comes from aspirations so lofty that they have grown
30 fantastic and have become impossible and indeed undesirable to realize. The impracticable visionary is far less often the guide and precursor than he is the embit-

tered foe of the real reformer, of the man who, with stumblings and shortcomings, yet does in some shape, in practical fashion, give effect to the hopes and desires of those who strive for better things. Woe to the empty phrasemaker, to the empty idealist, who, instead of making 5 ready the ground for the man of action, turns against him when he appears and hampers him as he does the work! Moreover, the preacher of ideals must remember how sorry and contemptible is the figure which he will cut, how great the damage that he will do, if he does not 10 himself, in his own life, strive measurably to realize the ideals that he preaches for others. Let him remember also that the worth of the ideal must be largely determined by the success with which it can in practice be realized. We should abhor the so-called "practical" men whose 15 practicality assumes the shape of that peculiar baseness which finds its expression in disbelief in morality and decency, in disregard of high standards of living and conduct. Such a creature is the worst enemy of the body politic. But only less desirable as a citizen is his nominal 20 opponent and real ally, the man of fantastic vision who makes the impossible better forever the enemy of the possible good.

We can just as little afford to follow the doctrinaires of an extreme individualism as the doctrinaires of an ex- 25 treme socialism. Individual initiative, so far from being discouraged, should be stimulated; and yet we should remember that, as society develops and grows more complex, we continually find that things which once it was desirable to leave to individual initiative can, under the 30 changed conditions, be performed with better results by common effort. It is quite impossible, and equally unde-

sirable, to draw in theory a hard and fast line which shall
always divide the two sets of cases. Thus every one who
is not cursed with the pride of the closet philosopher will
see, if he will only take the trouble to think about some of
5 our commonest phenomena. For instance, when people
live on isolated farms or in little hamlets, each house can
be left to attend to its own drainage and water supply;
but the mere multiplication of families in a given area
produces new problems which, because they differ in
10 size, are found to differ not only in degree but in kind from
the old; and the questions of drainage and water supply
have to be considered from the common standpoint. It
is not a matter for abstract dogmatizing to decide when
this point is reached; it is a matter to be tested by prac-
15 tical experiment. Much of the discussion about socialism
and individualism is entirely pointless, because of failure
to agree on terminology. It is not good to be the slave
of names. I am a strong individualist by personal habit,
inheritance and conviction; but it is a mere matter of
20 common sense to recognize that the state, the community, the citizens acting together, can do a number of
things better than if they were left to individual action.
The individualism which finds its expression in the abuse
of physical force is checked very early in the growth of
25 civilization, and we of to-day should in our turn strive to
shackle or destroy that individualism which triumphs by
greed and cunning, which exploits the weak by craft instead of ruling them by brutality. We ought to go with
any man in the effort to bring about justice and the equal-
30 ity of opportunity, to turn the tool user more and more
into the tool owner, to shift burdens so that they can be
more equitably borne. The deadening effect on any race

of the adoption of a logical and extreme socialistic system could not be overstated; it would spell sheer destruction; it would produce grosser wrong and outrage, fouler immorality, than any existing system. But this does not mean that we may not with great advantage adopt certain 5 of the principles professed by some given set of men who happen to call themselves socialists; to be afraid to do so would be to make a mark of weakness on our part.

But we should not take part in acting a lie any more than in telling a lie. We should not say that men are 10 equal where they are not equal, nor proceed upon the assumption that there is an equality where it does not exist; but we should strive to bring about a measurable equality, at least to the extent of preventing the inequality which is due to force or fraud. Abraham Lincoln,° a 15 man of the plain people, blood of their blood and bone of their bone, who all his life toiled and wrought and suffered for them, and at the end died for them, who always strove to represent them, who would never tell an untruth to or for them, spoke of the doctrine of equality with his 20 usual mixture of idealism and sound common sense. He said (I omit what was of merely local significance): "I think the authors of the Declaration of Independence intended to include all men, but that they did not mean to declare all men equal in all respects. They did not 25 mean to say all men were equal in color, size, intellect, moral development or social capacity. They defined with tolerable distinctness in what they did consider all men created equal—equal in certain inalienable rights, among which are life, liberty and the pursuit of happiness. This 30 they said, and this they meant. They did not mean to assert the obvious untruth that all were then actually enjoying that equality, or yet that they were about to confer it immediately upon them. They meant to set up a standard maxim for free society which should be familiar to all—constantly looked to, constantly labored for, 5 and, even though never perfectly attained, constantly approximated, and thereby constantly spreading and deepening its influence, and augmenting the happiness and value of life to all people, everywhere."

We are bound in honor to refuse to listen to those men 10 who would make us desist from the effort to do away with the inequality which means injustice; the inequality of right, of opportunity, of privilege. We are bound in honor to strive to bring ever nearer the day when, as far as is humanly possible, we shall be able to realize the 15 ideal that each man shall have an equal opportunity to show the stuff that is in him by the way in which he renders service. There should, so far as possible, be equality of opportunity to render service; but just so long as there is inequality of service there should and must be inequality 20 of reward. We may be sorry for the general, the painter, the artist, the worker in any profession or of any kind, whose misfortune rather than whose fault it is that he does his work ill. But the reward must go to the man who does his work well; for any other course is to create a 25 new kind of privilege, the privilege of folly and weakness; and special privilege is injustice, whatever form it takes.

To say that the thriftless, the lazy, the vicious, the incapable ought to have the reward given to those who are farsighted, capable and upright is to say what is not true 30 and cannot be true. Let us try to level up, but let us beware of the evil of leveling down. If a man stumbles, it is a good thing to help him to his feet. Every one of us needs a helping hand now and then. But if a man lies down, it is a waste of time to try to carry him; and it is a very bad thing for every one if we make men feel that the same reward will come to those who shirk their work and to those who do it. 5

Let us then take into account the actual facts of life, and not be misled into following any proposal for achieving the millennium, for recreating the golden age, until we have subjected it to hard-headed examination. On the other hand, it is foolish to reject a proposal merely be- 10 cause it is advanced by visionaries. If a given scheme is proposed, look at it on its merits and in considering it disregard formulas. It does not matter in the least who proposes it or why. If it seems good, try it. If it proves good, accept it; otherwise reject it. There are plenty of 15 men calling themselves socialists with whom up to a certain point it is quite possible to work. If the next step is one which both we and they wish to take, why of course take it, without regard to the fact that our views as to the tenth step may differ. But, on the other hand, keep clearly 20 in mind that, though it has been worth while to take one step, this does not in the least mean that it may be highly disadvantageous to take the next. It is just as foolish to refuse all progress because people demanding it desire at some points to go to absurd extremes as it would be to 25 go to these absurd extremes simply because some of the measures advocated by the extremists were wise.

The good citizen will demand liberty for himself, and, as a matter of pride, he will see to it that others receive the liberty which he thus claims as his own. Probably the 30 best test of true love of liberty in any country is the way in which minorities are treated in that country. Not only should there be complete liberty in matters of religion and opinion, but complete liberty for each man to lead his life as he desires, provided only that in so doing he does not wrong his neighbors.   Persecution is bad because it is 5 persecution, and without reference to which side happens at the moment to be the persecutor and which the persecuted.   Class hatred is bad in just the same way, and without any regard to the individual who at a given time substitutes loyalty to a class for loyalty to the nation or 10 substitutes hatred of men because they happen to come in a certain social category for judgment awarded them according to their conduct.   Remember always that the same measure of condemnation should be extended to the arrogance which would look down upon or crush any man 15 because he is poor and to the envy and hatred which would destroy a man because he is wealthy.   The over-bearing brutality of the man of wealth or power and the envious and hateful malice directed against wealth or power are really at root merely different manifestations of the same 20 quality, merely the two sides of the same shield.

The man who, if born to wealth and power, exploits and ruins his less fortunate brethren is at heart the same as the greedy and violent demagog who excites those who have not property to plunder those who have.   The 25 gravest wrong upon his country is inflicted by that man, whatever his station, who seeks to make his countrymen divide primarily on the line that separates class from class, occupation from occupation, men of more wealth from men of less wealth, instead of remembering that the only 30 safe standard is that which judges each man on his worth as a man, whether he be rich or poor, without regard to his profession or to his station in life.   Such is the only true democratic test, the only test that can with propriety be applied in a republic. There have been many republics in the past, both in what we call antiquity and in what we call the Middle Ages. They fell, and the prime factor in their fall was the fact that the parties 5 tended to divide along the line that separates wealth from poverty. It made no difference which side was successful, it made no difference whether the republic fell under the rule of an oligarchy or the rule of a mob. In either case, when once loyalty to a class had been sub- 10 stituted for loyalty to the republic the end of the republic was at hand. There is no greater need to-day than the need to keep ever in mind the fact that the cleavage between right and wrong, between good citizenship and bad citizenship, runs at right angles to, and not parallel with, 15 the lines of cleavage between class and class, between occupation and occupation. Ruin looks us in the face if we judge a man by his position instead of judging him by his conduct in that position.

In a republic to be successful we must learn to combine 20 intensity of conviction with a broad tolerance of difference of conviction. Wide differences of opinion in matters of religious, political and social belief must exist if conscience and intellect alike are not to be stunted, if there is to be room for healthy growth. Bitter internecine 25 hatreds, based on such differences, are signs not of earnestness of belief but of that fanaticism which, whether religious or anti-religious, democratic or anti-democratic, is itself but a manifestation of the gloomy bigotry which has been the chief factor in the downfall of so many, 30 many nations.

Of one man in especial, beyond any one else, the citizens

of a republic should beware, and that is of the man who appeals to them to support him on the ground that he is hostile to other citizens of the republic, that he will secure for those who elect him, in one shape or another,
5 profit at the expense of other citizens of the republic. It makes no difference whether he appeals to class hatred or class interest, to religious or anti-religious prejudice. The man who makes such an appeal should always be presumed to make it for the sake of furthering his own interest. The
10 very last thing that an intelligent and self-respecting member of a democratic community should do is to reward any public man because that public man says he will get the private citizen something to which this private citizen is not entitled, or will gratify some emotion or animos-
15 ity which this private citizen ought not to possess. Let me illustrate this by one anecdote from my own experience. A number of years ago I was engaged in cattle ranching on the great plains of the western United States. There were no fences. The cattle wandered free, the owner-
20 ship of each being determined by the brand; the calves were branded with the brand of the cows they followed. If on the round-up an animal was passed by, the following year it would appear as an unbranded yearling, and was then called a maverick. By the custom of the coun-
25 try these mavericks were branded with the brand of the man on whose range they were found. One day I was riding the range with a newly hired cowboy and we came upon a maverick. We roped and threw it, then we built a little fire, took out a cinch ring, heated it at the fire and
30 the cowboy started to put on the brand. I said to him: "It is So-and-so's brand," naming the man on whose range we happened to be. He answered: "That's all

right, boss; I know my business." In another moment I said to him: "Hold on; you are putting on my brand!" To which he answered: "That's all right; I always put on the boss's brand." I answered: "Oh, very well. Now, you go straight back to the ranch and get what is owing 5 to you; I don't need you any longer." He jumped up and said: "Why, what's the matter? I was putting on your brand." And I answered: "Yes, my friend, and if you will steal for me you will steal from me."

Now, the same principle which applies in private life 10 applies also in public life. If a public man tries to get your vote by saying that he will do something wrong in your interest, you can be absolutely certain that if ever it becomes worth his while he will do something wrong against your interest.   15

So much for the citizenship of the individual in his relations to his family, to his neighbor, to the state. There remain duties of citizenship which the state, the aggregation of all the individuals, owes in connection with other states, with other nations. Let me say at once that I am 20 no advocate of a foolish cosmopolitanism. I believe that a man must be a good patriot before he can be, and as the only possible way of being, a good citizen of the world. Experience teaches us that the average man who protests that his international feeling swamps his national feeling, 25 that he does not care for his country because he cares so much for mankind, in actual practice proves himself the foe of mankind; that the man who says that he does not care to be a citizen of any one country because he is a citizen of the world, is in very fact usually an exceedingly 30 undesirable citizen of whatever corner of the world he happens at the moment to be in. In the dim future all

moral needs and moral standards may change; but at
. present, if a man can view his own country and all other
countries from the same level with tepid indifference, it is
wise to distrust him, just as it is wise to distrust the man
5 who can take the same dispassionate view of his wife and
his mother. However broad and deep a man's sympathies,
however intense his activities, he need have no fear that
they will be cramped by love of his native land.

Now, this does not mean in the least that a man should
10 not wish to do good outside of his native land. On the
contrary, just as I think that the man who loves his family
is more apt to be a good neighbor than the man who does
not, so I think that the most useful member of the family
of nations is normally a strong patriotic nation. So far
15 from patriotism being inconsistent with proper regard for
the rights of other nations, I hold that the true patriot,
who is as jealous of the national honor as a gentleman of his own honor, will be careful to see that the nation neither inflicts nor suffers wrong, just as a gentle-
20 man scorns equally to wrong others or to suffer others to
wrong him. I do not for one moment admit that political
morality is different from private morality, that a promise
made on the stump differs from a promise made in private
life. I do not for one moment admit that a man should
25 act deceitfully as a public servant in his dealings with
other nations, any more than that he should act deceitfully
in his dealings as a private citizen with other private citizens. I do not for one moment admit that a nation should
treat other nations in a different spirit from that in which
30 an honorable man would treat other men.

In practically applying this principle to the two sets
of cases there is, of course, a great practical difference to

be taken into account. We speak of international law; but international law is something wholly different from private or municipal law, and the capital difference is that there is a sanction for the one and no sanction for the other; that there is an outside force which compels in-5 dividuals to obey the one, while there is no such outside force to compel obedience as regards the other. International law will, I believe, as the generations pass, grow stronger and stronger until in some way or other there develops the power to make it respected. But as yet 10 it is only in the first formative period. As yet, as a rule, each nation is of necessity obliged to judge for itself in matters of vital importance between it and its neighbors and actions must of necessity, where this is the case, be different from what they are where, as among private 15 citizens, there is an outside force whose action is all-powerful and must be invoked in any crisis of importance.

It is the duty of wise statesmen, gifted with the power of looking ahead, to try to encourage and build up every movement which will substitute or tend to substitute some 20 other agency for force in the settlement of international disputes. It is the duty of every honest statesman to try to guide the nation so that it shall not wrong any other nation. But as yet the great civilized peoples, if they are to be true to themselves and to the cause of humanity and 25 civilization, must keep ever in mind that in the last resort they must possess both the will and the power to resent wrongdoing from others. The men who sanely believe in a lofty morality preach righteousness; but they do not preach weakness, whether among private citizens or among 30 nations. We believe that our ideals should be high, but not so high as to make it impossible measurably to realize them. We sincerely and earnestly believe in peace; but if peace and justice conflict, we scorn the man who would not stand for justice, though the whole world came in arms against him.

5   And now, my hosts, a word in parting. You and I belong to the only two republics among the great Powers of the world. The ancient friendship between France and the United States has been, on the whole, a sincere and disinterested friendship. A calamity to you would 10 be a sorrow to us. But it would be more than that. In the seething turmoil of the history of humanity certain nations stand out as possessing a peculiar power or charm, some special gift of beauty or wisdom or strength, which puts them among the immortals, which makes them rank 15 forever with the leaders of mankind. France is one of these nations. For her to sink would be a loss to all the world. There are certain lessons of brilliance and of generous gallantry that she can teach better than any of her sister nations. When the French peasantry sang of 20 Malbrook,° it was to tell how the soul of this warrior foe took flight upward through the laurels he had won. Nearly seven centuries ago Froissart, writing of a time of dire disaster, said that the realm of France was never so stricken that there were not left men who would valiantly fight 25 for it. You have had a great past. I believe that you will have a great future. Long may you carry yourselves proudly as citizens of a nation which bears a leading part in the teaching and uplifting of mankind!

LAST WORDS ON AMERICANISM

I CANNOT be with you, and so all I can do is to wish you Godspeed. There must be no sagging back in the fight for Americanism merely because the war is over. There are plenty of persons who have already made the assertion that they believe the American people have a 5 short memory, and that they intend to revive all the foreign associations which most directly interfere, with the complete Americanization of our people.

Our principle in this matter should be absolutely simple. In the first place we should insist that if the im- 10 migrant who comes here does in good faith become an American and assimilates himself to us, he shall be treated on an exact equality with every one else, for it is an outrage to discriminate against any such man because of creed, or birthplace, or origin. 15

But this is predicted upon the man's becoming in very fact an American and nothing but an American. If he tries to keep segregated with men of his own origin and separated from the rest of America, then he isn't doing his part as an American. 20

There can be no divided allegiance here. Any man who says he is an American but something else also isn't an American at all. We have room for but one flag, the American flag, and this excludes the red flag, which symbolizes all wars against liberty and civilization just as 25 much as it excludes any foreign flag of a nation to which we are hostile.

We have room for but one language here and that is the English language, for we intend to see that the crucible

243

turns our people out as Americans, of American nationality, and not as dwellers in a polyglot boarding house; and we have room for but one soul loyalty, and that is loyalty to the American people.

NATURAL HISTORY

MY LIFE AS A NATURALIST [1]

I AM asked to give an account of my interest in natural history, and my experience as an amateur naturalist. The former has always been very real; and the latter, unfortunately, very limited.

I don't suppose that most men can tell why their minds 5 are attracted to certain studies any more than why their tastes are attracted by certain fruits. Certainly, I can no more explain why I like "natural history" than why I like California canned peaches; nor why I do not care for that enormous brand of natural history which deals 10 with invertebrates any more than why I do not care for brandied peaches. All I can say is that almost as soon as I began to read at all I began to like to read about the natural history of beasts and birds and the more formidable or interesting reptiles and fishes. 15

The fact that I speak of "natural history" instead of "biology," and use the former expression in a restricted sense, will show that I am a belated member of the generation that regarded Audubon° with veneration, that accepted Waterton°—Audubon's violent critic—as the 20 ideal of the wandering naturalist, and that looked upon Brehm° as a delightful but rather awesomely erudite example of advanced scientific thought. In the broader field, thank Heaven, I sat at the feet of Darwin° and Huxley,° and studied the large volumes in which Marsh's° 25 and Leidy's° palæontological studies were embalmed, with a devotion that was usually attended by a dreary lack

[1] Reprinted by permission from the *American Museum Journal*, vol. xviii, p. 321 (May, 1918.)

of reward—what would I not have given fifty years ago for a writer like Henry Fairfield Osborn,° for some scientist who realized that intelligent laymen need a guide capable of building before their eyes the life that was, in-
5 stead of merely cataloguing the fragments of the death that is.

I was a very nearsighted small boy, and did not even know that my eyes were not normal until I was fourteen; and so my field studies up to that period were even more
10 worthless than those of the average boy who "collects" natural history specimens much as he collects stamps. I studied books industriously but nature only so far as could ·be compassed by a molelike vision; my triumphs consisted in such things as bringing home and raising—by the
15 aid of milk and a syringe—a family of very young gray squirrels, in fruitlessly endeavoring to tame an excessively unamiable woodchuck, and in making friends with a gentle, pretty, trustful white-footed mouse which reared her family in an empty flower pot. In order to attract
20 my attention birds had to be as conspicuous as bobolinks or else had to perform feats such as I remember the barn swallows of my neighborhood once performed, when they assembled for the migration alongside our house and because of some freak of bewilderment swarmed in through
25 the windows and clung helplessly to the curtains, the furniture, and even to our clothes.

Just before my fourteenth birthday my father—then a trustee of the American Museum of Natural History— started me on my rather mothlike career as a naturalist
30 by giving me a pair of spectacles, a French pin-fire double-barreled shotgun—and lessons in stuffing birds. The spectacles literally opened a new world to me. The

mechanism of the pin-fire gun was without springs and
therefore could not get out of order—an important point,
as my mechanical ability was nil. The lessons in stuffing and mounting birds were given me by Mr. John G.
Bell, a professional taxidermist and collector who had 5
accompanied Audubon on his trip to the "Far West."
Mr. Bell was a very interesting man, an American of the
before-the-war type. He was tall, straight as an Indian,
with white hair and smooth-shaven clear-cut face; a
dignified figure, always in a black frock coat. He had 10
no scientific knowledge of birds or mammals; his interest
lay merely in collecting and preparing them. He taught
me as much as my limitations would allow of the art of preparing specimens for scientific use and of mounting them.
Some examples of my wooden methods of mounting birds 15
are now in the American Museum: three different species
of Egyptian plover, a snowy owl, and a couple of spruce
grouse mounted on a shield with a passenger pigeon—the
three latter killed in Maine during my college vacations.

With my spectacles, my pin-fire gun, and my clumsy 20
industry in skinning "specimens," I passed the winter
of '72-75 in Egypt and Palestine, being then fourteen
years old. My collections showed nothing but enthusiasm
on my part. I got no bird of any unusual scientific value.
My observations were as valueless as my collections 25
save on just one small point; and this point is of interest
only as showing, not my own power of observation, but
the ability of good men to fail to observe or record the
seemingly self-evident.

On the Nile the only book dealing with Egyptian birds 30
which I had with me was one by an English clergyman,
a Mr. Smith, who at the end of his second volume gave

a short list of the species he had shot, with some comments
on their habits but without descriptions. On my way
home through Europe I secured a good book of Egyptian ornithology by a Captain Shelley.   Both books enu-
5 merated and commented on several species of chats—the
Old World chats, of course, which have nothing in common
with our queer warbler of the same name. Two of these
chats were common along the edges of the desert. One
species was a boldly pied black and white bird, the other
10 was colored above much like the desert sand, so that when
it crouched it was hard to see. I found that the strikingly
conspicuous chat never tried to hide, was very much on
the alert, and was sure to attract attention when a long
way off; whereas the chat whose upper color harmonized
15 with its surroundings usually sought to escape observation
by crouching motionless. These facts were obvious even
to a dull-sighted, not particularly observant boy; they
were essential features in the comparison between and in
the study of the life histories of the two birds. Yet neither
20 of the two books in my possession so much as hinted at
them.

    I think it was my observation of these, and a few sim-
ilar facts, which prevented my yielding to the craze that
fifteen or twenty years ago became an obsession with
25 certain otherwise good men—the belief that all animals
were protectively colored when in their natural surroundings. That this simply wasn't true was shown by a moment's thought of these two chats; no rational man could
doubt that one was revealingly and the other conceal-
30 ingly colored; and each was an example of what was true
in thousands of other cases. Moreover, the incident
showed the only, and very mild, merit which I ever de-

veloped as a "faunal naturalist." I never grew to have
keen powers of observation. But whatever I did see I saw
truly, and I was fairly apt to understand what it meant.
In other words, I saw what was sufficiently obvious, and
in such case did not usually misinterpret what I had seen. 5
Certainly this does not entitle me to any particular credit,
but the outstanding thing is that it does entitle me to some,
even although of a negative kind; for the great majority
of observers seem quite unable to see, to record, or to understand facts so obvious that they leap to the eye. My 10
two ornithologists offered a case in point as regards the
chats; and I shall shortly speak of one or two other cases,
as, for example, the cougar and the saddle-backed lechwi.

After returning to this country and until I was halfway
through college, I continued to observe and collect in the 15
fashion of the ordinary boy who is interested in natural
history. I made copious and valueless notes. As I said
above, I did not see and observe very keenly; later it interested and rather chagrined me to find out how much
more C. Hart Merriam° and John Burroughs° saw when 20
I went out with them near Washington or in the Yellowstone Park; or how much more George K. Cherrie° and
Leo E. Miller° and Edmund Heller° and Edgar A. Mearns°
and my own son Kermit saw in Africa and South America, on the trips I took to the Nyanza lakes and across the 25
Brazilian hinterland.

During the years when as a boy I "collected specimens"
at Oyster Bay or in the north woods, my contributions to
original research were of minimum worth—they were limited to occasional records of such birds as the dominica 30
warbler at Oyster Bay, or to seeing a duck hawk work
havoc in a loose gang of night herons, or to noting the

bloodthirsty conduct of a captive mole shrew—I think I
sent an account of the last incident to C. Hart Merriam.
I occasionally sent to some small ornithological publication a local list of Adirondack birds or something of the
sort; and then proudly kept reprinted copies of the list on
my desk until they grew dog-eared and then disappeared.
I lived in a region zoölogically so well known that the
obvious facts had all been set forth already, and as I lacked
the power to find out the things that were not obvious, my
work merely paralleled the similar work of hundreds of other
young collectors who had a very good time but who made
no particular addition to the sum of human knowledge.

Among my boy friends who cared for ornithology was a
fine and manly young fellow, Fred Osborn, the brother of
Henry Fairfield Osborn. He was drowned, in his gallant
youth, forty years ago; but he comes as vividly before my
eyes now as if he were still alive. One cold and snowy
winter I spent a day with him at his father's house at
Garrison-on-the-Hudson.   Numerous   northern   birds,
which in our eyes were notable rarities, had come down
with the hard weather, I spied a flock of crossbills in a
pine, fired, and excitedly rushed forward. A twig caught
my spectacles and snapped them I knew not where. But
dim though my vision was, I could still make out the red
birds lying on the snow; and to me they were treasures of
such importance that I abandoned all thought of my
glasses and began a nearsighted hunt for my quarry. By
the time I had picked up the last crossbill I found that I
had lost all trace of my glasses; my day's sport—or scientific endeavor, whatever you choose to call it—came to
an abrupt end; and as a result of the lesson I never again
in my life went out shooting, whether after sparrows or

elephants, without a spare pair of spectacles in my pocket. After some ranch experiences I had my spectacle cases made of steel; and it was one of these steel spectacle cases which saved my life in after years when a man shot into me in Milwaukee.° 5

While in Harvard I was among those who joined in forming the Nuttall Club, which I believe afterward became one of the parent sources of the American Ornithologists' Union.

The Harvard of that day was passing through a phase of 10 biological study which was shaped by the belief that German university methods were the only ones worthy of copy, and also by the proper admiration for the younger Agassiz,° whose interest was mainly in the lower forms of marine life. Accordingly it was the accepted doctrine 15 that a biologist—the word "naturalist" was eschewed as archaic—was to work toward the ideal of becoming a section cutter of tissue, who spent his time studying this tissue, and low marine organisms, under the microscope. Such work was excellent; but it covered a very small part 20 of the biological field; and not only was there no encouragement for the work of the field naturalist, the faunal naturalist, but this work was positively discouraged, and was treated as of negligible value. The effect of this attitude, common at that time to all our colleges, was detri- 25 mental to one very important side of natural history research. The admirable work of the microscopist had no attraction for me, nor was I fitted for it; I grew even more interested in other forms of work than in the work of a faunal naturalist; and I abandoned all thought of making 30 the study of my science my life interest.

But I never lost a real interest in natural history; and

I very keenly regret that at certain times I did not display this interest in more practical fashion. Thus, for the dozen years beginning with 1883, I spent much of my time on the Little Missouri, where big game was then plentiful. Most big game hunters never learn anything about the game except how to kill it; and most naturalists never observe it at all. Therefore a large amount of important and rather obvious facts remains unobserved or inaccurately observed until the species becomes extinct. What is most needed is not the ability to see what very few people can see, but to see what almost anybody can see, but nobody takes the trouble to look at. But I vaguely supposed that the obvious facts were known; and I let most of the opportunities pass by. Even so, many of my observations on the life histories of the bighorns, white goats, prongbucks, deer, and wapiti, and occasional observations on some of the other beasts, such as black-footed ferrets, were of value; indeed as regards some of the big game beasts, the accounts in" Hunting Trips of a Ranchman," " Ranch Life and the Hunting Trial," and " The Wilderness Hunter " gave a good deal of information which, as far as I know, is not to be found elsewhere.

To illustrate what I mean as "obvious" facts which nevertheless are of real value I shall instance the cougar. In the winter of 1910 I made a cougar hunt with hounds, spending about five weeks in the mountains of northwestern Colorado. At that time the cougar had been seemingly well known to hunters, settlers, naturalists, and novelists for more than a century; and yet it was actually impossible to get trustworthy testimony on such elementary points as, for instance, whether the male and female mated permanently, or at least until the young were reared (like foxes and wolves), and whether the animal caught its prey by rambling and stalking or, as was frequently asserted, by lying in wait on the branches of a tree. The facts I saw and observed during our five 5 weeks' hunt in the snow were obvious; they needed only the simplest powers of observation and of deduction from observation. But nobody had hitherto shown or exercised these simple powers! My narrative in the volume "Outdoor Pastimes of an American Hunter" gave the first 10 reasonably full and trustworthy life history of the cougar as regards its most essential details—for Merriam's capital Adirondack study had dealt with the species when it was too near the vanishing point and therefore when the conditions were too abnormal for some of these essential 15 details to be observed.

In South America I made observations of a certain value on some of the strange creatures we met, and these are to be found in the volume "Through the Brazilian Wilderness;" but the trip was primarily one of explora- 20 tion. In Africa, however, we really did some good work in natural history. Many of my observations were set forth in my book "African Game Trails;" and I have always felt that the book which Edmund Heller and I jointly wrote, the "Life Histories of African Game Animals," was a serious 25 and worth-while contribution to science. Here again, this contribution, so far as I was concerned, consisted chiefly in seeing, recording, and interpreting facts which were really obvious, but to which observers hitherto had been blind, or which they had misinterpreted partly be- 30 cause sportsmen seemed incapable of seeing anything except as a trophy, partly because stay-at-home system-

atists never saw anything at all except skins and skulls
which enabled them to give Latin names to new "species"
or "subspecies," partly because collectors had collected
birds and beasts in precisely the spirit in which other
5 collectors assembled postage stamps.

I shall give a few instances. In mid-Africa we came
across a peculiar bat, with a greenish body and slate
blue wings. Specimens of this bat had often been collected. But I could find no record of its really interesting
10 habits. It was not nocturnal; it was hardly even crepus-
cular. It hung from the twigs of trees during the day and
its activities began rather early in the afternoon. It did
not fly continuously in swallow fashion, according to the
usual bat custom. It behaved like a phœbe or other fly-
15 catcher. It hung from a twig until it saw an insect, then
swooped down, caught the insect, and at once returned
to the same or another twig—just as a phœbe or peewee
or kingbird returns to its perch after a similar flight.

On the White Nile I hunted a kind of handsome river
20 antelope, the white-withered or saddle-backed lechwi.
It had been known for fifty years to trophy-seeking
sportsmen, and to closet naturalists, some of whom had
called it a kob and others a water buck. Its nearest
kinsman was in reality the ordinary lechwi, which dwelt
25 far off to the south, along the Zambezi. But during that
half century no hunter or closet naturalist had grasped
this obvious fact. I had never seen the Zambezi lechwi,
but I had carefully read the account of its habits by
Selous°—a real hunter-naturalist, faunal naturalist. As
30 soon as I came across the White Nile river bucks, and
observed their habits, I said to my companions that they
were undoubtedly lechwis: I wrote this to Selous,° and

to another English hunter-naturalist, Migand; and even a slight examination of the heads and skins when compared with those of the other lechwi and of the kobs and water bucks proved that I was right.

A larger, but equally obvious group of facts was that connected with concealing and revealing coloration. As eminent a naturalist as Wallace,° and innumerable men of less note, had indulged in every conceivable vagary of speculative theory on the subject, largely based on supposed correlation between the habits and the shape or color patterns of big animals which, as a matter of fact, they had never seen in a state of nature. While in Africa I studied the question in the field, observing countless individuals of big beasts and birds, and comparing the results with what I had observed of the big game and the birds of North America (the result being borne out by what I later observed in South America). In a special chapter of the " Life, Histories of African Game Animals," as well as in a special number of the "American Museum Bulletin," I set forth the facts thus observed and the conclusions inevitably to be deduced from them. All that I thus set forth, and all the conclusions I deduced, belonged to the obvious; but that there was need of thus setting forth the obvious was sufficiently shown by the simple fact that large numbers of persons refused to accept it even when set forth.

I do not think there is much else for me to say about my anything but important work as a naturalist. But perhaps I may say further that while my interest in natural history had added very little to my sum of achievement, it has added immeasurably to my sum of enjoyment in life.

NATURE FAKERS

In the Middle Ages there was no hard-and-fast line drawn between fact and fiction even in ordinary history; and until much later there was not even an effort to draw it in natural history. There are quaint little books on
5 beasts, in German and in English, as late as the sixteenth century, in which the unicorn° and the basilisk° appear as real creatures; while to more commonplace animals there are ascribed traits and habits of such exceeding marvelousness that they ought to make the souls
10 of the "nature fakers" of these degenerate days swell with envious admiration.

As real outdoor naturalists, real observers of nature, grew up, men who went into the wilderness to find out the truth, they naturally felt a half-indignant and half-
15 amused contempt both for the men who invented preposterous fiction about wild animals, and for the credulous stay-at-home people who accepted such fiction as fact. A century and a half ago old Samuel Hearne,° the Hudson Bay explorer, a keen and trustworthy observer, while
20 writing of the beaver, spoke as follows of the spiritual predecessors of certain modern writers:

"I cannot refrain from smiling when I read the accounts of different authors who have written on the economy of these animals, as there seems to be a contest between them
25 who shall most exceed in fiction. But the compiler of the 'Wonders of Nature and Art' seems, in my opinion, to have succeeded best in this respect; as he has not only collected all the fictions into which other writers on the subject have run, but has so greatly improved on them,

258

that little remains to be added to his account of the beaver besides a vocabulary of their language, a code of their laws, and a sketch of their religion, to make it the most complete natural history of that animal which can possibly be offered to the public.   5

"There cannot be a greater imposition, or indeed a grosser insult on common understanding, than the wish to make us believe the stories [in question] . . . a very moderate share of understanding is surely sufficient to guard [any one] against giving credit to such marvelous 10 tales, however smoothly they may be told, or however boldly they may be asserted by the romancing traveler."

Hearne was himself a man who added greatly to the fund of knowledge about the beasts of the wilderness. We need such observers; much remains to be told about the 15 wolf and the bear, the lynx and the fisher, the moose and the caribou. Undoubtedly wild creatures sometimes show very unexpected traits, and individuals among them sometimes perform fairly startling feats or exhibit totally unlooked-for sides of their characters in their relations 20 with one another and with man. We much need a full study and observation of all these animals, undertaken by observers capable of seeing, understanding, and recording what goes on in the wilderness; and such study and observation cannot be made by men of dull mind and 25 limited power of appreciation. The highest type of student of nature should be able to see keenly and writer interestingly and should have an imagination that will enable him to interpret the facts. But he is not a student of nature at all who sees not keenly but falsely, who writes 30 interestingly and untruthfully, and whose imagination is used not to interpret facts but to invent them.

We owe a real debt to the men who truthfully portray
for us, with pen or pencil, any one of the many sides of
outdoor life; whether they work as artists or as writers,
whether they care for big beasts or small birds, for the
5 homely farmland or for the vast, lonely wilderness,
whether they are scientists proper, or hunters of game,
or lovers of all nature—which, indeed, scientists and
hunters ought also to be. John Burroughs and John Muir,
Stewart Edward White, and Frederic Remington, Olive
10 Thorne Miller,° Hart Merriam, William Hornaday,
Frank Chapman, J. A. Allen,° Ernest Ingersoll, Witmer
Stone, William Cram, George Shiras—to all of these and
to many like them whom I could name, we owe much,
we who love the breath of the woods and the fields, and
15 who care for the wild creatures, large or small. And the
surest way to neutralize the work of these lovers of truth
and nature, of truth in nature-study, is to encourage those
whose work shows neither knowledge of nature nor love
of truth.
20   The modern "nature faker" is of course an object of
derision to every scientist worthy of the name, to every
real lover of the wilderness, to every faunal naturalist,
to every true hunter or nature lover. But it is evident
that he completely deceives many good people who are
25 wholly ignorant of wild life. Sometimes he draws on his
own imagination for his fictions; sometimes he gets them
second-hand from irresponsible guides or trappers or
Indians.
     In the wilderness, as elsewhere, there are some persons
30 who do not regard the truth; and these are the very
persons who most delight to fill credulous strangers with
impossible stories of wild beasts. As for Indians, they live

in a world of mysticism, and they often ascribe super-
natural traits to the animals they know, just as the men
of the Middle Ages, with almost the same childlike faith,
credited the marvels told of the unicorn, the basilisk, the
roc,° and the cockatrice.°   5

It would take a volume merely to catalogue the comic
absurdities with which the books of these writers are filled.
There is no need of discussing their theories; the point is
that their alleged "facts" are not facts at all, but fancies.
Their most striking stories are not merely distortions of 10
facts, but pure inventions; and not only are they inventions, but they are inventions by men who know so little of
the subject concerning which they write, and who to ignorance add such utter recklessness, that they are not even
able to distinguish between what is possible, however 15
wildly improbable, and mechanical impossibilities. Be it
remembered that I am not speaking of ordinary mistakes,
of ordinary errors of observation, of differences of interpretation and opinion; I am dealing only with deliberate
invention, deliberate perversion of fact.   20

Now all this would be, if not entirely proper, at least
far less objectionable, if the writers in question were content to appear in their proper garb, as is the case with the
men who write fantastic fiction about wild animals for
the Sunday issues of various daily newspapers. Moreover, 25
as a writer of spirited animal fables, avowed to be such, any
man can gain a distinct place of some importance. But
it is astonishing that such very self-evident fiction as
that which I am now discussing should, when advertised
as fact, impose upon any person of good sense, no matter 30
how ignorant of natural history and of wild life.' Most
of us have enjoyed novels like "King Solomon's Mines," °

for instance. But if Mr. Rider Haggard° had insisted that
his novels were not novels but records of actual fact, we
should feel a mild wonder at the worthy persons who
accepted them as serious contributions to the study of
5 African geography and ethnology.

It is not probable that the writers in question have even
so much as seen some of the animals which they minutely
describe. They certainly do not know the first thing
about their habits, nor even about their physical structure.
10 Judging from the internal evidence of their books, I
should gravely doubt if they had ever seen a wild wolf
or a wild lynx. The wolves and lynxes and other animals
which they describe are full brothers of the wild beasts
that appear in "Uncle Remus" ° and "Reynard the
15 Fox," ° and deserve the same serious consideration from
the zoölogical standpoint. Certain of their wolves appear
as gifted with all the philosophy, the self-restraint, and
the keen intelligence of, say, Marcus Aurelius,° together
with the lofty philanthropy of a modern altruist; though
20 unfortunately they are hampered by a wholly erroneous
view of caribou anatomy.

Like the White Queen° in "Through the Looking-
Glass," these writers can easily believe three impossible
things before breakfast; and they do not mind in the least
25 if the impossibilities are mutually contradictory. Thus,
one story relates how a wolf with one bite reaches the
heart of a bull caribou, or a moose, or a horse—a feat
which, of course, has been mechanically impossible of performance by any land carnivore since the death of the
30 last saber-toothed tiger. But the next story will cheer-
fully describe a doubtful contest between the wolf and a
lynx or a bulldog, in which the latter survives twenty

slashing bites. Now of course a wolf that could bite into the heart of a horse would swallow a bulldog or a lynx like a pill.

In one story, a wolf is portrayed as guiding home some lost children, in a spirit of thoughtful kindness; let the overtrustful individual who has girded up his loins to believe this think of the way he would receive the statement of some small farmer's boy that when lost he was guided home by a coon, a possum, or a woodchuck. Again, one of these story-book wolves, when starving, catches a red squirrel, which he takes round as a present to propitiate a bigger wolf. If any man seriously thinks a starving wolf would act in this manner, let him study hounds when feeding, even when they are not starving.

The animals are alternately portrayed as actuated by motives of exalted humanitarianism, and as possessed of demoniac prowess and insight into motive. In one story the fisher figures in the latter capacity. A fisher is a big marten, the size of a fox. This particular story-book fisher, when pursued by hunters on snow-shoes, kills a buck by a bite in the throat, and leaves the carcass as a bribe to the hunters, hoping thereby to distract attention from himself! Now, foxes are continually hunted; they are far more clever than fishers. What rational man would pay heed to a story that a fox when hunted killed a good-sized calf by a bite in the throat, and left it as a bribe to the hounds and hunters, to persuade them to leave him alone? One story is just as possible as the other.

In another story, the salmon is the hero. The writer begins by blunders about the young salmon which a ten minutes' visit to any government fish hatchery would have enabled him to avoid; and as a climax, describes how the salmon goes up a fall by flopping from ledge to ledge of a cliff, under circumstances which make the feat about as probable as that the fish would use a stepladder. As soon as these writers get into the wilderness, they develop 5 preternatural powers of observation, and, as Mr. Shiras says, become themselves "invisible and odorless," so that the shyest wild creatures permit any closeness of intimacy on their part; in one recent story about a beaver colony, the alternative to the above proposition is that the beavers 10 were both blind and without sense of smell.

Yet these same writers, who see such marvelous things as soon as they go into the woods, are incapable of observing aright the most ordinary facts when at home. One of their stories relates how the eyes of frogs shine at night 15 in the wilderness; the author apparently ignoring the fact that frog-ponds are common in less remote places, and are not inhabited by blazing-eyed frogs. Two of our most common and most readily observed small mammals are the red squirrel and the chipmunk. The chipmunk has 20 cheek pouches, in which he stores berries, grain, and small nuts, whereas the red squirrel has no cheek pouches, and carries nuts between his teeth. Yet even this simple fact escapes the attention of one of the writers we are discussing, who endows a red squirrel with cheek pouches 25 filled with nuts. Evidently excessive indulgence in invention tends to atrophy the power of accurate observation.

In one story a woodcock is described as making a kind of mud splint for its broken leg; it seems a pity not to have added that it also made itself a crutch to use while 30 the splint was on. A Baltimore oriole is described as making a contrivance of twigs and strings whereby to attach its nest, under circumstances which would imply the mental ability and physical address of a sailor making a hammock; and the story is backed up by affidavits, as are others of these stories. This particular feat is precisely as possible as that a Rocky Mountain pack rat can throw the diamond hitch. The affidavits in support of these 5 various stories are interesting only because of the curious light they throw on the personalities of those making and believing them.

If the writers who make such startling discoveries in the wilderness would really study even the denizens of a 10 barnyard, they would be saved from at least some of their more salient mistakes. Their stories dwell much on the "teaching" of the young animals by their elders and betters. In one story, for instance, a wild duck is described as "teaching" her young how to swim and get 15 their food. If this writer had strolled into the nearest barnyard containing a hen which had hatched out ducklings, a glance at the actions of those ducklings when the hen happened to lead them near a puddle would have enlightened him as to how much "teaching" they needed. 20 But these writers exercise the same florid imagination when they deal with a robin or a rabbit as when they describe a bear, a moose, or a salmon.

It is half amusing and half exasperating to think that there should be excellent persons to whom it is necessary 25 to explain that books stuffed with such stories, in which the stories are stated as facts, are preposterous in their worthlessness. These worthy persons vividly call to mind Professor Lounsbury's comment on "the infinite capacity of the human brain to withstand the introduction of 30 knowledge." The books in question contain no statement which a serious and truth-loving student of nature can

accept, save statements which have already long been known as established by trustworthy writers. The fables they contain bear the same relation to real natural history that Barnum's° famous artificial mermaid bore to real
5 fish and real mammals. No man who has really studied nature in a spirit of seeking the truth, whether he be big or little, can have any controversy with these writers; it would be as absurd as to expect some genuine student of anthropology or archeology to enter into a controversy
10 with the clumsy fabricators of the Cardiff Giant.° Their books carry their own refutation; and affidavits in support of the statements they contain are as worthless as the similar affidavits once solemnly issued to show that the Cardiff "giant" was a petrified pre-Adamite man.
15 There is now no more excuse for being deceived by their stories than for being still in doubt about the silly Cardiff hoax.

Men of this stamp will necessarily arise, from time to time, some in one walk of life, some in another. Our
20 quarrel is not with these men, but with those who give them their chance. We who believe in the study of nature feel that a real knowledge and appreciation of wild things, of trees, flowers, birds, and of the grim and crafty creatures of the wilderness, give an added beauty and
25 health to life. Therefore we abhor deliberate or reckless untruth in this study as much as in any other; and therefore we feel that a grave wrong is committed by all who, holding a position that entitles them to respect, yet condone and encourage such untruth.

THE DEER OF NORTH AMERICA

WITH the exception of the bison, during the period of its plenty, the chief game animals followed by the American rifle-bearing hunter have always been the different representatives of the deer family, and, out on the great plains, the pronghorn antelope. They were the game 5 which Daniel Boone followed during the closing decades of the eighteenth century, and David Crockett during the opening decades of the nineteenth; and now, at the outset of the twentieth century, it is probably not too much to say that ninety-nine out of every hundred head 10 of game killed in the United States are deer, elk, or antelope. Indeed, the proportion is very much larger. In certain restricted localities black bear were at one time very numerous, and over large regions the multitudinous herds of the bison formed until 1883 the chief objects of 15 pursuit. But the bison have now vanished; and though the black bear has held its own better than any other of the larger carnivora, it is only very locally that it has ever been plentiful in the sense that even now the elk, deer, and antelope are still plentiful over considerable 20 tracts of country. Taking the United States as a whole, the deer have always been by far the most numerous of all game; they have held their own in the land better than any other kinds; and they have been the most common quarry of the hunter. 25

The nomenclature and exact specific relationships of American deer and antelope offer difficulties not only to the hunter but to the naturalist. As regards the nomenclature, we share the trouble encountered by all peoples of European descent who have gone into strange lands. The incomers are almost invariably men who are not accustomed to scientific precision of expression. Like other people, they do not like to invent names if they 5 can by any possibility make use of those already in existence, and so in a large number of cases they call the new birds, and animals by names applied to entirely different birds and animals of the Old World to which, in the eyes of the settlers, they bear some resemblance. 10 In South America the Spaniards, for instance, christened "lion" and "tiger" the great cats which are properly known as cougar and jaguar. In South Africa the Dutch settlers, who came from a land where all big game had long been exterminated, gave fairly grotesque names to 15 the great antelopes, calling them after the European elk, stag, and chamois. The French did but little better in Canada. Even in Ceylon the English, although belonging for the most part to the educated classes, did no better than the ordinary pioneer settlers, miscalling 20 the sambur stag an elk, and the leopard a cheetah. Our own pioneers behaved in the same way. Hence it is that we have no distinctive name at all for the group of peculiarly American game birds of·which the bob-white is the typical representative; and that, when we could not 25 use the words quail, partridge, or pheasant, we went for our terminology to the barn-yard, and called our fine grouse, fool-hens, sage-hens, and prairie-chickens. The bear and wolf our people recognized at once. The bison they called a buffalo, which was no worse than the 30 way in which every one in Europe called the Old World bison an aurochs. The American true elk and reindeer were rechristened moose and caribou—excellent names,

by the way, derived from the Indian. The huge stag
was called an elk. The extraordinary antelope of the high
Western peaks was christened the white goat; not un-
naturally, as it has a most goatlike look. The prongbuck of the plains, an animal standing as much alone 5
among ruminants as does the giraffe, was simply called
antelope. Even when we invented names for ourselves,
we applied them loosely. The ordinary deer is sometimes
known as the red deer, sometimes as the Virginia deer,
and sometimes as the whitetail deer,—the last being 10
by far the best and most distinctive term.

In the present condition of zoölogical research it is
not possible to state accurately how many "species" of
deer there are in North America, both because mammal-
ogists have not at hand a sufficient amount of material 15
in the way of large series of specimens from different
localities, and because they are not agreed among themselves as to the value of "species," or indeed as to exactly
what is denoted by the term. Of course, if we had a
complete series of specimens of extinct and fossil deer 20
before us, there would be an absolutely perfect inter-
gradation among all the existing forms through their
long-vanished ancestral types; for the existing gaps have
been created by the extinction and transformation of
these former types. Where the gap is very broad and 25
well marked no difficulty exists in using terms which
shall express the difference. Thus the gap separating
the moose, the caribou, and the wapiti from one another,
and from the smaller American deer, is so wide, and
there is so complete a lack of transitional forms, that 30
the differences among them are expressed by naturalists
by the use of different generic terms. The gap between

the whitetail and the different forms of blacktail, though much less, is also clearly marked. But when we come to consider the blacktail among themselves, we find two very distinct types which yet show a certain tendency to
5 intergrade; and with the whitetail very wide differences exist, even in the United States, both individually among the deer of certain localities, and also as between all the deer of one locality when compared with all the deer of another. Our present knowledge of the various forms
10 hardly justifies us in dogmatizing as to their exact relative worth, and even if our knowledge was more complete, naturalists are as yet wholly at variance as to the laws which should govern specific nomenclature. However, the hunter, the mere field naturalist, and the lover of
15 outdoor life, are only secondarily interested in the niceness of these distinctions, and it is for them that this volume is written. Accordingly, I shall make no effort to determine the number of different but closely allied forms of smaller deer which are found in North Temper-
20 ate America.

Disregarding the minor differences, there are in North America in addition to the so-called antelope, six wholly distinct kinds of deer: the moose, caribou, wapiti, whitetail, and the two blacktails.

25 The moose in its various forms reaches from the Atlantic to the Pacific, through the cold boreal forests of Canada, extending its range down into the United States in northern New England, Minnesota, and along the Rocky Mountains. It was exterminated from the Adirondacks
30 in the early sixties, about the time that the wapiti was exterminated in Pennsylvania, or very shortly before. It is the brother of the Old World elk, and its huge size,

shovel horns, short neck, swollen nose, and long legs distinguish it at a glance from any other animal.

The caribou is found throughout most of the moose's range, but it does not extend so far south, and in some of its forms reaches much farther north, being found on the 5 cold barrens, from Newfoundland to the shores of the Arctic. It is the only animal which is still at certain seasons found in enormous multitudes comparable to the vast herds of bison in the old days, and in parts of its range it is being slaughtered in the same butcherly spirit 10 that was responsible for the extinction of the bison. The different kinds of American caribou are closely akin to the reindeer of the Old World, and their long, irregularly branched antlers, with palmated ends, their big feet, coarse heads, and stout bodies, render them as easily dis- 15 tinguishable as the moose.

The wapiti or round-horned elk always had its centre of abundance in the United States, though in the West it was also found far north of the Canadian line. This splendid deer affords a good instance of the difficulty of deciding 20 what name to use in treating of our American game. On the one hand, it is entirely undesirable to be pedantic; and on the other hand, it seems a pity, at a time when speech is written almost as much as spoken, to use terms which perpetually require explanation in order to avoid confu- 25 sion. The wapiti is not properly an elk at all; the term wapiti is unexceptionable, and it is greatly to be desired that it should be generally adopted. But unfortunately it has not been generally adopted. From the time when our backwoodsmen first began to hunt the animal among the 30 foot-hills of the Appalachian chains to the present day, it has been universally known as elk wherever it has been

found. In ordinary speech it is never known as anything
else, and only an occasional settler or hunter would understand what the word wapiti referred to. The book name is
a great deal better than the common name; but after all,
5 it is only a book name. The case is almost exactly parallel
to that of the buffalo, which was really a bison, but which
lived as the buffalo, died as the buffalo, and left its name
imprinted on our landscape as the buffalo. There is little
use in trying to upset a name which is imprinted in our
10 geography in hundreds of such titles as Elk Ridge, Elk
Mountain, Elkhorn River. Yet in the books it is often
necessary to call it the wapiti in order to distinguish it
both from its different named close kinsfolk of the Old
World, and from its more distant relatives with which it
15 shares the name of elk. It is the largest of the true deer,
and the noblest and stateliest of the deer kind throughout the world. It is closely akin to the much smaller
European stag or red deer, and still more closely to certain
Asiatic deer, one of which so closely approaches it in size,
20 appearance, and stately presence as to be almost indistinguishable. Its huge and yet delicately moulded proportions, and its massive, rounded antlers, the beam of which
bends backward from the head, while the tines are thrust
forward, render it impossible to confound it with any
25 other species of American deer. Owing to its habitat it
has suffered from the persecution of hunters and settlers
more than any other of its fellows in America, and the
boundaries of its range have shrunk in far greater proportion. The moose and caribou have in most places greatly
30 diminished in numbers, and have here and there been
exterminated altogether from outlying portions of their
range; but the wapiti has completely vanished from nine-

tenths of the territory over which it roamed a century and a quarter ago. Although it was never found in any one place in such enormous numbers as the bison and the caribou, it nevertheless went in herds far larger than the herds of any other American game save the two mentioned, and was formerly very much more abundant within the area of its distribution than was the moose within the area of its distribution. It is now almost limited to certain mountainous areas in the Rockies and on the Pacific coast,—The Pacific coast form differing from the ordinary form.

The remaining three deer are much more closely connected with one another, all belonging to the same genus. The whitetail has always been, and is now, on the whole the commonest of American game, and it has held its own better than any other kind. It is found from southern Canada, in various forms, from the Atlantic to the Pacific, down into South America. It is given various names, and throughout most of its habitat is simply known as "deer"; but wherever it comes in contact with the blacktail it is almost invariably called whitetail. This is a very appropriate name, for its tail is habitually so carried as to be extremely conspicuous, being white and bushy, only the middle part above being dark colored. The antlers curve out and forward, the prongs branching from the posterior surface.

The Rocky Mountain blacktail or mule-deer is somewhat larger, with large ears, its tail short-haired and round, white excepting for a black tip, and with antlers which fork evenly like the prongs of a pitchfork,—so that it is difficult to say which prong should be considered the main shaft,—and each prong itself bifurcates again. In

the books this animal is called the mule-deer, but throughout its haunts it is almost always known simply as the
blacktail. It is found in rough, broken country from the
Bad Lands of the western Dakotas to the Pacific coast,
5 and is everywhere the characteristic deer of the Rocky
Mountains. The southern California form is peculiar,
especially in having a dark stripe on the tail above.

The true blacktail is found on the Pacific coast from
southern Alaska to northern California. Its horns are
10 like those of the Rocky Mountain blacktail; its tail is
more like that of the whitetail, but is not as large, and
the white is much reduced, the color above and on the
sides, to the very tip, being barely black.

The most striking and melancholy feature in connection
15 with American big game is the rapidity with which it
has vanished. When, just before the outbreak of the
Revolutionary War, the rifle-bearing hunters of the backwoods first penetrated the great forests west of the Alleghanies, deer, elk, black bear, and even buffalo swarmed
20 in what are now the states of Kentucky and Tennessee;
and the country north of the Ohio was a great and almost
virgin hunting-ground. From that day to this the shrink-
age has gone on, only partially checked here and there,
and never arrested as a whole. As a matter of historical
25 accuracy, however, it is well to bear in mind that a great
many writers in lamenting this extinction of the game
have, from time to time, anticipated or overstated the
facts. Thus as good an author as Colonel Richard Irving
Dodge spoke of the buffalo as practically extinct, while
30 the great northern herd still existed in countless thousands.
As early as 1880 very good sporting authorities spoke
not only of the buffalo but of the elk, deer, and antelope

as no longer to be found in plenty; and within a year one
of the greatest of living hunters has stated that it is no
longer possible to find any American wapiti bearing heads
comparable with the red deer of Hungary. As a matter
of fact, in the early eighties there were still great regions 5
where every species of game that had ever been known
within historic times on our continent were still to be
found as plentifully as ever. In the early nineties there
were still large regions in which this was true of all game
except the buffalo; for instance, it was true of the elk in 10
portions of northwestern Wyoming, of the blacktail in
northwestern Colorado, of the whitetail here and there
in the Indian Territory, and of the antelope in parts of
New Mexico. Even at the present day there are smaller,
but still considerable regions where these four animals 15
are yet found in great abundance, and I have seen antlers
of wapiti shot in 1900 far surpassing any of which there
is record from Hungary. In New England and New York,
as well as New Brunswick and Nova Scotia, the whitetail
deer is more plentiful than it was thirty years ago, and 20
in Maine (and to an even greater extent in New Brunswick
the moose and caribou have, on the whole, increased
during the same period. There is yet ample opportunity
for the big game hunter in the United States and Canada;
while not even in the old days was it possible to go on 25
any trip better worth taking than the recent successful
hunt of Mr. Dall DeWeese, of Cañon City, Colorado,
after the giant moose, giant bear, white sheep, and caribou
of Alaska.

While it is necessary to give this word of warning to 30
those who, in praising time past, always forget the opportunities of the present, it is a thousand fold more necessary

to remember that these opportunities are, nevertheless,
vanishing; and if we are a sensible people, we will make
it our business to see that the process of extinction is
arrested.   At the present moment the great herds of
5 caribou are being butchered as in the past the great herds
of bison and wapiti have been butchered.   Every believer
in manliness, and therefore in manly sport, and every
lover of nature, every man who appreciates the majesty
and beauty of the wilderness and of wild life, should
10 strike hands with the far-sighted men who wish to preserve our material resources, in the effort to keep our
forests and our game beasts, game birds, and game fish—
indeed all the living creatures of prairie, and woodland,
and seashore—from wanton destruction.

THE WHITETAIL DEER

THE whitetail deer is now, as it always has been, the most plentiful and most widely distributed of American big game. It holds its own in the land better than any other species, because it is by choice a dweller in the thick forests and swamps, the places around which the tide of 5 civilization flows, leaving them as islets of refuge for the wild creatures which formerly haunted all the country. The range of the whitetail is from the Atlantic to the Pacific, and from the Canadian to the Mexican borders, and somewhat to the north and far to the south of these 10 limits. The animal shows a wide variability, both individually and locally, within these confines; from the hunter's standpoint it is not necessary to try to determine exactly the weight that attaches to these local variations.

There is also a very considerable variation in habits. 15 As compared with the mule-deer, the whitetail is not a lover of the mountains. As compared with the prong-buck, it is not a lover of the treeless plains. Yet in the Alleghanies and the Adirondacks, at certain seasons especially, and in some places at all seasons, it dwells high 20 among the densely wooded mountains, wandering over their crests and sheer sides, and through the deep ravines; while in the old days there were parts of Texas and the Indian Territory where it was found in great herds far out on the prairie. Moreover, the peculiar nature of its 25 chosen habitat, while generally enabling it to resist the onslaught of man longer than any of its fellows, sometimes exposes it to speedy extermination. To the westward of the rich bottom-lands and low prairies of the

Mississippi Valley proper, when the dry plains country
is reached, the natural conditions are much less favorable for whitetail than for other big game.   The black
bear, which in the East has almost precisely the same
5 habitat as the whitetail, disappears entirely on the great
plains, and reappears in the Rockies in regions which the
whitetail does not reach.   All over the great plains, into
the foot-hills of the Rockies, the whitetail is found, but
only in the thick timber of the river bottoms.   Through-
10 out the regions of the Upper Missouri and Upper Platte,
the Big Horn, Powder, Yellowstone, and Cheyenne, over
all of which I have hunted, the whitetail lives among the
cottonwood groves and dense brush growth that fringe the
river beds and here and there extend some distance up the
15 mouths of the large creeks.   In these places the whitetail
and the mule-deer may exist in close proximity; but normally neither invades the haunts of the other.

Along the ordinary plains river, such as the Little Missouri, where I ranched for many years, there are three
20 entirely different types of country through which a man
passes as he travels away from the bed of the river.   There
is first the alluvial river bottom covered with cottonwood
and box-elder, together with thick brush.   These bottoms
may be a mile or two across, or they may shrink to but a
25 few score yards.   After the extermination of the wapiti,
which roamed everywhere, the only big game animal
found in them was the whitetail deer.   Beyond this level
alluvial bottom the ground changes abruptly to bare,
rugged hills or fantastically carved and shaped Bad Lands
30 rising on either side of the river, the ravines, coulies,
creeks, and canyons twisting through them in every direction.   Here there are patches of ash, cedar, pine, and

occasionally other trees, but the country is very rugged, and the cover very scanty. This is the home of the mule-deer, and, in the roughest and wildest parts, of the big-horn. The absolutely clear and sharply defined line of demarkation between this rough, hilly country, flanking 5 the river, and the alluvial river bottom, serves as an equally clearly marked line of demarkation between the ranges of the whitetail and the mule-deer. This belt of broken country may be only a few hundred yards in width; or it may extend for a score of miles before it changes into the 10 open prairies, the high plains proper. As soon as these are reached, the prongbuck's domain begins.

As the plains country is passed, and the vast stretches of mountainous region entered, the river bottoms become narrower, and the plains on which the prongbuck is found 15 become of very limited extent, shrinking to high valleys and plateaus, while the mass of rugged foot-hills and moun-tains add immensely to the area of the mule-deer's habitat.

Given equal areas of country, of the three different types alluded to above, that in which the mule-deer is 20 found offers the greatest chance of success to the rifle-bearing hunter, because there is enough cover to shield him and not enough to allow his quarry to escape by stealth and hiding. On the other hand, the thick river bottoms offer him the greatest difficulty. In consequence, 25 where the areas of distribution of the different game ani-mals are about equal, the mule-deer disappears first be-fore the hunter, the prongbuck next, while the whitetail holds out the best of all. I saw this frequently on the Yellowstone, the Powder, and the Little Missouri. When 30 the ranchman first came into this country the mule-deer swarmed, and yielded a far more certain harvest to the

hunter than did either the prongbuck or the whitetail. They were the first to be thinned out, the prongbuck lasting much better. The cowboys and small ranchmen, most of whom did not at the time have hounds, then fol-
5 lowed the prongbuck; and this, in its turn, was killed out before the whitetail. But in other places a slight change in the conditions completely reversed the order of destruction. In parts of Wyoming and Montana the mountainous region where the mule-deer dwelt was of such
10 vast extent, and the few river bottoms on which the whitetail were found were so easily hunted, that the whitetail was completely exterminated throughout large districts where the mule-deer continued to abound. Moreover, in these regions the tablelands and plains upon which
15 the prongbuck was found were limited in extent, and although the prongbuck outlasted the whitetail, it vanished long before the herds of the mule-deer had been destroyed from among the neighboring mountains.

The whitetail was originally far less common in the
20 forests of northern New England than was the moose, for in the deep snows the moose had a much better chance to escape from its brute foes and to withstand cold and starvation. But when man appeared upon the scene he followed the moose so much more eagerly than he followed
25 the deer that the conditions were reversed and the moose was killed out. The moose thus vanished entirely from the Adirondacks, and almost entirely from Maine; but the excellent game laws of the latter state, and the honesty and efficiency with which they have been executed during
30 the last twenty years, has resulted in an increase of moose during that time. During the same period the whitetail deer has increased to an even greater extent. It is doubt-

less now more plentiful in New York and New England than it was a quarter of a century ago. Stragglers are found in Connecticut, and, what is still more extraordinary, even occasionally come into wild parts of densely populated little Rhode Island,—my authority for the last 5 statement being Mr. C. Grant La Farge. Of all our wild game, the whitetail responds most quickly to the efforts for its protection, and except the wapiti, it thrives best in semi-domestication; in consequence, it has proved easy to preserve it, even in such places as Cape Code in Mas- 10 sachusetts and Long Island in New York; while it has increased greatly in Vermont, New Hampshire, and Maine, and has more than held its own in the Adirondacks. Mr. James R. Sheffield, of New York City, in the summer of 1899, spent several weeks on a fishing trip through north- 15 ern Maine. He kept count of the moose and deer he saw, and came across no less than thirty-five of the former and over five hundred and sixty of the latter; in the most lonely parts of the forest deer were found by the score, feeding in broad daylight on the edges of the ponds. Deer 20 are still plentiful in many parts of the Alleghany Mountains, from Pennsylvania southward, and also in the swamps and cane-brakes of the South Atlantic and Gulf states.

Where the differences in habitat and climate are so 25 great there are may changes of habits, and some of them of a noteworthy kind. Mr. John A. McIllhenny, of Avery's Island, Louisiana, formerly a lieutenant in my regiment,° lives in what is still a fine game country. His plantation is in the delta of the Mississippi, among the vast marshes, 30 north of which lie the wooded swamps. Both the marshes and the swamps were formerly literally thronged with

whitetail deer, and the animals are still plentiful in them. Mr. McIllhenny has done much deer-hunting, always using hounds. He informs me that the breeding times are unexpectedly different from those of the northern
5 deer. In the North, in different localities, the rut takes place in October or November, and the fawns are dropped in May or June. In the Louisiana marshes around Avery's Island the rut begins early in July and the fawns are dropped in February. In the swamps immediately
10 north of these marshes the dates are fully a month later. The marshes are covered with tall reeds and grass, and broken by bayous, while there are scattered over them what are called "islands" of firmer ground overgrown with timber. In this locality the deer live in the same
15 neighborhood all the year round, just as, for instance, they do on Long Island. So on the Little Missouri, in the neighborhood of my ranch, they lived in exactly the same localities throughout the entire year. Occasionally they would shift from one river bottom to another, or go
20 a few miles up or down stream because of scarcity of food. But there was no general shifting.

On the Little Missouri, in one place where they were not molested, I knew a particular doe and fawn with whose habits I became quite intimately acquainted.
25 When the moon was full they fed chiefly by night, and spent most of the day lying in the thick brush. When there was little or no moon they would begin to feed early in the morning, then take a siesta, and then—what struck me as most curious of all—would go to a little willow-
30 bordered pool about noon to drink, feeding for some time before and after drinking. After another siesta they would come out late in the afternoon and feed until dark.

In the Adirondacks the deer often alter their habits completely at different seasons. Soon after the fawns are born they come down to the water's edge, preferring the neighborhood of the lakes, but also haunting the stream banks. The next three months, during the hot weather, 5 they keep very close to the water, and get a large proportion of their food by wading in after the lilies and other aquatic plants. Where they are much hunted, they only come to the water's edge after dark, but in regions where they are little disturbed they are quite as often diurnal 10 in their habits. I have seen dozens feeding in the neighborhood of a lake, some of them two or three hundred yards out of the shallow places, up to their bellies; and this after sunrise, or two or three hours before sunset. Before September the deer cease coming to the water, and 15 go back among the dense forests and on the mountains. There is no genuine migration, as in the case of the mule-deer, from one big tract to another, and no entire desertion of any locality. But the food supply which drew the animals to the water's edge during the summer months 20 shows signs of exhaustion toward fall; the delicate water-plants have vanished, the marsh-grass is dying, and the lilies are less succulent. An occasional deer still wanders along the shores or out into the lake, but most of them begin to roam the woods, eating the berries and the leaves 25 and twig ends of the deciduous trees, and even of some of the conifers, although a whitetail is fond of grazing, especially upon the tips of the grass itself. I have seen moose feeding on the tough old lily stems and wading after them when the ice had skimmed the edges of the 30 pool. But the whitetail has usually gone back into the woods long before freezing time.

From Long Island south there is not enough snow to make the deer alter their habits in the winter. As soon as the rut is over, which in different localities may be from October to December, whitetail are apt to band together—
5 more apt than at any other season, although even then they are often found singly or in small parties. While nursing, the does have been thin, and at the end of the rut the bucks are gaunt, with their necks swollen and distended. From that time on bucks and does alike put
10 on flesh very rapidly in preparation for the winter. Where there is no snow, or not enough to interfere with their travelling, they continue to roam anywhere through the woods and across the natural pastures and meadows, eating twigs, buds, nuts, and the natural hay which is
15 cured on the stalk.

In the northern woods they form yards during the winter. These yards are generally found in a hardwood growth which offers a supply of winter food, and consist simply of a tangle of winding trails beaten out through the snow
20 by the incessant passing and repassing of the animal. The yard merely enables the deer to move along the various paths in order to obtain food. If there are many deer together, the yards may connect by interlacing paths, so that a deer can run a considerable distance through them.
25 Often, however, each deer will yard by itself, as food is the prime consideration, and a given locality may only have enough to support a single animal. When the snows grow deep the deer is wholly unable to move, once the yard is left, and hence it is absolutely at the mercy of a
30 man on snow-shoes, or of a cougar or a wolf, if found at such times. The man on snow-shoes can move very comfortably; and the cougar and the wolf, although

hampered by the snow, are not rendered helpless like the
deer. I have myself scared a deer out of a yard and seen
it flounder helplessly in a great drift before it had gone
thirty rods. When I came up close it ploughed its way
a very short distance through the drifts, making tremen- 5
dous leaps. But as the snow was over six feet deep, so
that the deer sank below the level of the surface at each
jump, and yet could not get its feet on the solid ground,
it became so exhausted that it fell over on its side and
bleated in terror as I came up; after looking at it I passed 10
on. Hide hunters and frontier settlers sometimes go out
after the deer on snow-shoes when there is a crust, and
hence this method of killing is called crusting. It is simply
butchery, for the deer cannot, as the moose does, cause
its pursuer a chase which may last days. No self-respect- 15
ing man would follow this method of hunting save from
the necessity of having meat.

In very wild localities deer sometimes yard on the ice
along the edges of lakes, eating off att the twigs and
branches, whether of hardwood trees or of conifers, which 20
they can reach.

At the beginning of the rut the does flee from the bucks,
which follow them by scent at full speed. The whitetail buck rarely tries to form a herd of does, though
he will sometimes gather two or three. The mere fact 25
that his tactics necessitate a long and arduous chase after
each individual doe prevents his organizing herds as the
wapiti bull does. Sometimes two or three bucks will be
found strung out one behind the other, following the same
doe. The bucks wage desperate battle among them- 30
selves during this season, coming together with a clash;
and then pushing and straining for an hour or two at a

time, with their mouths open, until the weakest gives
way. As soon as one abandons the fight he flees with all
possible speed, and usually escapes unscathed.   While
head to head there is no opportunity for a disabling thrust,
5 but if, in the effort to retreat, the beaten buck gets caught,
he may be killed. Owing to the character of the antlers
whitetail bucks are peculiarly apt to get them interlocked
in such a fight, and if the efforts of the two beasts fail to
disentangle them, both ultimately perish by starvation.
10 I have several times come across a pair of skulls with
interlocked antlers. The same thing occurs, though far
less frequently, to the mule-deer and even the wapiti.

The whitetail is the most beautiful and graceful of all
our game animals when in motion. I have never been
15 able to agree with Judge Caton that the mule-deer is
clumsy and awkward in his gait. I suppose all such
terms are relative. Compared to the moose or caribou
the mule-deer is light and quick in his movements, and
to me there is something very attractive in the poise and
20 power with which one of the great bucks bounds off, all
four legs striking the earth together and shooting the
body upward and forward as if they were steel springs.
But there can be no question as to the infinitely superior
grace and beauty of the whitetail when he either trots
25 or runs. The mule-deer and blacktail bound, as already
described. The prongbuck gallops with an even gait,
and so does the bighorn, when it happens to be caught
on a flat; but the whitetail moves with an indescribable
spring and buoyancy. If surprised close up, and much
30 terrified, it simply runs away as hard as it can, at a gait
not materially different from that of any other game animal under like circumstances, while its head is thrust for-

ward and held down, and the tail is raised perpendicularly. But normally its mode of progression, whether it trots or gallops, is entirely unique. In trotting, the head and tail are both held erect, and the animal throws out its legs with a singularly proud and free motion, bringing the 5 feet well up, while at every step there is an indescribable spring. In the canter or gallop the head and tail are also held erect, the flashing white brush being very conspicuous. Three or four low, long, marvellously springy bounds are taken, and then a great leap is made high in the air, 10 which is succeeded by three or four low bounds, and then by another high leap. A whitetail going through the brush in this manner is a singularly beautiful sight. It has been my experience that they are not usually very much frightened by an ordinary slow trackhound, and 15 I have seen a buck play along in front of one, alternately trotting and cantering, head and flag up, and evidently feeling very little fear.

OBSERVATIONS ON CONCEALING COLORATION IN AFRICAN ANIMALS [1]

In Africa I was able to study for nearly a year the habits of the teeming myriads of great game, and many of my observations were made with special reference to this question of concealing coloration. The first, and by far
5 the most important, fact brought home to any competent observer is that as regards the great majority of these animals the question of cover infinitely outweighs the question of coloration in the problem of concealment; this being so true that when there is no adequate cover
10 most of the big animals do not trust to concealment at all, and concealment, whether of coloration or otherwise, plays no part in making their lives successful. Next comes the fact that there are some animals, chiefly the cats, whose peculiar physical address in hiding and in stealthy
15 approach and escape is such that their ability in this respect far outweighs the question of coloration, and even the question of cover, provided the cover is in any way adequate. Finally, there are some animals as to which it is possible that the coloration does have a concealing
20 effect of some importance.

The game that dwells in thick cover is extremely hard, not merely to shoot, but even to see; and it is the cover, and not the coloration of the animals, that is responsible for this. Indeed mere size seems to have a far greater
25 effect on visibility than does color; the bigger the animal,

[1] Reprinted by permission from "Revealing and Concealing Coloration in Birds and Mammals" in *Bulletin of the American Museum of Natural History*, vol. xxx, p. 119.

the easier it is to see. But sufficiently heavy cover shields even the heaviest game. In the high elephant grass, and in bamboos, as well as in dense forest, elephants disappear so completely that they can only be procured by following on their trail, and even their giant bodies, looming black 5 and large, are not visible to the peering, expectant hunter until but a few yards away. The buffalo, big, black, easily trailed, are, just because smaller, even more difficult to follow and see in thick cover, whether of reeds or jungle. Neither animal gets the slightest advantage from its color; 10 indeed the coloration of both is advertising; but in such cover the coloration is of no consequence, one way or the other. The hunter follows the trail, and if the beast does not hear or wind him, he finally catches a glimpse of it close up—just as the weasel follows the trail of a rabbit 15 or mouse until close enough for the jump. The difference is merely that the hunter follows the trail by sight, and the weasel by scent; doubtless the latter's sharp eyes come in use when the scent warns it that its quarry is close by; and there is no more warrant for supposing that the weasel 20 is misled by the "white stern sky pattern" on such of his victims as happen to possess such a pattern than for supposing that the hunter would be misled if an elephant were similarly ornamented.

Those rhinoceroses that dwell in the bush are hard to 25 see and hunt, whereas in the plains they are, next to the elephant and the giraffe, the most conspicuous animals. In the bush they owe their invisibility solely to the cover; their coloration is of no consequence one way or the other.

The lesser game animals of the thick cover vary so 30 widely in coloration as to render it impossible that the coloration of any one of them can be of real protective or concealing value. In the gloomy, wet mountain forests, choked with vines and undergrowth and down timber, the giant hog and the bongo are the two typical big game animals. The giant hog is almost black; the bongo, an antelope as big as an alderney cow, is brilliantly colored. The coloration of the bongo is, if anything, advertising rather than concealing—it is certainly advertising under any conditions which make the color of its co-dweller in the same haunts, the giant hog, concealing. But as a matter of fact the coloration has not the slightest effect in either revealing or concealing the presence of either animal. Each is so wary, and the extreme thickness of the cover serves each as such a complete shield, that they are hardly ever seen or shot by the best and most persevering white hunters, and only rarely killed by the wild, naked wood men themselves, unless with the assistance of dogs. The same is true as regards the effect of the coloration of the smaller animals found in the edges of the heavy timber, or in the lighter forests; the bush buck, reed buck, water buck, and bush pig. The bush buck in all its phases is a brilliantly colored antelope, bright chestnut or reddish, varied with white. Its coloration is always advertising. At first I thought the reed buck's coloration was under certain circumstances concealing, but further experience made me come to the conclusion and this was not so, and that I had been misled by the fact that its coloration was not so boldly advertising as the bush buck's. When driven out of a reed bed or thicket or when startled and dashing through one, the advertising effect on the vivid coloration was at once evident. The reed buck was much the easier of the two to see or shoot simply because it was generally found in

more open ground. Both owed their invisibility purely
to the thick cover in which they dwelt and to their own
ability in lying close or skulking stealthily off; their coloration, where it had any effect, was revealing and not
concealing. But the effect of the coloration is probably 5
negligible. It was practically impossible to see the grass-
dwelling reed buck while the grass was really long; and
it became quite conspicuous as soon as the grass was
burned. It was the grass and not the coloration which
determined whether it should be visible to the eyes of its 10
foes. When it ran it showed its white flag much like a
whitetail deer. The water bucks, of two species, were
sometimes found in thin forest or patches of dense forest,
and in papyrus beds, but more commonly in comparatively
open country. When in thick cover they often tried to 15
escape notice by standing motionless or sneaking quietly
off, and their coloration was certainly less conspicuous
than that of the two smaller antelope; but they themselves
were always more conspicuous because of their larger
size, their greater clumsiness in skulking, and especially 20
the more open nature of their haunts. One of the two
kinds of water buck had a white patch round the rump;
which was advertising. The bush pig was a dark colored
beast, less conspicuous than the antelope.

We found two antelopes dwelling in the thick swamps, 25
the situtunga and the white-withered lechwe. Both are
handsome, striking looking antelopes. The situtunga has
a shaggy, dark, nearly monocolored coat. Its coloration
is not advertising, in the sense that black or white is
advertising, but neither is it concealing, save as any nearly 30
uniform rather dull color is concealing, the extreme difficulty in seeing it—and save its cousin the bongo it is the

most difficult of all the big antelopes of East Africa to see—
arises practically exclusively from its secretive, stealthy
nature, and the impenetrable cover afforded by the beds
of reeds and papyrus in which it dwells. It ventures be-
5 yond the edges only at night, and then for but a short
distance. The white-withered lechwe dwells in the reed
beds and the edges of the papyrus swamps of the middle
White Nile. Its coloration is advertising instead of concealing, the old bucks in particular being very conspicuous
10 because of the white of their withers and the upper sides
of their necks; and it is a noisy creature, grunting continually. But it is not nearly as easy to see or to shoot as
are the antelope of the open plains, for it lives in dense
cover and seeks to avoid observation; it will stand motion-
15 less in the thick reeds or sneak off through them with
neck outstretched and head held low; it does not habitually jump up on ant hills to look about as is the custom
of its cousin the kob. The coloration of the doe is almost
exactly the same as that of the kob doe, although the
20 habitat and surroundings are different; the kob dwelling
on the open plains or among sparsely scattered clumps of
grass, bush and trees, where it is very visible, and makes
little effort to avoid observation, usually trusting to its
vigilance and sharp sight to enable it to see its foes at a
25 distance (although occasionally lying close like a reed
buck, in long grass); while the white-withered lechwe
spends its whole time in the reed beds, trusting to its
surroundings to shield it from the sight of any foe, these
surroundings being such that its coloration probably
30 makes no difference either way as far as concealment goes.
At any rate the bright red of the does, and the brilliant
white back and neck markings of the old bucks, seen

against the dark green of the endless reeds, must always be advertising where they have any effect at all.

Here are two water, or swamp, antelope, each trusting for safety mainly to eluding observation, and both living in practically the same surroundings, yet totally different 5 in color; and the one with the less concealing coloration is the one which lives under conditions that would make it more important to have a concealing coloration. The coloration in these cases must be a well-nigh or altogether negligible element from the concealing standpoint. A 10 similar lesson was impressed on me by my experience with the various antelope in the Lado, on the west bank of the upper White Nile, during our hunt after the white rhinoceros. For miles around our camp country was open, covered with tall grass and a sparse, scattering growth of 15 thorn trees, with occasional patches of brush and scrub. During our stay most of the grass was burnt. Where the grass was very long it was almost impossible to see or find any of the antelope, but where it was short or sparse, and especially where it was burnt, the difficulty vanished. 20 Hartebeest, water buck, kob, bush buck, oribi, and dyker were abundant. The bush buck's red coat was marked with white stripes and spots making the "checkered sun-fleck and leaf-shadowed" pattern which Mr. Thayer considers so potently obliterative. The other species 25 were almost uniformly colored—bright foxy red, straw-tinted, gray, brown. Of course if any one of these coloration patterns was concealing the others must have been advertising. But the difference in coloration sank into insignificance, so far as giving concealment was concerned, 30 compared to the difference in size. The bush buck was harder to see and kill than the water buck, kob or harte-

beest, simply because it kept closer to the thickets and
patches of long grass and was more given to skulking; but
the dyker was harder to see and kill than the bush buck,
in the Lado, although its coat was uniform in color with-
5 out any of the (purely fanciful) advantages Mr. Thayer
believes to come from such a "checkered" pattern as the
bush buck's; and this merely because the dyker was
smaller and was an even greater adept at twisting and
skulking through the grass and underbrush. All the ante-
10 lope were frequently found in exactly the same country;
although as a rule the water buck was the only one of the
bigger antelope which habitually wandered into the places
most affected by the bush buck and dyker—and it was
also habitually found in the favorite haunts of the kob
and hartebeest. The utterly different colorations of the
15 different animals had, in reality, no effect whatever as
regards rendering any one of them more invisible than the
others; but of these antelopes those that normally dwell
in the open plains were more visible than the others, under
like conditions, because they did not try to hide them-
20 selves.

So much for the animals which seek to conceal themselves, and which owe their escape from notice to the
cover in which they dwell and their ability to hide and
skulk. The majority of the big game of the parts of Africa
25 which I traversed dwell in the open, or very sparsely
wooded, plains, and do not seek to elude observation at
all. One thing that struck me about these animals was the
fact that the "countershading" on which Mr. Thayer
lays such stress played, so far as I could see, practically no
30 part whatever in concealing them. The animals of the
open plain were just as much countershaded as those of the

jungle; and, exactly as the animals with least counter-shading in the jungle were nevertheless as hard to see as the others, so on the open plain those with most counter-shading were no more concealed than those with practically none. The color itself, the hue of the animal, was of 5 infinitely more consequence than the countershading; although, if the ground was flat and the grass short, the color was of no consequence, because the animal, if stand-ing up, could be seen as far as the eye had power. Of two different species, both countershaded—zebras or harte- 10 beests, for instance and oryx or common eland—the first, if colored conspicuously, would be seen a mile or two off, while the other was still invisible; the difference of course being due to the difference in tint, the countershading being the same, and having practically no effect. I do not mean 15 that the countershading could have been neglected from the artistic or pictorial standpoint. Under certain cir-cumstances, it did make the animal lose its sharpness of outline at a slightly less distance than would otherwise have been the case. But it was of no consequence com- 20 pared to the general hue of coloration; and of course, if this general hue was unlike the surroundings, if there was no cover of bushes or of tall grass, and if the ground was flat, the animal could be made out anyhow, by any hunter, brute or human, at a long distance; within a few hundred 25 yards or less, the outlines were so vivid that the counter-shading was of no consequence whatever.

The giant eland of the Lado dwelt in a dry sunburnt country, covered with a sparse open growth of scantily leaved trees and bushes; the general tint of the coat, like 30 the general tint of the coat of the roan antelope which in the same locality, merged well with that of the general

landscape; but neither animal sought to skulk or hide,
or trusted to concealment, each placing reliance only on
its keen senses, and wariness. In East Africa, a buck
Grant's gazelle—not the doe or young, which have the
5 conspicuous lateral black stripe—an ordinary eland, a
roan, or an oryx, except when either of the latter animals
was looking round, so as to show the highly advertising
face coloring, might be difficult for the eye to pick up at
a distance, even when the wildebeest, topi, hartebeest or
10 zebra in the same landscape were plainly visible; but this
was merely because the coats of the four animals first
named were of much less conspicuous color than the coats
of the second four. The countershading on a wildebeest,
which shows dark against the green or brown or yellowish
15 plains, had, not merely practically, but absolutely, no
effect whatever in rendering it invisible, for it could be
seen as far as a black tree stump, for instance, could be
seen. Among leafless bushes and small thickets, and
clumps of tall dried grass, an oryx or roan or buck Grant
20 might if motionless, for a short time escape the notice of
untrained eyes, not because of the countershading, but
simply because in the flood of bright sunlight, the light,
washed-out color of the surrounding objects prevented
any vivid contrast and made the eye hesitate in picking
25 out the motionless antelope from its accidented, motionless, shaded and lighted, not very differently colored,
surroundings, although these surroundings were solid
objects. In other words, the reason for even this partial
invisibility was the direct reverse of what Mr. Thayer
30 claims; it was not in the least because the animals were
countershaded, for if their general color was in contrast
to that of their surroundings they stood out in bold re-

lief; it was simply because the eye was inattentive to individual objects in the multiplicity of objects, the effects of light and shade being practically the same on the buck and its surroundings, so that among the rocks and bushes and grass clumps and small euphorbias, the body of the 5 buck was not readily picked out.   It was chiefly to my own eyes, however, that the trouble was due; the native hunters who were with me could usually pick out the animal at once if within any reasonable distance.   Doubtless the same is true of a beast of prey, for evidently none 10 of these antelope, even when they ventured off the open bare plain into the brush, trusted to concealment; they made no effort to hide, and were constantly on the alert to detect foes.   But if in very thick and tall grass they did hide, lying still, in confidence that they could not be seen 15 unless stumbled upon; here of course their coloration had nothing to do with their concealment, which was due purely to the dense cover.   The only occasions when they were ever in any degree difficult to make out while in the bare open plains was when they laid down, when of course 20 the countershading was at a minimum compared to when they were standing up; the resting antelope looking like some inanimate object.   But in the open, even where lying down the antelope were watchful, and trusted in no way to concealment; only the very young fawns sought 25 safety in trying to escape observation, lying motionless with head and neck outstretched.

It was instructive to study the habits of the oribi under changed conditions.   The oribi is a small, graceful, swift antelope, well countershaded, with a neutral tinted back, 30 and no advertising marks.   Where the grass is long its habits are substantially those of the reed buck, stein-buck

and dyker; it lies close, trusting to the protection of the
thick cover, and is very difficult to see. But when the
grass has been burned, unlike the stein-buck and dyker
it takes to the bare open plains, and shows itself as much at
5 home on them as if it were a gazelle. Under these changed
conditions it ceases to make any effort to conceal itself,
or to trust in any way to concealment for protection,
relying purely on its eyesight, wariness, and speed. Although without such advertising markings as those of
10 the Tommy Gazelle, the oribi becomes conspicuous, simply because any animal is conspicuous when on a bare
plain, the "counter-gradation" of so-called obliterative
shadings entirely failing to conceal any creature, when
it alone is in question. Where fire had passed over the
15 plains shooting oribi was like shooting the small gazelle;
the little creature was easy to make out a long way off,
but great care was needful in order to stalk it within
rather long rifle range without being noticed.

Of the game habitually seen on the plains I have already
20 spoken of the elephant, rhinoceros, and then the buffalo,
all of which are also found—and in places much more frequently found—in forest or dense jungle. The giraffe
is ordinarily a beast of the open plains, feeding where
there is a sparse growth of thorn trees. Mr. Thayer states
25 that the giraffe's countershading and pattern "adequately
obliterate" it. As a matter of fact the giraffe is never
"adequately obliterated" by countershading or coloration pattern, or by anything else. It is, except the elephant, the most conspicuous of all animals. Its size and
30 shape advertise it unerringly to the dullest sighted lion
or native hunter; it can escape observation only if at such
a distance that no detail of its coloration would by any

chance be visible. The giraffe never under any circumstances seeks to avoid observation. Its one concern is to be so placed that it can itself observe any possible foe. We often found it in the same country with the rhinoceros, a monocolored beast; and in speaking of leopards 5 and giraffe (beasts by the way, which it is as absurd to treat together as so to treat lions and elephants) Mr. Thayer especially dwells on their invisibility as compared with beasts which are "monochrome objects." But the rhinoceros more often eluded hasty observation than did 10 the giraffe, and was less often seen at a very long distance, simply because the height and shape of the giraffe, and the fact that it hardly ever lies down, made it the more conspicuous object of the two. Any animal, of any size, shape or color, may under certain circumstances 15 escape observation, and a man of poor or untrained vision may fail to see animals which could not possibly elude keen eyes, brute or human, if accustomed to the wilderness. But save under wholly exceptional circumstances no brute or human foe of the giraffe could possibly fail to 20 see the huge creature if fairly close by; and at a distance the pattern of the coloration would be lost. The giraffe owes nothing to concealment; its coloration has not the slightest concealing or obliterative effect so far as its foes are concerned. 25

The zebra has also, very absurdly, been taken as an example of "concealing coloration." Men unused to the consideration of the subject are often surprised when they go outdoors to discern how difficult it is to see any animal— just as a raw city-bred recruit, during his first campaigns, 30 finds it difficult to locate even a civilized foe, and impossible to locate a savage foe, such as an Indian. The more

conspicuous the animal the greater is the surprise of the
average man when he fails to find it as conspicuous in the
landscape as he had supposed; he thinks of a zebra, for instance, as jumping to the eye as it does in a menagerie;
5 and when he finds this not to be the case, he goes to the
opposite extreme and supposes that the zebra's coloration
is concealing. As a matter of fact it is not concealing,
it is highly advertising, when close at hand; but when
over three or four hundred yards off the black and white
10 stripes merge together, and the coat becomes monocolored, but catches the sunlight in such shape as still to
render the bearer conspicuous. The narrow stripes of the
big Grévey's zebra fade together at a shorter distance
than is the case with the broader stripes of the smaller
15 zebra; the broad bands on the rump of the latter can be
seen at a long distance. The zebra is purely a beast of the
open plains; it never seeks to conceal itself, but trusts always to seeing its foes. When under or among thin
leaved, scattered thorn trees it is still usually conspicuous;
20 although now and then a peculiar light and shadow effect
may conceal it. It never goes into thick cover save at
drinking places, and then only if it is unavoidable; it does
not come down stealthily to drink, but openly and warily,
always on the watch and continually galloping off on false
25 alarms; it returns to the plains as soon as it has drank;
and as such an animal can never escape observation when
in motion, and as it is never motionless when at or near
the drinking places, it is impossible that its coloration
can in any way conceal it at such times. Mr. Thayer's
30 ingenious theories of how all the various stripings on a
zebra obliterate it are without the smallest foundation in
fact. So far as the coloration of the zebra has any effect

at all, as regards beasts of prey, it is an advertising, not a concealing, effect. The wildebeest and topi, which are found in company with it, are more conspicuous; the hartebeests sometimes more and sometimes less, according to the sunlight; the eland and oryx and gazelle less. 5 A moment's thought ought to show Mr. Thayer and his adherents that animals so differently colored as these, all leading their lives under similar conditions, cannot possibly all be concealingly colored. As a matter of fact none of them owe their safety to concealing coloration, 10 and the majority of them are advertisingly colored. In East Africa the lion preys chiefly on zebra and hartebeest, which live under precisely the same conditions, have the same habits and associate in the same herds; yet two more differently colored animals cannot be im- 15 agined, and neither is concealed in the slightest degree by its coloration. Among the hunter-naturalists to whom we owe most of our knowledge of the enthrallingly interesting life-histories of African big game, Captain Stigand comes second only to Mr. Selous. When I wrote of pro- 20 tective coloration in "African Game Trails," I had had opportunity only to glance at Stigand's admirable book on the game of British East Africa. In this he discusses the subject in masterly fashion, and with a knowledge that could only come to a trained big game hunter and 25 field naturalist gifted with exceptionally keen powers of observation and analysis. I quote a few lines: "Very few animals seem to rely on protective coloration as a means of escaping observation, however they may be colored. They appear to rely on fleetness of foot, quick- 30 ness of eye and ear, or on scenting powers . . . (the animals that do trust to hiding) seem to rely more on cover

and concealment or partial concealment than on any great
similarity to natural objects . . . even if (the larger game
of the plains) were perfect examples of protective har-
mony, which I do not admit, it would avail them little
5 when their lives are spent in walking about in the open.
For a moving object even if it assimilates in color to its
surroundings always catches the eye of a practiced observer. The two most absurd, but often quoted, examples
of wonderful instances of protective coloration are the
10 zebra and the giraffe. It is true that the zebra in very
long grass is sometimes difficult to pick out, but so is any
animal almost entirely concealed from view—even an
elephant if the grass in long enough. In their usual East
African habitat (the plains) zebras are strikingly con-
15 spicuous, turning from black to white as they move and
their sides are alternately in shadow or exposed sunlight. . . . A giraffe near, or even in the far distance,
when not screened from view, is a most conspicuous object to the practiced eye."

ANIMALS OF CENTRAL BRAZIL [1]

WHEN I contemplated going on this trip° the first thing I did was to get in touch with Dr. Frank M. Chapman of the American Museum. I wanted to get from him information as to what we could do down there and whether it would be worth while for the Museum to send a couple 5 of naturalists with me. On any trip of this kind—on any kind of a trip I have ever taken—the worth of the trip depends not upon one man but upon the work done by several men in co-operation. This journey to South America would have been not worth the taking, had it 10 not been for the two naturalists from the American Museum who were with me, and for the Brazilian officers° skilled in cartographical work who joined the expedition.

I thought of making the trip a zoölogical one only, when I started from New York, but when I reached Rio Janeiro 15 the Minister of Foreign Affairs, Mr. Lauro Müller, whom I had known before, told me that he thought there was a chance of our doing a piece of geographical work of importance. In the course of the work of the telegraph commission under Colonel Rondon, a Brazilian engineer, 20 there had been discovered the headwaters of a river running north through the center of Brazil. To go down that river, and put it on the map would be interesting, but he wanted to tell me that one cannot guarantee what may happen on unknown rivers—there might be some 25

[1] A lecture delivered before the members of the American Museum of Natural History, December 10, 1914. Reprinted by permission from the *American Museum Journal*, vol. xv, page 35, (February, 1915.)

303

surprises before we got through. Of course we jumped at
the chance, and at once arranged to meet Colonel Rondon
and his assistants at the head of the Paraguay, to go down
from there with them.

5   We touched at Bahia and Rio Janeiro and then came
down by railway across southern Brazil and Uruguay to
Buenos Aires and went through the Argentine over to
Chili. We traveled south through Chili and then crossed
the Andes. That sounds a very elaborate thing to do, but
10 as a matter of fact it was pure pleasure. It was a wonderful trip. The pass through which we crossed was like the
Yosemite, with snow-capped volcanic mountains all
about. Afterward we went across Patagonia by auto-
mobile and then started up the Paraguay. Our work did
15 not begin until we were inside the Tropic of Capricorn.
We took mules at Tapirapoan and went up through the
high central plateau of Brazil—not a fertile country but
I have no question but that great industrial communities
will grow up there.

20   The hard work on the unknown river came during the
first six weeks. In those forty-two days we made only an
average of about a mile and a half a day and toward the
end we were not eating any more than was necessary and
that was largely monkey and parrot. The parrots were
25 pretty good when they were not tough but I can assure
Mr. Hornaday that he could leave me alone in the monkey
cage at the New York Zoölogical Gardens with perfect
safety.

Both of the naturalists who were with me and I myself
30 were interested primarily in mammalogy and ornithology.
We were not entomologists and studied only those insects
that forced themselves upon our attention. There were

two or three types that were welcome. The butterflies were really wonderful. I shall never forget the spectacle in certain places on the Unknown River where great azure blue butterflies would fly about up and down through the glade or over the river. Some of the noises made by insects were extraordinary. One insect similar to a katydid made a noise that ended with a sound like a steamboat whistle.

We found the mosquitoes bad in only two or three places. On the Paraguay marshes there were practically no mosquitoes. In that great marsh country where I should suppose mosquitoes would swarm, there were scarcely any. Our trouble was chiefly with gnats. These little flies were at times a serious nuisance. We had to wear gauntlets and helmets and we had to tie the bottom of our trouser legs. When we stopped on one occasion to build canoes, two or three of our camaradas were so crippled with the bites of the gnats that they could hardly walk. The wasps and stinging bees were also very obnoxious and at times fairly dangerous. There were ants we called foraging ants that moved in dense columns and killed every living thing that could not get out of the way. If an animal is picketed in the line of march of these foraging ants, they are likely to kill it in short time.

There is also a peculiar ant called the leaf ant which doesn't eat a man but devours his possessions instead. I met with a tragedy one night myself. We had come down the Unknown River and had lost two or three canoes and had to portage whatever we had over the mountain. We had to throw away everything that was not absolutely necessary. I reduced my own baggage to one change of clothing. We got into camp late and Cherrie and I had

our two cots close together and did not get the fly up until after dark.   My helmet had an inside lining of green
and I had worn a red handkerchief around my neck.   At
night I put my spectacles and the handkerchief in the
5 hat.   The next morning I looked out of bed preparing
to get my spectacles.   I saw a red and green line.   It was
moving.   There was a procession of these leaf-bearing ants
with sections of my handkerchief and hat.   I had had one
spare pair of socks and one spare set of underclothing and
10 I needed them both.   By morning I had part of one sock
and the leg and waistband of the underwear and that was
all.   It is amusing to look back at but it was not amusing
at the time.

The most interesting fish that we became acquainted
15 with was called the "cannibal fish," ° the "man-eating
fish."   It is about the size of our shad with a heavily
undershot jaw and very sharp teeth.   So far as I know,
it is the only fish in the world that attacks singly or in
shoals animals much larger than itself.   Cannibal fishes
20 swarm in most of the rivers of the region we passed
through, in most places not very dangerous, in others
having the custom of attacking man or animals, so that
it is dangerous for anyone to go into the water.   Blood
maddens them.   If a duck is shot, they will pull it to pieces
25 in a very few minutes.

This side of Corumba a boy who had been in swimming
was attacked in midstream by these fishes and before
relief could get to him, he had not only been killed but
half eaten.   Two members of our party suffered from them.
30 Colonel Rondon after carefully examining a certain spot
in the river went into the water and one of these fishes
bit off his little toe.   On another occasion on the Unknown

River,° Mr. Cherrie went into the water thinking he could take his bath right near shore and one of the fish bit a piece out of his leg.

One of the most extraordinary things we saw was this. On one occasion one of us shot a crocodile. It rushed 5 back into the water. The fish attacked it at once and they drove that crocodile out of the water back to the men on the bank. It was less afraid of the men than the fish.

We were interested one day in a certain big catfish, 10 like any other big catfish except that it had a monkey inside of it. I had never heard that a catfish could catch monkeys but it proved to be a fact. The catfish lives at the bottom of the water. The monkeys come down on the ends of branches to drink and it seems to be no un- 15 common thing for the fish to come to the surface and attack the monkey as it stoops to drink. Our Brazilian friends told us that in the Amazon there is a gigantic catfish nine feet long. The natives are more afraid of it than of the crocodile because the crocodile can be seen 20 but the catfish is never seen until too late. In the villages, poles are stacked in the water so that women can get their jars filled with water, these stockades of poles keeping out the giant crocodile and catfish. I had never seen in any book any allusions to the fact that there is 25 a man-eating fish of this type in the Amazon.

One day when we were going down the Unknown River Mr. Cherrie and I in the same canoe, we saw a flying fish. Of course everyone knows about the flying fish on the ocean but I had no idea there were flying fish on the 30 South American streams. I very much wish that some ichthyologist would go down to South America and come back with not not only a collection of the fishes but also full notes on their life histories.

We did not see very many snakes, I suppose only about twenty venomous ones. The most venomous are 5 those somewhat akin to our rattle-snakes but with no rattles. One of the most common is the jararaca, known in Martinique as the fer-de-lance. One of the biggest is called the bushmaster and attains a length of about ten feet. These snakes are very poisonous and very dan- . 10 gerous. The mussurama is another South American snake, and it lives on poisonous snakes. It habitually kills and eats dangerous reptiles, its most common prey being the jararaca. I saw the feat performed at a lab- oratory where poisonous snakes are being studied to secure 15 antidotes to the poisons and to develop enemies to the snakes themselves. Such an enemy is this mussurama which must be like our king snake—but larger. The king snake is a particularly pleasant snake; it is friendly toward mankind, not poisonous and can be handled 20 freely. The scientists at the laboratory brought out a big good-natured mussurama which I held between my arm and coat. Then they brought out a fairly large fer-de- lance about nine inches shorter than. the mussurama and warning me to keep away, put it on the table. Then they 25 told me to put my snake where it could get at the fer-de- lance. I put down my snake on the table and it glided up toward the coiled fer-de-lance. My snake was perfectly free from excitement and I did not suppose it meant to do anything, that it was not hungry. It put its "nose" 30 against the body of the fer-de-lance and moved toward the head. The fer-de-lance's temper was aroused and it coiled and struck. The return blow was so quick that

I could not see just what happened. The mussurama had the fer-de-lance by the lower jaw, the mouth wide open. The latter struck once again. After that it made no further effort to defend itself in any way. The poisonous snake is a highly specialized creature and practically helpless 5 when once its peculiarly specialized traits are effectively nullified by an opponent. The mussurama killed the snake and devoured it by the simple process of crawling outside of it. Many snakes will not eat if people interfere with them, but the mussurama had no prejudices in this 10 respect. We wanted to take a photograph of it while eating, so I took both snakes up and had them photographed against a white cloth while the feast went on uninterruptedly.

Birds and mammals interested me chiefly, however. I 15 am only an amateur ornithologist but I saw a great deal there that would be of interest to any of us who care for birds. For instance there are two hundred and thirteen families of birds very plentiful there, either wholly unknown to us, or at least very few of them known.   20

The most conspicuous birds I saw were members of the family of tyrant flycatchers, like our kingbird, great crested flycatcher and wood pewee. All are birds that perch and swoop for insects. One species, the bientevido, is a big bird like our kingbird, but fiercer and more power- 25 ful than any northern kingbird. One day I saw him catching fish and little tadpoles and also I found that he would sometimes catch small mice. Another kind of tyrant, the red-backed tyrant, is a black bird with reddish on the middle of the back. We saw this species first out on the 30 bare Patagonian plains. It runs fast over the ground exactly like our pippit or longspur.

Curved-bill wood-hewers, birds the size and somewhat the coloration of veeries, but with long, slender sickle-bills were common about the gardens and houses.

Most of the birds build large nests. The oven-birds 5 build big, domed nests of mud. Telegraph poles offer splendid opportunities for building nests. Sometimes for miles every telegraph pole would have an oven-bird's nest upon it. These birds come around the houses. They look a little bit like wood thrushes and are very interest- 10 ing in that way they have all kinds of individual ways. The exceedingly beautiful honey creepers are like clusters of jet. They get so familiar that they come into the house and hop on the edge of the sugar bowl.

The people living on many of the ranches in Brazil 15 make us rather ashamed for our own people. The ranch-men protect the birds and it is possible to see great jabiru storks nesting not fifty yards from the houses, and not shy.

Most of the birds in Brazil are not musical although 20 some of them have very prettty whistles. The oven-bird has an attractive call. The bell-bird of the gray hue (contrasted with the white bell-bird) has a ringing whistle which sounds from the topmost branches of the trees.

25   The mammals were a great contrast to what I had seen in Africa. Africa is the country for great game. There is nothing like that in South America. The animals in South America are of interest to the naturalist more than to the person who is traveling through the country and 30 takes the ordinary layman's point of view. Only two of the animals found there are formidable. One of these is the jaguar, the king of South American game, ranking

on an equality with the noblest beasts of the chase of North America, second only to the huge and fierce creatures which stand at the head of the big game of Africa and Asia. The great spotted creatures are very beautiful. Like all cats they are easily killed with a pack of hounds, but they are very difficult to come upon otherwise. They will charge men and sometimes become man-eaters.

Another big mammal of the Brazilian forest is the white-lipped peccary. The white-lipped peccaries herd together in the dense jungles in packs of thirty or forty or sometimes as many as two or three hundred. They are formidable creatures. The young ones may be no larger than a setter dog but they have tremendous tusks. They surge and charge together and I think that they may legitimately be called dangerous. On one occasion Cherrie was hunting peccaries and the peccaries treed him. He was up there four hours. He found those four hours a little monotonous, I judge. I never had any adventure with them myself. They make queer moaning grunts. We spent a couple of days in getting the specimens that we brought back. We had four dogs with us. The ranchman had loaned them to us although I doubt whether they really wished to let us have them, for the big peccary is a murderous foe of dogs. One of them frankly refused to let his dogs come, explaining that the fierce wild swine were "very badly brought up" and that respectable dogs and men ought not to go near them. We might just as well not have taken any dogs, however. Two of them as soon as they smelled the peccaries went home. The third one made for a thicket about a hundred yards away and stayed there until he was sure which would come out ahead. The fourth advanced only when there was a man ahead of him. The dangerous little peccaries made fierce moaning grunts on their way through the jungle and rattled their tusks like castanets whenever we came up.

Armadillos were unexpectedly interesting because they ran so fast. Once on a jaguar hunt we came upon two of the big nine-banded armadillos, which are called the "big armadillos." The dogs raced at them. One of the armadillos got into the thick brush. The other ran for a hundred yards with the dogs close upon it, wheeled and came back like a bullet right through the pack. Its wedged-shaped snout and armored body made the dogs totally unable to seize or stop it. It came back right toward us and got into the thick brush and so escaped. Other species of armadillo do not run at all.

The anteaters, most extraordinary creatures of this latter-day world, are found only in South America. The anteater is about the size of a small black bear and has a long narrow toothless snout, a long bushy tail and very powerful claws on its fore feet. It walks on the sides of its fore feet with the claws curved in under the foot. These powerful claws make it a formidable enemy for the dogs. But it goes very slowly. Anteaters were continually out in the open marshes where we got the two specimens that we sent to the Museum. They were always on muddy ground, and in the papyrus swamp we found them in several inches of water. I do not see how they continue to exist in a country with jaguars and pumas. They are too slow to run away and they are very conspicuous and make no effort to conceal themselves.

The great value of our trip will be shown only when full studies have been made of the twenty-five hundred and more specimens of birds and mammals brought back.

We will be able to give for the first time an outline of the mammalogy and ornithology of central Brazil.

Probably the most important feature of the trip was going down the Unknown River, because, of course, at this stage of geographical history it is a rare thing to 5 be able to put on the map a new river, a river never explored, a river the length of the Rhine of which not a line is to be found on any map.

It was a journey well worth taking, a rough trip of course, but I shall always be more grateful than I can say 10 to Professor Osborn and Dr. Chapman of the American Museum for having sent Mr. Cherrie and Mr. Miller with me, thus enabling me to take part in a zoö-geographical reconnaissance of a part of the Brazilian wilderness.

NOTES

AUTOBIOGRAPHY

In 1913 Roosevelt published his autobiography under the title *Theodore Roosevelt, An Autobiography.* " Naturally," he wrote in the Preface, " there are chapters in my autobiography which cannot now be written," but incomplete though the book is, it covers the greater part of his career. Appearing as it did while he was still active in politics, the book is in large measure a defense of political acts and policies. Still there is a great deal that is purely personal, and it must be said that if one could read but one book of Roosevelt's, it would be the book to select for this purpose. The chapters represented in this book have been condensed without destroying their connectedness.

BOYHOOD AND YOUTH

1 : 5. Curtis. George William Curtis (1824–92) was an American writer noted for his pleasing sketches and essays. Among these was the *Potiphar Papers* (1853), a series of satirical sketches of New York society.

2 : 13. moujik. A Russian peasant.

2 : 14. malachite. A green stone, the finest specimens of which come from Siberian mines.

2 : 28. Grant. Ulysses S. Grant (1822–85) was the commander-in-chief of the Union forces in the latter part of the Civil War.

315

3 : 21. Roosevelt. Theodore Roosevelt, Senior (1831–1878), was a glass importer in New York City, widely known for his philanthropy and activity in charitable and reform movements.

5 : 11. Martha Bulloch. On his mother's side, Roosevelt was descended from some of the best-known families of the South, combining in his veins the blood of both Scotch-Irish and Huguenot ancestors. His great-great-grandfather, Archibald Bulloch, was a member of the Continental Congress, and the first State Governor of Georgia. One of his great-grandfathers, Daniel Stewart, was a brigadier-general in the Continental army. His mother, Martha Bulloch, married Theodore Roosevelt, Sr., at her father's home at Roswell, Cobb County, Georgia, in 1853. Mrs. Roosvelt's brother, James D. Bulloch, was an officer of the Confederate navy, and acted during the greater part of the war as a secret agent for the Confederacy in England, where he contracted for the purchase of the privateers *Florida* and *Georgia*.

5 : 13. " Unreconstructed." The expression means that Roosevelt's mother never gave up her belief in the justness of the political ideals for which her section, the South, contended in the Civil War.

6 : 16. Boone and Crockett. The horses were named for Daniel Boone (1735–1820) and David Crockett (1786–1836), both famous American backwoodsmen and pioneers.

6 : 18. Buena Vista. The battle of Buena Vista, fought February 22 and 23, 1847, resulted in a decisive victory for the Americans over the Mexicans.

6 : 20. " Br'er Rabbit " stories. The animal stories popular among the negroes make the rabbit oftentimes the hero. Many of these stories were first collected by

Joel Chandler Harris and published in his " Uncle Remus " books. Roosevelt's aunt, however, had learned the stories first-hand from Georgia negroes.

6 : 23. " Harper's." *Harper's Monthly* is one of the oldest and most distinguished of American literary periodicals.

6 : 24. genius. Joel Chandler Harris (1848–1908). The negro folk-tales which Harris collected and published were told by an imaginary negro named Uncle Remus. Hence the name was applied to the writer, although it was not in any wise the author's *nom de plume*.

7 : 11. interest in natural history. For a fuller account of Roosevelt's early interest in natural history, see the selection given in this book entitled " My Life as a Naturalist."

7 : 19. Reid's Books. Mayne Reid (1818–83). An English writer of hunting romances and stories of adventure. He himself led a wandering and adventurous life, and his books often are based on his own experiences. Although born in England, he spent many years of his life in the United States, and his books oftentimes have that country as a background. In his later years he returned to England. Some of his best known books are *The Rifle Rangers* (1850), *Scalp Hunters* (1851), *White Chief* (1859), *Afloat in the Forest* (1865) and *The Castaways* (1870).

9 : 4. Audubon's. John James Audubon (1780–1851) was an American naturalist who especially devoted himself to the study of birds. He eventually gave up all business pursuits and spent his time roaming hither and thither in the forests making observation of bird and animal life. His greatest production, *Birds of North America* (1831–39), consisted of five volumes of drawings and descriptions of American birds, the drawings, of which there were over four hundred, being life-size.

9 : 5. Mr. Venus's Shop. The description of the queer, cluttered-up shop of this taxidermist and " articulator of human bones " may be found in Chapter VII of Dickens's *Our Mutual Friend.*

9 : 32. Spencer Baird (1823–87). An American naturalist who was for many years connected with the Smithsonian Institution. Among the most important of his publications were *Catalogue of North American Reptiles* (1853), *Birds of North America* (1860), *Mammals of North America* (1859), and *History of North American Birds* (1874–84).

10 : 4. Europe. Roosevelt's first trip to Europe was a short one made when he was ten years old. The second one was four years later. His account of it, which is here omitted, shows that he devoted much of his time to bird collecting, especially while he was in Egypt.

10 : 16. Harvard. Harvard University at Cambridge, Massachusetts, is the oldest as well as one of the most influential universities in the United States.

10 : 23. Mr. Cutler. Roosevelt completed his preparation for Harvard under Mr. Arthur Cutler, who afterwards founded the Cutler School in New York.

10 : 24. Hill. Adams Sherman Hill (1833–1910) was for many years professor of rhetoric in Harvard University. He was a remarkably stimulating teacher in this subject.

10 : 26. Eliot. Charles William Eliot (1834–), has been for many years one of the foremost figures in American education. During the larger part of his career he was president of Harvard University, a position which he filled with notable distinction until his retirement in 1909.

10 : 28. Forensics. College exercises in spoken or written discussion.

11 : 9. Gracchi. Two Roman brothers who were upholders of the interests of the people. The older one, Tiberius Sempronius, endeavored to restore to the peasant class their small holdings of land. The younger, Caius Sempronius, endeavored to establish in Rome more of a pure democracy than existed under the aristocratic republican form of government. Both brothers lost their lives in insurrections resulting from their political activities, the former in 133 B. C., the latter in 121 B. C.

12 : 19. Phi Beta Kappa. A Greek letter organization existing in many American colleges, admission to which is granted upper classmen who attain a superior average of scholarship.

12 : 22. Wilson. Alexander Wilson (1766–1813) was an American ornithologist. He emigrated from Scotland to the United States where for several years he worked as weaver, peddler, and school teacher. Finally his interest in birds led him to undertake to make a comprehensive collection of drawings of American birds. To collect material and gather subscriptions, the author travelled extensively in all parts of the country and endured many hardships. Seven volumes of his projected work were prepared by him during his lifetime, but his death left to other hands the completing of the work.

12 : 23. Coues. Eliot Coues (1842–99) was an American naturalist particularly known for his researches in ornithology.

12 : 23. Merriam. Clinton Hart Merriam (1855–). An American naturalist. From 1885–1910, he was chief of the United States Biological Survey. This position he resigned in order to conduct biological investigations under a special trust fund established by Mrs. E. H. Harriman.

12 : 24. Chapman. Frank Michler Chapman (1864–). An American ornithologist. He has written many books about birds of a popular scientific character.

12 : 24. Hornaday. William Temple Hornaday (1854–). An American zoölogist who has been since 1896 director of the New York Zoölogical Park. He has been active in promoting game preserves and new laws for the protection of wild life generally. He has spent much time in travelling in the United States and other countries on scientific expeditions and has written delightfully about his experiences.

15: 12. Dark Ages. A designation sometimes given to the Middle Ages (approximately 476–1453), or, more especially to the earlier part of this period. It was the time of feudalism and civilization was generally ruder and more barbaric than during the preceding Classical Age. In the political theories of the time the individual was held to be higher than the state.

The Vigor of Life

16 : 6. Valley Forge. The Pennsylvania village where Washington and the American Army passed the winter of 1777–78 amid great privations.

16 : 7. Morgan's riflemen. The Revolutionary riflemen under General Daniel Morgan (1736–1802) fought bravely at the battle of Saratoga in 1777.

16 : 16. Moosehead Lake. A large lake, about thirty-five miles long, in Northern Maine.

17 : 11. Heenan. In 1860, there was an international

boxing bout between Tom Sayers, the English champion, and John Heenan. The contest was declared a draw, when, after two hours of fighting, the spectators rushed into the ring and ended the fight.

18 : 27. Aroostook. A river in northern Maine.

18 : 29. Matterhorn. A peak of the Alps, noted for its steepness. It is 14,703 feet high.

18 : 30. Jungfrau. One of the chief peaks in the Alps, having a height of 13,670 feet.

19 : 2. Sagamore Hill. Roosevelt's home on Long Island. See page 67 for an account of the origin of the name.

19 : 4. South African War. From 1899–1902, there was a conflict for supremacy in South Africa between Great Britain and the Boer republics of the Transvaal and the Orange Free State. The outcome was a victory for the British.

19 : 7. Stewart Edward White (1873–), the author of several books on Western life, is himself an experienced hunter and woodsman.

20 : 1. " buck fever." Nervous excitement on the part of a hunter, especially an inexperienced one, when he finds a deer or other game approaching.

22 : 11. Governor. Roosevelt was Governor of New York State from 1899 to 1900.

In the fall of 1898, politics in New York State were in an upheaval. Governor Black's administration was unpopular, and unless a candidate could be found so popular on his own account as to pull the Republicans through, the chances were that the Democrats would repeat their success of the past year. Because of the widespread popularity that had come to Roosevelt in connection with his

Rough Rider regiment and its part in the Spanish-American War, he seemed the most suitable man, and the Republican State Convention nominated him. After an exciting campaign between Augustus Van Wyck, the Democratic candidate, Theodore Bacon, the independent candidate, and Roosevelt, the latter was elected.

Of Roosevelt's administration, it has been said that his two years at Albany saw more constructive and reconstructive legislation placed on the statute books than the entire decade which had preceded it. The Civil Service Law was amended and enforced strictly—" putting the starch into it," Roosevelt called it. He personally investigated the tenement-house problem of New York City, and then secured the passage of a radical act that went far toward its solution. Among the laws enacted affecting the laboring classes were an eight-hour law, a law providing for the licensing of employment agencies, and stringent factory laws, which, by the establishment of a licensing system, practically wiped out the worst abuses of the " sweat-shops."

No piece of legislation was more earnestly pressed by Governor Roosevelt than the Corporation Franchise Tax law. It was his first step in the development of a policy which he afterwards advocated in a wider field—namely, the requirement that wealthy corporations should be required to pay their just proportion of the expenses of running the Government.

As the time drew near for the Republican National Convention in 1900, it was evident that there was a strong movement on foot to nominate Roosevelt for Vice-President on the same ticket with President McKinley. Those who were engaged in promoting his candidacy were not, however, all actuated by the same motives. Especially was this true of the advocates of his nomination in his own State. During his administration he had been a thorn in the flesh to Senator Platt, the Republican leader of New York State, and the machine politicians. It was their desire to eliminate him from State politics, and shelve him in the office of Vice-President for the time being at least. Roosevelt perceived this intention and was very reluctant to accept the nomination. But party pressure brought him in the end to consent to the plan. In the fall he and McKinley were easily elected.

23 : 5. Single stick. The art of attack and defence with single sticks, i. e., a staff fitted with a guard like that of a saber.

23 : 5. Wood. Leonard Wood (1860–). See Roosevelt's account of his early career, page 60. In recent years he has risen to the highest rank in the American Army.

23 : 13. jiu-jitzu. A form of wrestling practiced by the Japanese.

23 : 27. Hayes. An American athlete who won the Marathon race in the international Olympic games of 1908, held at London.

24 : 4. " The Strenuous Life." An extract from this address may be found in this volume, page 166. The entire address may be found in Roosevelt's book entitled *The Strenuous Life*.

24 : 8. Manchurian. The military operations of the Russo-Japanese War (1904–05) were chiefly on Manchurian soil.

25 : 2. "Ode on a Grecian Urn." A notable poem by John Keats (1795–1821).

25 : 2. The Gettysburg Speech. Lincoln's speech delivered at the dedication of the Gettysburg National Cemetery, November 19, 1863.

25 : 3. Frederick. Frederick the Great (1620–1688) King of Prussia, won at Leuthen, December 5, 1757, a notable victory over an Austrian army under Prince Charles of Lorraine.

25 : 3. Nelson. Admiral Nelson (1758–1805), in command of the British fleet, won the famous victory over the French in the battle off Cape Trafalgar, October 19, 1805.

26 : 14. Marryat's books. Frederick Marryat (1792–1848) was an English novelist who wrote many stories of sea life. He was himself an officer in the English navy for many years. *Peter Simple* and *Mr. Midshipman Easy* are among his best known stories.

ENTERING POLITICS

Roosevelt began his political career under the following circumstances: In the fall of 1881, he was nominated by the Republicans of the old Twenty-first District of New York City as their candidate for the state assembly. The nomination came to him unexpectedly and unsought. There had been a revolt against the district leader, "Jake" Hess, in which young Roosevelt had taken an active part. Hess's candidate was turned down and the opposition settled upon Roosevelt, less than a year and a half out of college, and with no political record to hamper him. Roosevelt had already identified himself with the reform element in the city, and belonged to a club devoted to the furthering the principles of free trade, which he had accepted in college, but as he was "regular" so far as party affiliations were concerned, Hess acquiesced in his choice. After a spirited campaign, Roosevelt was elected.

28 : 3. Thayer. Ezra Ripley Thayer (1866–1915) was an American lawyer and educator. For many years he was Dane professor of law at Harvard University and dean of the Law School. Roosevelt studied law at the Columbia University Law School and in the office of his uncle, Robert B. Roosevelt.

28 : 8. Caveat emptor. A legal phrase signifying that the purchaser of land or goods takes his chances as to the title or quality of the property acquired by him.

30 : 7. Elected to the Legislature. For awhile, as Roosevelt states in his *Autobiography*, he took little part in the debates, but watched and learned. Suddenly, about the middle of the session, he dumbfounded the party leaders by demanding the investigation of a certain judge. He was voted down and his friends urged him to drop the matter, assuring him that such independence would mean his political death. He persisted in his demand stubbornly day after day until he got a majority of the Assembly with him, and the investigation was provided for.

This was his first personal political victory, and from then on in the Legislature, he was a force to be reckoned with. In 1882, he was reëlected by a large majority, despite the fact that this was a year which saw the Democratic party triumphant in the state, especially in the election of Grover Cleveland as Governor. In 1883, Roosevelt was elected for a third term. During his second term he was the Republican floor leader, and in his third, was a candidate for the Speakership, but was defeated.

The struggle over the Republican Presidential nomination of 1884 began in New York on the choice of delegates to the State Convention. Roosevelt had to defeat his old opponent, Jacob Hess, before he himself could secure a place as delegate to the State Convention at Utica. This he was able to do, and he went to the Convention an enthusiastic partisan of Edmunds, of Vermont, who was the candidate supported by the reform element of the Republican party. The Convention was divided between supporters of Arthur, Blaine, and Edmunds, and the delegates to the National Convention, of whom Roosevelt was one, were uninstructed.

In the proceedings of the National Convention at Chicago, he took a prominent part. During the bitter struggle among these three candidates for the nomination, he worked and voted steadfastly for Edmunds, and was one of those who voted for him upon the final ballot which gave the nomination to Blaine.

After the Convention Roosevelt went West to his ranch in North Dakota to think over the situation in quiet and make up his mind what course to take. Many of his friends among the reform element in his party were announcing that they would carry their opposition to the nominee, Blaine, to the extent of voting for the Democratic candidate.

But to Roosevelt the idea of breaking with his party did not appear to be tenable. Having reached this decision he gave out the following public statement: " I intend to vote the Republican presidential ticket. A man cannot act both without and within the party; he can do either, but he cannot possibly do both. I went in with my eyes open to do what I could within the party; I did my best and got beaten, and I propose to stand by the result. I am by inheritance and by education a Republican; whatever good I have been able to accomplish in public life has been accomplished through the Republican party; I have acted with it in the past, and I wish to act with it in the future." Following this declaration he returned to the East, where he took a rather inactive part in the campaign.

This disappointment in politics together with personal reasons led Roosevelt to spend the greater part of the following years up to 1889, when he accepted the appointment as Civil Service Commissioner, in the West on his ranch. There he enjoyed to the full outdoor life and found time in which to do a good deal of writing.

30 : 13. Duke of Wellington. Arthur Wellesley, Duke of Wellington (1769–1852) was the British general who won at the battle of Waterloo, June 18, 1815, a decisive victory over Napoleon's army.

31 : 25. Hamilton. Alexander Hamilton (1757–1804) was an American statesman who, in the early days of the nation when disintegrating tendencies were pronounced, contended for a strong, centralized government.

34 : 11. Josh Billings. The pen name of Henry W. Shaw (1818–1885), one of the early American humorists. His chief works were his *Farmer's Allminax* (1870–1880), *Every Boddy's Friend* (1876), and *Josh Billings' Spice Box* (1881).

In Cowboy Land

38 : 2. Territory of Dakota. In 1889, the large Territory of Dakota was divided into two sections and these were admitted into the Union as the States of North and of South Dakota.

38 : 7. Owen Wister's stories. This American novelist has written vividly about the Far West which he knew
from intimate experience. His *The Virginian* (1902) is
acknowledged to be one of our best portrayals of Western
life. For Roosevelt's estimate of it, see page 49.

38 : 8. Frederic Remington's drawings. Frederic
Remington (1861–1909) was an American artist who embodied in his drawings and paintings, in a remarkable way
Western life. He had lived for several years as a cowboy
on a ranch and had thus absorbed the spirit of Western
life in a first-hand way.

38 : 11. Atlantis. A large island, which, according to
an ancient tradition was at one time situated in the Atlantic near the Pillars of Hercules (now in the Strait of
Gibraltar).

39 : 28. Duffle-Bag. A bag, usually of canvas, in which
is carried a sportsman's or camper's outfit.

40 : 13. Old sledge. A game of cards more generally
known as *all-fours*.

46 : 14. maverick. A Western expression designating
cattle found without an owner's brand.

48 : 23. Bryce. Viscount Bryce (1838–) was ambassador from England to the United States from 1907 to
1913.

The Rough Riders

55 : 2. Assistant Secretary of the Navy. Roosevelt
was recalled from his ranch in the fall of 1886 to become
a candidate for Mayor of New York City. He was the
nominee of the Independent Committee of One Hundred
and of the Republican party. His opponents were Henry
George, running on a Labor and Single-Tax Platform, and

Abram S. Hewitt whom Tammany had nominated. The result of the contest was that Hewitt was chosen Mayor.

In May, 1889, Roosevelt was appointed a member of the National Civil Service Commission by President Harrison. He served through Harrison's administration, and was retained in office by President Cleveland, whom he had helped, ten years before, to establish civil service on a firmer basis in New York State. The six years that Roosevelt spent in Washington in this position gave him splendid training in a wider field than he had hitherto entered. He won the friendship and regard of public men from all parts of the country, and even those who were not in entire sympathy with the reforms he represented recognized his sincerity, fairness, and energy.

Roosevelt resigned from the Civil Service Commission in May, 1895, and accepted one of the Police Commissionerships tendered him by Mayor Strong of New York City. Roosevelt was chosen president of the Board, and from the first stamped his personality on the Department. The new board found the police force in a thoroughly demoralized and disorganized condition, but it was able to bring order out of chaos and enforce a strict discipline which soon improved the morale of the force. Roosevelt resigned his position as Police Commissioner in March, 1897, to return to Washington as Assistant Secretary of the Navy.

55 : 3. Lodge. Henry Cabot Lodge (1850–) is a prominent American politician. He has been United States Senator from Massachusetts since 1893.

58 : 2. Captain Mahan. Alfred Thayer Mahan (1840–1914) was an eminent American naval officer who wrote several important books on naval history and strategy.

58 : 15. Jefferson. Thomas Jefferson (1743–1826) was the author of the Declaration of Independence and third President of the United States.

60 : 1. the Maine. The blowing up of the United States battleship *Maine* in Havana harbor on the evening of February 15, 1898, with the loss of 266 men was the critical incident that provoked hostilities between the United States and Spain.

60 : 15. Apaches. One of the Western Indian tribes, formerly living chiefly in New Mexico and Arizona, which gave a great deal of trouble in the early settlement of the West.

61 : 1. Alger. Russell Alexander Alger (1836–1907) was an American soldier and politician. He was at one time Governor of Michigan and in President McKinley's cabinet he was Secretary of War. His administration of the War Department during the Spanish-American War was severely criticized, but an investigating committee in the main exonerated him.

62 : 7. San Antonio. The leading city in western Texas.

63 : 3. Tampa. Tampa, Florida, situated on Tampa Bay, was an embarkation point during the Spanish-American War.

64 : 6. good record. In the first conflict with the Spanish at Las Guasimas on June 24, 1898, the Rough Riders saw severe fighting and conducted themselves well. Before another engagement, Wood was promoted to the rank of brigadier-general, and Roosevelt became commander of the regiment. In the fighting in connection with the assault of Santiago, July 1, 1898, Roosevelt displayed great bravery, leading his men in person. Before the fighting was over, the death or wounding of the other commanding officers left him the ranking officer of the brigade. The regiment was under fire all the next day and night, but maintained the position on the hills it had won. The regiment lay in the trenches before the city until its surrender, Roosevelt being in command of the second brigade of the cavalry division, from the middle of July.

It was during this period that the incident of the famous "round robin" letter occurred. The officers and men who had undergone the hardships of the campaign were anxious to return North to recuperate, now that the fighting was over for the time being. The damp summer season with its malaria and yellow fever was approaching. They had not complained when there was fighting to be done, but they objected to being sacrificed to no good purpose. On August 4, all the general officers of General Shafter's command united in a letter of protest asking that the troops be moved North, and declaring that the "army must be moved at once or perish."

Although there was a tendency to criticize the letter, which had been composed by Roosevelt, as unmilitary and subversive of good discipline, yet it accomplished the end sought. General Shafter concurred in its request and transmitted it to the War Department with the result that in three days the entire command was ordered North. Colonel Roosevelt and his Rough Riders were ordered to Camp Wyckoff, at Montauk Point, where they arrived on August 15 and were shortly afterwards mustered out.

THE PRESIDENCY

65 : 1. President McKinley. William McKinley (1843–1901) was the twenty-fifth President of the United States. After his first term (1897–1901) he had been re-elected for a second term. While he was taking part in a public reception at the Pan-American Exposition at Buffalo, New York, on September 6, 1901, he was shot by an anarchist, Leon Czolgosz.

65 : 24. Loeb. William Loeb, the private secretary of President McKinley who served Roosevelt in the same capacity during his Presidency.

66 : 19. to show my competence by my deeds. That Roosevelt fulfilled this expectation is shown by the fact that after completing the unexpired term of McKinley, he was nominated in 1904 to succeed himself. He was elected by the largest popular majority ever given for any Presidential candidate.

Space does not permit an account of Roosevelt's administration. Suffice it to say that the seven and a half years which he spent in the White House were crowded with achievements of national and international significance. His relation to " big business " and to labor, his policy regarding the conservation of natural resources, his upholding of the Monroe doctrine in the Venezuela affair, his service as peace-maker between Japan and Russia, his interest in developing the efficiency of the navy, his securing the enactment of laws controlling the matter of railway rates, and his steps toward the building of the Panama Canal, were some of the outstanding features of his administration.

In the fall of 1913 Roosevelt left the United States for his second extended hunting and exploring expedition. This time he went to South America and after many months in the jungle emerged to tell the world that he had discovered a river one thousand miles long, which he named the Rio Duvido, or River of Doubt.

In 1914 Roosevelt refused the Progressive nomination for Governor of New York, and between that time and 1916 he became reconciled to the Republican party. He was a candidate for the Presidential nomination in 1916, but when Charles E. Hughes was nominated he supported him vigorously.

Though denied an active part in the war Roosevelt, despite failing health, from time to time made addresses urging a tireless prosecution of the war. On the day the armistice was signed, he had to go to the hospital on account of inflammatory rheumatism. Happily he was able to be at home for Christmas and spent a happy holiday season with those of his children and grandchildren who could be present.

The last day of his life, January 5th, was spent in reading and writing at his home. He spent the evening with his family and went to bed at eleven o'clock. Shortly after four o'clock the next morning, his personal attendant, who was sleeping in the next room, noticed that his breathing was unnatural. He hurriedly called the trained nurse who was sleeping nearby, but when they reached Roosevelt's beside, they found that a clot of blood, settling upon a vital spot, had brought him peaceful death. His burial was without pomp and circumstance, his last resting place being a beautiful spot on a knoll looking over Long Island Sound. There among the woods and hills which he had loved since boyhood he was fittingly left to lie.

The public life of Roosevelt should not obscure his family life in the memory of the American people. As has been well said, " His family life was as intense as his public life. His wife and children and home were next

to his heart, together with his country.   He believed that
the strength of the nation lay in the tenderness and in the
fine love of American parents and children for one another,
and in his own life he practiced his belief."   It seems fitting
therefore to close these selections from his Autobiography
with a portion of the chapter in which he drew a most
engaging picture of his life at Sagamore Hill.   As a supple-
ment to this chapter, Roosevelt's *Letters to his Children*
should be read.

Outdoors and Indoors

69 : 16. Burroughs.   John Burroughs (1836–) is an
American nature-lover and writer between whom and
Roosevelt there was a warm friendship.

71 : 1. Harris.   Roosevelt had great admiration for
Joel Chandler Harris, author of the Uncle Remus books.
In a letter included in Mrs. Julia Collier Harris's life of
her father-in-law, Roosevelt has written as follows: " When
I became President, I set my heart on having Joel Chandler
Harris a guest at the White House.   But to get him there
proved no easy task.   He was a very shy, sensitive, re-
tiring man, who shrank from all publicity, and to whom
it was really an agony to be made much of in public.   But
I knew that he liked me; and I had the able assistance of
Julian (Harris's son), who remarked to me: ' I'll get father
up to see you if I have to blindfold him and back him
into the White House.'   Fortunately such extreme measures were not necessary; but I shall never forget the smile
of triumph with which Julian did actually deliver the
somewhat deprecatory ' father ' inside the White House
doors.   But I think he soon felt at home.   He loved the
children, and at dinner that evening we had no outsider

except Fitzhugh Lee, who was a close family friend, and with whom I knew he would get on well.

" In a little while he was completely at ease; . . . and after half an hour he was talking and laughing freely, and exchanging anecdotes and comparing reminiscences. When he left next morning all of our family agreed that we had never received at the White House a pleasanter friend or a man whom we more delighted to honor." (*Joel Chandler Harris*, pages 514 and 515.)

71 : 15. the Sequoias. The *Sequoia gigantea*, found in California, is the largest American forest tree. The average height of the trees is about 275–300 feet and the trunk diameter 30–35 feet near the ground.

71 : 16. Muir. John Muir (1838–1914) was an American naturalist and writer. He did much exploring not only in the far West and in Alaska, but also in other remote and unfamiliar parts of the world. He found time to write entertainingly articles and books about his experiences and his observations in the field of natural history.

71 : 19. Emerson. Ralph Waldo Emerson (1803–1882) was a famous American poet and essayist. In 1871, he made a lecture tour as far west as California.

74 : 18. Poe. Edgar Allan Poe (1809–1849) was the famous American poet and prose-writer.

75 : 21. Gaston Phœbus. Gaston III (1331–1391) was one of the counts of Foix, an old and distinguished French family which flourished from the eleventh to the fifteenth century. Gaston III was surnamed Phœbus (Apollo) on account of his beauty. He was very fond of hunting and wrote a book entitled *Pleasures of Hunting Wild Beasts and Birds of Prey.*

75 : 22. Emperor Maximilian. Maximilian I (1459–1519) was the Emperor of the Holy Roman Empire from 1493–1519. He was the author of books on the art of war, hunting, gardening, etc.

76 : 10. Gibbon. Edward Gibbon (1737–1794), the English historian whose *The History of the Decline and Fall of the Roman Empire* is one of the greatest histories ever written.

76 : 10. Macaulay. Thomas Babington Macaulay (1800–1859), an English historian and essayist, whose chief historical work is *History of England* covering the reigns of James II and William III.

76 : 10. Herodotus. A celebrated Greek historian (?484–?424 B. C.), sometimes called " the Father of History " who wrote a history of the Persian invasion of Greece.

76 : 11. Thucydides. A noted Greek historian (?471–?401 B. C.) who began an elaborate *History of the Peloponnesian War*, which, however, he did not live to finish.

76 : 11. Tacitus. A celebrated Roman historian (?55–?after 117) whose *Germania* gives an account of the German tribes.

76 : 11. Heimskringla. An important prose history of the Norse Kings from the earliest times to the battle of Re in 1177. The author was an Icelander, Snorri Sturlusow (1178–1241).

76 : 11. Froissart. Jean Froissart (1337–?1410) was a celebrated French historian whose great work is *Chronicles of France, England, Italy, and Spain* relating the historical events from 1332 till 1400.

76 : 12. Joinville. Jean de Joinville (?1224–1317) was a French chronicler, author of *History of St. Louis*.

76 : 12. Villehardouin. Geoffroi de Villehardouin (?1150–?1212) was a French historian who has left a valuable account of the Fourth Crusade (1198–1207) in which he was an active participant.

76 : 12. Parkman. Francis Parkman (1823–1893) was an American historian whose works include *Conspiracy of Pontiac, Pioneers of France in the New World, Jesuits in North America, Discovery of the Great West, The Old Régime in Canada, Montcalm and Wolfe*, and *The California and Oregon Trail*, to mention only the more important.

76 : 12. Mahan. See above **58 : 2.**

76 : 13. Mommsen. Theodor Mommsen (1817–1903), a celebrated German historian, whose principal work is *Roman History*.

76 : 13. Ranke. Leopold von Ranke (1795–1886), a German historian, author of several noted historical works, dealing with different phases of European history, especially with Germany.

76 : 16. Darwin. Charles Robert Darwin (1809–1882), a celebrated English scientist, whose chief work, *Origin of Species* (1859), propounded the theory of biological evolution.

76 : 16. Huxley. Thomas Henry Huxley (1825–1895) was one of the great English scientists. He became the champion of Darwin's evolutionary theories and defended them stoutly in his writings and speeches. He had a remarkable gift for popularizing in his writings scientific facts and theories.

76 : 17. Carlyle. Thomas Carlyle (1795–1881) was a noted English essayist and historian of Scotch descent. Among his best known books are *Sartor Resartus, The*

French Revolution, Heroes and Hero-Worship, Past and Present, and *History of Frederick the Great.*

76 : 17. Emerson. Ralph Waldo Emerson (1803–1882) was the great American essayist, whose various writings have stimulated many in an ethical way.

76 : 17. Kant. Immanuel Kant (1724–1804) was a noted German philosopher.

76 : 18. Sutherland's. Alexander Sutherland (1852–1902) was an Australian journalist. Roosevelt refers here to his *Origin and Growth of the Moral Instinct* (1898).

76 : 19. Acton. Lord Acton (1834–1902) was a noted English historian who in the latter part of his life was Regius Professor of Modern History at Oxford University.

76 : 19. Lounsbury. Thomas Raynesford Lounsbury (1838–) was for a long time professor of English at Yale University. Among his writings were *Studies in Chaucer* and several volumes of Shakespearean studies.

77 : 10. One Hundred Best Books. Sir John Lubbock, an English scientist of the nineteenth century, drew up a list of the " hundred best books " in the world's literature which attracted much attention.

77 : 10. Five-Foot Library. Several years ago President Eliot of Harvard made the statement that all the books really necessary to culture could be gathered together on a shelf five feet long. Later, he made this statement explicit by drawing up a list of the books to be included in this library.

77 : 21. Milton. John Milton (1608–1674), a celebrated English poet, author of *Paradise Lost,* regarded as the most sublime poem in English literature.

77 : 22. Pope. Alexander Pope (1688–1744), a famous English poet, noted for his success in brilliant, epigrammatic satiric verse.

77 : 22. Whitman. Walt Whitman (1819–1892), an American poet, whose formless but vigorous poetry as represented in *Leaves of Grass* was a forerunner of the modern free verse.

77 : 23. Browning. Robert Browning (1812–1889), an English poet, whose poetry is difficult to read but very stimulating.

77 : 23. Lowell. James Russell Lowell (1819–1891), an American poet.

77 : 24. Tennyson. Alfred Tennyson (1809–1892), a celebrated English poet.

77 : 24. Kipling. Rudyard Kipling (1865–), an English poet popular for vivid, vigorous verse.

77 : 24. Körner. Karl Theodor Körner (1791–1813), a German lyric poet whose short life closed on the battlefield. Many of his poems were written while in army service, the appropriate title of his volume of verse, published after his death, being *Lyre and Sword*.

77 : 24. Heine. Heinrich Heine (1797–1856), a German lyric poet of Hebrew descent.

77 : 25. Bard of the Dimbovitza. The title of an interesting collection of Roumanian folk-songs collected from the peasants in the valley of the Dimbovitza by Helena Vacaresco and published in an English translation in 1908.

77 : 25. Tolstoy's. Count Leo Tolstoy (1828–1910), a Russian novelist and social reformer, whose chief novels are *War and Peace* and *Anna Karénina*.

77 : 26. Sienkiewicz. Henryk Sienkiewicz (1845–)

was a Polish novelist. *Quo Vadis?*, a picture of Roman life in the time of Nero, being his best known book.

77 : 27. " Salammbo." A novel by the French novelist Flaubert based upon the history of Hannibal's sister Salammbo.

77 : 27. " Tom Brown." The two famous books by Thomas Hughes, *Tom Brown's School-days* and *Tom Brown at Oxford*, illustrating respectively public school and collegiate life in England.

77 : 28. " Two Admirals." A novel of sea adventure by James Fenimore Cooper.

77 : 28. " Quentin Durward." A historical romance by Sir Walter Scott.

77 : 29. " Artemus Ward." The pseudonym of C. F. Browne (1834–1867), an American humorist.

77 : 29. " Ingoldsby Legends." A series of satirical stories in prose and verse written about the middle of the nineteenth century by Barham, whose pen-name was Thomas Ingoldsby, Esq.

77 : 30. " Pickwick." *The Posthumous Papers of the Pickwick Club* by Charles Dickens.

77 : 30. " Vanity Fair." The most representative novel of William Makepeace Thackeray (1811–1863).

78 : 17. Macbeth. One of Shakespeare's tragedies dealing with deep passions that lead to violence and crime.

78 : 17. Hamlet. Another of Shakespeare's tragedies which is more thoughtful and poetic than *Macbeth*.

82 : 20. Farragut. David Glasgow Farragut (1801–1870), a celebrated American admiral, who directed many brilliant naval campaigns during the Civil War. August 5, 1864, with eighteen ships, four of them monitors, Farragut ran past the batteries guarding entrance to Mobile bay, and engaged the Confederate fleet within the bay. His defeat of the Confederate ironclad, Tennessee, was the notable achievement of this expedition.

85 : 15. Jonathan Edwards. The bear derived his name from an eminent American theologian of the eighteenth century whose doctrines represented the extreme views of the New England Puritans on points of Calvinistic theology.

88 : 15. " Kim." The hero of a story by Kipling telling the adventures of an Irish waif in India who acquired marvelous knowledge of the Orient.

HISTORY

THE BACKWOODSMEN OF THE ALLEGHANIES

IT was with historical writing that Roosevelt began his literary career, his first volume being *The History of the Naval War of 1812*. Although this was the work of a young man just twenty-three years old it was an exceedingly meritorious performance in that it corrected many mistakes of earlier historians and showed an impartiality of judgment.

His longest and most painstaking historical work is *The Winning of the West*, the four volumes of which were written from 1889 to 1896. So excellent is this account of our territorial expansion from 1769–1807 and of the men to whom it was due that many regard it as Roosevelt's most enduring contribution to literature. When one considers the difficulty of finding and collecting material in this field thirty years ago, he cannot fail to feel that Roosevelt's achievement was a remarkable one. One of the most striking chapters in this book is the one here reprinted which gives vivid picture of the life and character of the men who played so large a part in the development of American civilization.

93 : 22. Fort Pitt. Located at what is now Pittsburg.

93 : 23. Cherokees. An Indian tribe which occupied the mountainous section of North Carolina and Georgia.

94 : 8. Quakers. Members of the religious denomination known as the Society of Friends which took its rise in England about the middle of the seventeenth century.

94 : 23. Scotch-Irish. This term does not indicate, as many people suppose, mixed Scotch and Irish descent. It denotes the descendants of the early Scotch Presbyterian who settled, for a hundred years or more after 1600, with their wives and families in Ulster, in the north of Ireland. For a hundred years after 1700 their descendants seeking to escape civil and religious burdens that were intolerable, sought a more promising home in America. They became an important ingredient in the American population.

94 : 24. Roundhead. A member of the Puritan party during the English Civil War in the seventeenth century. This nickname was applied to the Puritans because of their custom of wearing their hair cut short in contrast to the general custom of the time.

94 : 24. Cavalier. The adherents of Charles I of England during the Civil War in the seventeenth century.

94 : 27. Huguenot. The French Calvinists were known as Huguenots. During the 16th and 17th centuries they were subjected to much persecution on account of their Protestant faith. To escape these persecutions thousands of the Huguenots left France and settled in other countries, many going to America.

94 : 30. Knox. John Knox (1505–1572) was a Scotch

divine who was a leader in the establishment of Presbyterianism in Scotland.

94 : 30. Calvin. John Calvin (1509–1564) was the noted Protestant reformer and founder of Presbyterianism.

94 : 31. Covenanters. Those in Scotland who in the seventeenth century bound themselves by a solemn covenant to uphold and maintain the Presbyterian doctrine and scheme of church government against Catholicism and Anglicanism.

95 : 13. Milesian Irish. Descendants of the original Gaelic colonists of Ireland who were called Milesians because according to the legend they sprang from the three sons of Mil, or Milesius, who came from Spain or Gaul and conquered the preceding inhabitants some centuries before the Christian era.

95 : 20. Cromwell. Oliver Cromwell (1599–1658) was the Puritan leader who became ruler of England from 1653–1658 with the title of Lord Protector.

95 : 21. Derry. The city of Derry (now known more commonly as Londonderry) was successfully defended by the Irish Protestants when James II of England attacked it during his expedition into Ireland, 1689.

95 : 22. Boyne. A river in Ireland on whose banks in 1690 the army of James II was heavily defeated.

95 : 22. Aughrim. An Irish village where in 1691 the English defeated an army of the Irish and French.

96 : 11. independence. The reference is to the Mecklenburg Declaration drawn up by the citizens of Mecklenburg County, North Carolina, in 1775. It is believed by some to have antedated the Philadelphia Declaration but this view is not generally held by historians.

105 : 17. **pankräition.** Among the Olympic games of the Greeks this was a contest involving a combination of boxing and wrestling. The combatants fought naked, their bodies being oiled and sprinkled with sand for the sake of a better hold. It seems to have been very much of the nature of a rough-and-tumble fight although there were rules governing the contest.

105 : 24. **Kenton.** Simon Kenton (1755–1836) was an American pioneer whose fame as a frontier hero was second only to that of Daniel Boone.

105 : 32. **pillion.** A pad or cushion placed behind a saddle as a seat for a second person, usually a woman.

107 : 18. **noggins.** Wooden mugs.

THE HISTORIAN OF THE FUTURE

THIS selection is from Roosevelt's address as president of the American Historical Association, delivered at the Boston meeting, December 27, 1912. The title, "History as Literature," indicated that Roosevelt was discussing the topic whether history should be treated in a cold and dispassionate scientific manner or whether it should be presented as a vivid story with emphasis on man as the principal factor. His position is sufficiently indicated in the portion of the address which is here given. The last two or three paragraphs of the selection have been much admired as one of the most striking and eloquent passages in all Roosevelt's writings.

121 : 8. **Ten Thousand.** In the campaign of Cyrus the Younger against the Persians, the Greek army of 10,000 was forced to retreat after the death of Cyrus in the battle of Cunaxa. "At last one day—in the fifth month—February 400 B. C.—Xenophon, who was with the rearguard, heard a great shouting among the men who had reached the top of a hill in front. He thought they saw an enemy. He mounted his horse, and galloped forward with some cavalry. As they came nearer, they could make out the shout: it was "*The sea! the sea!* There, far off was the silver gleam of the Euxine. After the long, intense strain of toil and danger, the men burst into tears: like true Greek children of the sea they knew now that they were in sight of home." (Jebb's *Greek Literature*, p. 110.)

121 : 10. Jehu. See Bible, *II Kings* IX. In his usurpation of the throne of Israel, Jehu killed Jezebel, the queen-mother.

121 : 11. Ahab. See Bible, *I Kings* XXII, 29–40. Ahab was a King of Israel who was killed in battle with Jehoshaphet, King of Judah.

121 : 12. Josiah. See Bible, *II Kings* XXII–XXIII and *II Chronicles* XXXIV, XXXV. When Pharaoh-Necho went from Egypt to carry on his war with Assyria, Josiah, King of Judah, opposèd his march. In the subsequent battle Josiah was killed.

121 : 19. Shalmaneser. Shalmaneser and Sargon were Assyrian rulers, Amenhotep and Rameses, Egyptian.

121 : 23. Peloponnesian War. A war extending from 431 to 404 B. C. between the Athenians and their allies and the Peloponnesian Confederacy embracing the Spartans and their allies. The result was a victory for Athens.

122 : 3. Richard III. In the play *Richard III*, Shakespeare has represented this king as more cruel and bloodthirsty than modern historians believe him to have been. This was due to Shakespeare's use of a biassed history popular in his day. But so vivid is his portrayal of Richard that most persons hold their ideas of him from the play.

122 : 4. Keats. In Keats' poem *On First Looking into Chapman's Homer*, he made the mistake of referring to Cortez as the discoverer of the Pacific Ocean when he should have said Balboa.

122 : 11. Napier. Sir William F. P. Napier (1785–1860) was a British general who saw service in the Peninsular campaigns. Afterwards he wrote a full account of the campaign, in six volumes, entitled *History of the Peninsular War,* which described vividly the deeds of the English in such engagements as Roosevelt mentions.

122 : 13. Parkman. See note **76 : 12.**

122 : 14. Montcalm. Marquis de Montcalm (1712–1759) was the general commanding the French forces in the struggle around Quebec in 1759. An account of his death together with that of Wolfe may be found in Parkman's *France and England in North America,* Part VII.

122 : 14. Wolfe. James Wolfe (1727–1759) was an English general commanding the English forces in the attack on Quebec in 1759. As he led the decisive charge, he was killed.

122 : 15. Fitzgerald. Edward Fitzgerald (1809–1883) was an English poet whose fame is due almost wholly to his translation, from the Persian, of the *Rubáiyát* of Omar Khayyám. His rendering of this old poem seems final so far as English literature is concerned.

122 : 20. Gibbon. See note **76 : 10.**

123 : 3. Maspero. Sir Gaston Camille Charles Maspero (1846–) is a distinguished French authority on Egyptian history.

123 : 4. Breasted. James Henry Breasted (1865–) is an American authority on Oriental history. He has written several books, his *Ancient Records of Egypt* being one of his most notable.

123 : 4. Weigall. Arthur Edward P. B. Weigall (1880–) is an English authority on Egyptian history.

123 : 7. Heimskringla. See note **76 : 10.**

123 : 7. Sagas. The sagas are prose accounts of the deeds of ancient Icelandic heroes. The accounts are always vivid and forceful, the events happening mostly between 874 and 1030.

123 : 11. Mount Vernon. The burial place of George Washington some fifteen miles down the Potomac river from Washington.

125 : 18. Ivan the Terrible. Ivan IV, Czar of Russia from 1547–1584. His conquests were accompanied by so many cruelties that he was surnamed The Terrible.

125 : 31. Jenghiz Khan. A Mongolian king who conquered northern China and central Asia 1215–1221.

126 : 4. Touaregs. A powerful tribe inhabiting that portion of the Sahara lying south of Algeria and between Morocco and Senegal. They control the principal caravan routes.

126 : 7. Moslem. The followers of Mohammedism.

126 : 7. Buddhist. A follower of the religious system founded by Buddha in India in the sixth century.

127 : 20. Agincourt. In the battle of Agincourt, October 25, 1415, between the French and the English the skill of the English with the long bow was a decisive factor in the victory.

127 : 21. Alexander. Alexander the Great (356–323 B. C.), King of Macedon, pushed his conquests eastward as far as an invasion of India.

127 : 23. Low-Dutch sea-thieves. The Anglo-Saxon

conquerors of England were from Teutonic tribes living around the mouth of the river Elbe.

127 : 25. Unknown continents. The reference is to the peopling of North America and Australia by the descendants of the early Anglo-Saxons.

127 : 25. Hannibal. The Carthaginian general, Hannibal, carried his conquests up through Spain to the gates of Rome itself. He was defeated by Scipio Africanus in 202.

128 : 9. Memphis. The early capital of Egypt, situated on the Nile, south of Cairo. It continued to exist down to Roman times, but was gradually abandoned and ruined after the Mohammedan conquest.

128 : 10. Babylon. The capital of ancient Babylonia, situated on the Euphrates, and one of the oldest cities of the East. The famous Hanging Gardens, one of the seven wonders of the world, seem to have been a building on the roof of which were planted trees, flowers, and shrubs, and are said to have been constructed by Nebuchadnezzar for the gratification of his queen because the level scenery around Babylon was dreary to her in comparison with that of her mountain home in Media.

128 : 11. Nineveh. The capital of the ancient Assyrian Empire. It was situated on the upper Tigris.

128 : 12. Queen Maeve. A famous warrior-queen in the early Irish sagas.

128 : 14. Olaf. One of the most famous of the Norwegian Kings (995–1030).

128 : 20. Samurai. The military class in Japan during the prevalence of the feudal system in that country.

128 : 24. Timur the Lame (1333–1405). The Tartar conqueror who became ruler of a great empire embracing the larger part of Asia. His name is more usually given as Tamburlane.

128 : 25. Gustavus. Gustavus Adolphus (1594–1632), King of Sweden.

128 : 26. Frederick. Frederick the Great (1712–1786), King of Prussia.

128 : 26. Napoleon. Napoleon Bonaparte (1769–1821), Emperor of the French, 1804–1814.

129 : 15. Wilderness. This westward expansion of the United States has been vividly portrayed by Roosevelt in *The Winning of the West*.

ADVENTURE

Bear Hunting Experiences

ʻRoosevelt's ranch life in the 80's resulted in several books descriptive of his experiences in the Far West, especially on his hunting trips. Among his books in this class is *Hunting Trips of a Ranchman* (1886) from which the selection here given is taken. Other books of the same general character are *The Wilderness Hunter* (1887), *Ranch Life and Hunting Trail* (1888) and *American Big Game Hunting* (1893).

136 : 4. grisly. Although both the spelling *grizzly* and *grisly* are sanctioned, yet the first is the older. It originated from the color of the animal which is usually a grizzled gray but is very variable, being sometimes whitish, blackish, or brownish. The word *grizzled* was especially in Elizabethan days used to denote a grayish color, for example, a grizzled beard (Cf. *Hamlet* i, 2, 240), and this adjective was applied to this species of bear. The second form of spelling originated in the way suggested by Roosevelt; that is, it came through association with the adjective *grisly* which was connected with the ferocious disposition of the animal.

Getting Christmas Dinner on a Ranch

Accompanying the selection from Roosevelt's hunting books may be placed this little sketch which was reprinted in *Everybody's Magazine* with a note to the effect that it was written twenty years before and published in a paper of small circulation, which was now defunct. Because it is a vividly written bit of writing in Roosevelt's best style, it seems worthy of being more widely known.

CITIZENSHIP

True Americanism

During the earlier part of his political life, Roosevelt wrote several magazine articles and addresses embodying his ideals of citizenship. These he collected in 1897 into a volume with the title *American Ideals and Other Essays, Social and Political.* In a subsequent edition he added several of his later discussions of such topics, thus making this volume, together with *Addresses and Presidential Addresses, 1902–1904,* important sources from which may be gathered his ideas on politics and government. As yet his later addresses in this field have not been collected and added to the authorized edition of his works.

The essay chosen from *American Ideals* for inclusion here presents his views upon a topic which has become identified closely with his name because it was the cornerstone of his theory of citizenship.

149 : 3. **Johnson.** Dr. Samuel Johnson (1709–1784)

was the noted English essayist and poet. Boswell in his *Life of Johnson*, records this remark about patriotism as follows: "Patriotism having become one of our topics, Johnson suddenly uttered, in a strong determined tone, an apothegm, at which many will start: 'Patriotism is the last refuge of a scoundrel.' But let it be considered, that he did not mean a real and generous love of our country, but that pretended patriotism which so many, in all ages and countries, have made a cloak for self-interest."

150 : 26. Manchester. A manufacturing city in England.

152 : 20. Ancient republics of Greece. Ancient Greece was largely a country of individual states each fired with a desire for independence and freedom. The two most prominent were Athens and Sparta. Both of these developed a government by the people, or democracy.

152 : 20. mediæval republics of Italy. During the Middle Ages, Italy was largely a country of city republics such as Venice, Florence, and Genoa.

152 : 21. petty states of Germany. Until the Congress of Vienna in 1815, what is now the German Empire had consisted of thirty-nine independent states.

153 : 16. Harris. See note **6 : 24.**

153 : 17. Mark Twain. Samuel Langhorne Clemens (1835–1910), the noted American humorist.

162 : 24. Jay. John Jay (1745–1829) was a distinguished American lawyer and statesman.

162 : 24. Sevier. John Sevier (1745–1815) was a famous pioneer who participated in the battle of King's Mountain (1779) as the leader of a band of mountain men and who afterwards became Governor of Tennessee.

162 : 24. Marion. Francis Marion (1732–1795) was a noted American leader in the Revolutionary War. He was known as the Swamp Fox because he made the swamps of South Carolina the rendezvous from which he harassed the British.

162 : 24. Laurens. Henry Laurens (1724–1792) was a South Carolinian prominent in Revolutionary days.

162 : 32. Schuyler. Philip Schuyler (1733–1804) was in command of the expedition into Canada in 1775 and of the forces sent against Burgogne in 1777. After the close of the Revolutionary War, he was for two terms senator from New York.

163 : 1. Van Buren. Martin Van Buren (1782–1862) was the eighth President of the United States (1837–1841).

163 : 12. Mühlenburgs. H. M. Mühlenburg (1711–1787) was a German-American clergymen who founded the Lutheran Church in the United States. His sons, J. P. G. Mühlenburg, F. A. Mühlenburg, and G. H. E. Mühlenburg, all distinguished themselves as citizens.

163 : 16. Carroll. Charles Carroll (1737–1832) one of the signers of the Declaration of Independence for Maryland.

163 : 16. Sullivan. John Sullivan (1740–1795) was an American general in Revolutionary times.

163 : 17. Sheridan. Philip Henry Sheridan (1831–1888) was a prominent general on the Union side in the Civil War.

163 : 17. Shields. General James Shields (1810–1879) served both in the Mexican War and the Civil War.

164 : 22. Samoan trouble. Owing to disturbances in Samoa in 1889, the joint protectorate which England, Germany, and the United States had been exercising for several years was terminated and the islands partitioned among these three powers. In this connection there was friction between the United States and Germany.

The Strenuous Life

Another early collection of essays similar to *American Ideals* was the volume entitled *The Strenuous Life* (1900). The latter volume took its title from the first essay which had been originally a speech delivered by Roosevelt when he was before the Hamilton Club of Chicago, April 10, 1899. In reprinting the essay in this book, portions of it that dealt particularly with some of the domestic and foreign problems arising out of the Spanish-American War which had just closed are omitted, but enough is given to show the essential spirit of the address.

Our Responsibilities as a Nation

When Roosevelt became President in his own right on March 4, 1905, he delivered this brief inaugural address. Short though it is, the reader may find in it the touchstone by which to interpret the foreign and domestic policies of his administration.

The Man with the Muck-Rake

The occasion of this address was the laying of the cornerstone of the Office Building of the House of Representatives, April 14, 1906. Just at that time, criticism was rife in the press, especially on the part of some of the popular magazines, regarding public evils and the actions of those in authority. Roosevelt took this occasion to indicate that there was a difference between legitimate criticism and the exaggeration in which many journals were indulging. After discussing this topic he passed to the matter of the accountability to the community of those who had accumulated large property.

177 : 2. Capitol. The capitol at Washington was begun in 1793 and substantially completed in 1811.

177 : 20. Bunyan's. John Bunyan (1628–1688) was a celebrated English preacher who wrote the prose allegory *The Pilgrim's Progress* 1678 (second part 1684). The success of the allegory has come not merely from its exposition of the Protestant theory of the plan of salvation as from the vivid representation of persons and places and the effective narrative.

177 : 21. Man with the Muck-rake. This character appears in the Second Part of *Pilgrim's Progress.* The Interpreter conducts Christian into a room " where was a man that could look no way but downwards, with a muck-rake in his hand. There stood also one over his head with a celestial crown in his hand, and proffered him that crown for his muck-rake: but the man did neither look up, nor regard, but raked to himself the straws, the small sticks, and dust of the floor."

179 : 14. Aristides. A celebrated Athenian statesman and general who lived in the fourth century B. C.

179 : 31. Panama Canal. The building of a ship canal across the Isthmus of Panama is one of the greatest tangible results of Roosevelt's Presidency. For over four hundred years there had been discussion of the project and a few attempts at accomplishing it. Roosevelt's interest in the scheme led to the United States beginning the work of constructing the canal in 1904. It was completed in 1914, the cost being approximately $375,000,000.

181 : 19. Crackling of thorns, etc. See Bible, *Eccle-*

siastes VII, 6. The image is from the Eastern use of thorns for fuel. A fire of such material burns up quickly. In this passage in the Bible it is used as a comparison to show how futile was mirth which was merely frivolous.

182 : 11. " Ecclesiastical Polity." This book was written by the English theologian, Richard Hooker (1553–1600).

THE DEVELOPMENT OF THE AMERICAN NATION

This speech delivered at the opening of the Jamestown Exposition is representative of Roosevelt's occasional speeches made for various political and social occasions. It contains a significant review of the factors in the development of the American nation. In this respect it illustrates the truth of the statement made about Roosevelt that, " With him, love of country was based upon complete knowledge. He knew his country's history as few men know it."

189 : 3. celebrating. In 1907, the Jamestown Exposition was held on Hampton Roads, Virginia, in commemoration of the three hundredth anniversary of the first permanent English settlement in America.

189 : 5. first settled. The first permanent settlement of the English was in 1607 at Jamestown, on the banks of the James river in Virginia, about thirty-two miles from its mouth. On the site of the settlement, are at present ruins of the fort, a church, and two or three houses.

189 : 17. the Cavalier and the Puritan. See note **94 : 24.**

196 : 5. Martin Chuzzlewit. In this novel by Charles Dickens, the portions descriptive of the hero's experiences in America are Chapters XV–XVII, XXI–XXIII, XXXIII and XXXIV. The description of Eden may be found in Chapters XXI, XXIII, and XXXIII.

196 : 11. Andrew Jackson (1767–1845). The seventh President of the United States (1829–1837).

196 : 27. Jefferson. See note **58 : 15.**

196 : 28. Marshall. John Marshall (1755–1835) was a celebrated American jurist, who was chief justice of the United States Supreme Court (1801–1835).

197 : 19. Grant. See note **2 : 28.**

197 : 20. Lee. Robert E. Lee (1807–1870) was commander-in-chief of the Confederate Army in the Civil War.

199 : 15. Sketch. The reference is to the life of Edmund Burke, the English statesman of the eighteenth century, which John Morley, the English statesman and author, wrote in 1879 for the English Men of Letters Series.

Conservation of Natural Resources

Roosevelt's name will always be associated with the movement for the conservation of natural resources. All during his Presidential career, this attempt to foster foresight and restraint in man's use of the primary sources of wealth,—the earth's surface, the forests and waters upon it, and the minerals beneath it,—and to secure their equal enjoyment by the people of this and of future generations received his constant and enthusiastic attention. In 1908, he called a conference of all the state governors and other delegates to consider the conservation of natural resources in all its aspects. To this conference, which met at the White House, May, 1908. Roosevelt delivered the address which is here given.

210 : 27. Pinchot. Gifford Pinchot (1865–) is an American forestry expert who served as Chief of the Forestry Bureau during Roosevelt's administration.

The Duties of the Citizen

On his way back to the United States after his African expedition, Roosevelt visited several of the European capitals and delivered at each some notable address. One of the most interesting of these addresses was the one here reprinted which was delivered in Paris before a large and representative body of French scholars and other notables.

215 : 12. famous university. The Sorbonne was founded about 1250.

217 : 21. Gamaliel. A famous Jewish rabbi who was the teacher of the Apostle Paul. "To sit at the feet of Gamaliel" has become a common expression for being a disciple or learner.

221 : 8. Hotspur. Henry Percy, an English nobleman, who was killed in the battle of Shrewsbury, 1403. His impetuous nature and his fiery temper won for him the nickname Hotspur. Shakespeare gives an engaging picture of him in *Henry IV*, Part I.

221 : 26. French epic. The *Chanson de Roland*.

242 : 20. Malbrook. A popular French song beginning "Malbrook has gone to war." The authorship is unknown but the song is supposed to have originated about 1780.

Last Words on Americanism

It is significant that Roosevelt's last message to the American people was upon the theme of Americanism.

He had been invited to speak at a meeting under the auspices of the American Defence Society on the evening of January 5th, 1919. Not being able to attend on account of his health, he wrote and sent the letter here given which was read at the meeting.

NATURAL HISTORY

MY LIFE AS A NATURALIST

247 : 19. Audubon. See note **9 : 4.**

247 : 20. Waterton. Charles Waterton (1782–1865) was an English naturalist who spent many years in wandering about in South America having no other object than the pursuit of natural history. His adventures in South America are graphically described in his *Wanderings in South America, the Northwest of the United States, and the Antilles in 1812, 1816, 1820, and 1824.*

247 : 22. Brehm. Christian Ludwig Brehm (1787–1864) was a German ornithologist.

247 : 24. Darwin. See note **76 : 16.**

247 : 25. Huxley. See note **76 : 16.**

247 : 25. Marsh. Othniel Charles Marsh (1831–1899) was an American zoölogist and paleontologist who accomplished a great amount of valuable scientific work in the discovery of fossil vertebrates in the geological formations of the Western states.

247 : 26. Leidy's. Joseph Leidy (1823–1891) was an American naturalist who made many important contributions to paleontology and other branches of natural science.

248 : 2. Osborn. Henry Fairfield Osborn is a noted American paleontologist.

251 : 20. Merriam. See note **12 : 23.**

251 : 20. Burroughs. See note **69 : 16.**

251 : 22. Cherrie. One of the scientists sent by the American Museum of Natural History with Roosevelt on the South American trip.

251 : 23. Miller. Another scientist sent by the American Museum of Natural History with Roosevelt's South American trip.

251 : 23. Heller. One of Roosevelt's companions on the African trip.

251 : 23. Mearns. Another of Roosevelt's companions on the African trip.

253 : 5. Milwaukee. During the violent campaign of 1912, Roosevelt, while speaking in Milwaukee, was shot by a fanatic just three weeks before the election, but he was not seriously injured.

253 : 14. Agassiz. Alexander Agassiz (1835–1910) was the son of Louis Agassiz and himself a naturalist of distinction, his special interest being marine zoölogy.

256 : 29. Selous. Frederick C. Selous (1851–) is an English hunter and explorer who has spent much time in South Africa. He has written several books upon his experiences and his observations.

257 : 7. Wallace. Alfred Russel Wallace (1822–1913) was an English scientist. Simultaneously with Darwin he announced the theory of natural selection which he had arrived at independently.

NATURE FAKIRS

One of the surest indications that Roosevelt possessed the spirit of a true naturalist was his impatience with the faulty observations and false deductions of others. Again and again in his writings he insists upon care and accuracy in observation as well as in the interpretation of observations, even though there may thereby be lost some of the sensational features which a too vivid imagination or a looseness regarding veracity may so easily impart to accounts of natural phenomena. As a designation for these unscrupulous persons, he coined the term " nature fakirs " and voiced his indignation toward them in the magazine article which is here reprinted.

258 : 6. **unicorn.** A fabulous animal with one horn.

258 : 6. **basilisk.** A fabulous serpent whose breath, and even its look, was fatal.

258 : 18. **Hearne.** Samuel Hearne (1745–1792) was an English explorer who between 1769 and 1772 visited many parts of British North America.

260 : 10. **Miller.** Olive Thorne Miller (1831–), author of several bird books.

260 : 11. **J. A. Allen,** etc. These are all American naturalists who have written interestingly and accurately about outdoor life and wild creatures.

261 : 5. **roc.** A mythical Arabian bird of such immense size that it bore off elephants to feed its young.

261 : 5. **cockatrice.** A fabulous monster believed to have been hatched by a serpent from a cock's egg, and supposed to possess characteristics of both these animals. Like the basilisk, its breath was believed to be fatal.

261 : 32. **" King Solomon's Mines."** A highly colored romance of adventure in the wilds of Africa in quest of King Solomon's Ophir—the country mentioned in Biblical passages such as *I Kings* IX, 26 and X, 11, whence Solomon received treasures. The exact location of this country is unknown, scholars differing in the conjectures.

262 : 1. Haggard. Sir Henry Rider Haggard (1856–) is an English novelist.

262 : 14. " Uncle Remus." See note **6 : 25.**

262 : 15. " Reynard the Fox." A poem, widely popular in the Middle Ages, in which the characters are animals, the hero being the fox Reynard.

262 : 18. Marcus Aurelius. A celebrated Roman Emperor living between 121 and 180 A. D. who was greatly devoted to philosophy. His work, " The Meditations of Marcus Aurelius," exhibits his acute, reflective mind.

262 : 22. White Queen. One of the characters in Lewis Carroll's *Through the Looking Glass.*

266 : 4. Barnum's. Phinias Taylor Barnum (1810–1891) was a famous American showman.

266 : 10. Cardiff Giant. In 1868 a rude statue of a man was found buried near Cardiff, New York. It was given out that this was a petrified prehistoric giant. It turned out that the whole matter was a hoax.

THE DEER OF NORTH AMERICA

As shown in the *Autobiography,* Roosevelt's ambition in early life was to become a naturalist of the type of Audubon, Wilson, Baird, or Coues—an outdoor student of birds and mammals. The laboratory study of natural science as conducted in the colleges had little interest for him. He preferred the study of the living animal in its habitat to the study of its dead body. He felt that the pursuit of this sort of knowledge might be intimately connected with love of the chase and enjoyment of outdoor life without being overshadowed by them and lost sight of. This double purpose he tried to indicate by the title " hunter-naturalist " which he was fond of applying to himself. On his various expeditions he found as keen satisfaction in clearing up even in some slight degree the imperfect life-history of some animal by observations upon its habits as he did in securing trophies of the chase.

While Roosevelt himself almost never referred to himself as a naturalist, yet it may be said that he achieved the goal he set for himself in youth of becoming an outdoor naturalist such as Audubon or Wilson or Coues. In 1907 no less authority than Dr. C. Hart Merriam said: " Theodore Roosevelt is the world's authority on the big game mammals of North America. His writings are fuller and his observations are more complete and accurate than those of any other man who has given the subject study." In 1902, Roosevelt had contributed to a volume entitled *The Deer Family* several chapters dealing with the deer and antelope of North America as he had studied them in the West. It is from this book that the two selections here included are taken. From them it is easy to discover the qualities that made him an authority in this field.

OBSERVATIONS ON CONCEALING COLORATION IN AFRICAN ANIMALS

As indicated above in the selection " My Life as a Naturalist," one of the scientific problems that especially interested Roosevelt was that of concealing, or as it is frequently called, protective coloring. The question at issue was, To what extent does the coloration of an animal, by resembling the background against which it is seen, render it inconspicuous and thereby protect it from its enemies? Some writers on the subject have claimed that all forms of animals are concealingly colored and that this underlying principle is the explanation of the development of color in the animal kingdom. Roosevelt took issue with so sweeping a generalization, especially as it was presented by G. H. and Abbott H. Thayer in their book *Concealing Coloration in the Animal Kingdom.* The extract here given from Roosevelt's paper, " Revealing and Concealing Coloration in Birds and Mammals " states his general position as well as indicates the range and accuracy of the observations upon which he based his views, especially in connection with data gathered on his African trip.

ANIMALS OF CENTRAL BRAZIL

303 : 1. trip. In the winter of 1913–1914, Roosevelt made an exploring and collecting trip through the valley of the Amazon River,—the heart of South America. Such a trip has been suggested to him in the last year of his Presidency by Father Zahm, a Catholic priest who was himself fond of exploration and was acquainted with South America, but for the time being such a trip was put aside for the African trip of 1909–1910. Finding himself invited to deliver several addresses in South American countries, Roosevelt decided not to return home without exploring the depths of the Brazilian wilderness. The American Museum of Natural History in New York was glad to send two naturalists, George K. Cherrie and Leo E. Miller, to accompany the expedition. Father Zahm also joined it. Among the others in the party were Roosevelt's son, Kermit, who had been with his father on the African trip, and Anthony Fiala, a former Arctic explorer. The object of the expedition was to secure animal and plant specimens from the central plateau of Brazil, which lies between the headwaters of the Amazon and Paraguay rivers.

After Roosevelt's speaking engagements had been fulfilled, the expedition started on December 9, 1913, into the wilds. It was the latter part of April when it emerged into civilization. The achievements were noteworthy not only from a zoölogical standpoint but also from a geographical. A full and vivid account of it is to be found in Roosevelt's book *Through the Brazilian Wilderness*. In lieu of an extract from that book, there is given here a resumé of the trip in a lecture delivered before the members of the American Museum of Natural History, December 10, 1914.

303 : 12. Brazilian officers. The Brazilian Government sent with the Roosevelt expedition Colonel Rondon, a noted army engineer and explorer, and a number of assistants and scientific men.

306 : 15. " Cannibal Fish." The piranha. Roosevelt says of this fish in his *Through the Brazilian Wilderness:* " South America makes up for its lack, relatively to Africa and India, of large man-eating carnivores by the extraordinary ferocity or bloodthirstiness of certain small creatures of which the kinsfolk elsewhere are harmless. It is only here that fish no bigger than trout kill swimmers, and bats the size of the ordinary ' flittermice ' of the northern hemisphere drain the life-blood of big beasts and of man himself."

307 : 2. The Unknown River. Roosevelt claimed that he had put on the map an unknown river in length and volume roughly corresponding to the Rhone, the Elbe, or the Rhine. The upper course, he asserted, had never been traversed, although the lower course, he admitted, was known to a few rubber-men but was not known to geographers. This announcement caused much discussion in scientific circles and learned opinion was divided as to the validity of his claim. However this may be, Roosevelt and several of his party had an exciting and perilous trip down the River of Doubt as they called it. An account of this may be read in *Through the Brazilian Wilderness.*

Printed in the United States of America